SHIFTING THE BURDEN

American Politics and Political Economy Series
Edited by Benjamin I. Page

SHIFTING THE BURDEN

The Struggle over Growth and
Corporate Taxation

Cathie J. Martin

The University of Chicago Press
Chicago and London

Cathie J. Martin is assistant
professor of political science
at Boston University.

The University of Chicago Press, Chicago 60637
The University of Chicago Press, Ltd., London
© 1991 by The University of Chicago
All rights reserved. Published 1991

Printed in the United States of America

00 99 98 97 96 95 94 93 92 91   5 4 3 2 1

Library of Congress Cataloging-in-Publication Data

Martin, Cathie J.
Shifting the burden : the struggle over growth and corporate taxation / Cathie J. Martin.
p.   cm.—(American politics and political economy series)
Includes index.
ISBN 0-226-50832-3 (cloth).—ISBN 0-226-50833-1 (pbk.)
1. Income tax—United States. 2. Corporations—Taxation—United States. 3. Corporations—Taxation—Law and legislation—United States. I. Title. II. Series: American politics
and political economy.
HJ4653.C7M334 1991
336.24′3′0973—dc20   90-24497
                                            CIP

∞ The paper used in this publication meets the minimum requirements of the American National Standard for Information Sciences—Permanence of Paper for Printed Library Materials,
ANSI Z39.48-1984.

Contents

For James R. Milkey
Thank you for true love and great happiness

And for my parents
Thank you for your unflagging faith in me

Acknowledgments

This book has been something of a joint venture: many friends and colleagues have contributed ideas, citations, and emotional support. The project began with the help of a wonderful thesis committee. Walter Dean Burnham's enthusiasm for the project produced reams of comments that would be the envy of most graduate students. Joshua Cohen repeatedly read the manuscript; he deserves major credit for the coherence and clarity of the piece. Michael Lipsky's unconditional support and good advice helped me to maintain my perspective. Thomas Ferguson initially sparked my interest in business. Ben Page, my colleague at Northwestern and the editor of this series, became godfather to the manuscript and deserves a standing ovation for his many contributions. Ongoing conversations with Jim Shoch and Jimmy Grey Pope helped me to think through many theoretical concerns. Others who have contributed to the development of this project include Alan Altshuler, Karl Henrik Bentzen, Suzanne Berger, Dennis Chong, Peter Monk Christiansen, Steve Elkin, Christine Herrington, Joel Krieger, Herb Jacob, Dave Jacobs, Tim Knudsen, Richard Lester, Jenny Mansbridge, Ann Markussen, Michael McCann, Guy Molyneux, Hans Jørgen Nilsen, David Olson, Dennis Quinn, Bent Schou, John and Evie Stephen, David Vogel, Dick Weatherley, and Jung-En Woo.

I would also like to acknowledge others working in the tax field and urge you to read their books as well: Jeff Birnbaum, Susan Hansen, Dennis Ippolito, Ron King, Margaret Levi, Catherine Rudder, Stein Steinmo, Randy Strahan, and John Witte. I benefited greatly from discussions with my fellow graduate students at MIT (and Harvard): Catherine Boone, Carol Conoway, Charles Ferguson, Vicky Hattam, Sylvia Maxfield, Greg Nowell, Jenny Purnell, Gretchan Ritter, Peter Truboitz, Joe Schwartz, and Ashu Varshney. Thanks also to my supportive colleagues at Northwestern and Boston University. John Tryneski has been a terrific editor at the University of Chicago Press. I greatly appreciate the financial help of the National Science Foundation's Doctoral Dissertation Improvement Program, and Northwestern University's university research grant program and Center for Urban Affairs and Policy Research. Lee Williams and the National Retail Federation (formerly the American Retail Federation) were very kind to provide me with the photograph in the Introduction. My deepest thanks go to the several hundred individuals in business and government who took the time to give me their insights about the tax policy process.

Just as this book was a joint venture with colleagues, it was also a family project. My mother, Mary MacKenzie, enthusiastically doubled as a research assistant and editor. Bob and Patty Martin publicized the forthcoming piece throughout the Midwest. Mary and Jim Kozlowski donated airline passes to do research. Robin and John Hanley provided a weekend retreat during the Chicago years. Jimmy and Julie Martin promised to coerce their friends into buying copies. Polly Taylor marveled at the project. Katy, Michael, Patty, Joey, Jay, and Christina wished that Aunt Coco would work less and play more. Bob and Ruth Milkey, Joanne and Michael Ertel, John Milkey, and Lindley Boegehold enthusiastically welcomed an academic to the family. Kari Moe's adventures in real politics have provided fodder for the intellectual gristmill over many years. Nora Dudwick's studies of political anthropology have opened my mind to new directions. Gary Humes provided bed and breakfast during many trips to Washington. The Brewer family, Janice Mallman, Janice Kettler, Florence Cohen, and Jennifer Phillips reminded me that there was more to my life than political science. Kuniko Shiotani, Marianne and Jørgen Ole Børch, Jens and Lisa Koch, Maryse Igout Pedersen, Ib Hørlyck, and Elisabeth Møller have sought to broaden my distinctly American world view.

In a class by himself (in many ways) I come to my husband, James R. Milkey. His love has given me the strength and peace of mind to write this book. With all of this help, I have no one but myself to blame for its shortcomings.

Introduction: Corporate Taxation in Pursuit of Growth

Her eyes were open, but she still beheld,
Now wide awake, the vision of her sleep:
There was a painful change, that nigh expell'd
The blisses of her dream so pure and deep.
John Keats, "The Eve of St. Agnes"

Paradigm shifts are intriguing: those Saint Agnes Eve moments when Porphyro suddenly appears to one in the flesh, stripped of dream-state interpretations and disappointing in comparison. The "What did I ever see in this guy?" syndrome boggles the mind. How can one enthusiastically embrace a choice, belief, or style, only to equally resolutely abandon one's preference or understanding later? If transitions in the personal realm are baffling, shifts in national policy are even more so. The mass exodus of elite and public opinion from one worldview to another both challenges one's sense of the rational and disrupts policy and politics as usual.

U.S. corporate income taxation is a compelling example of policy-making at its least consistent. Since the Second World War the progressive and universal tax structure has been eroded by selective incentives to achieve economic goals, contributing over time to a much smaller corporate share of the total tax burden. Yet this trend toward long-term decline has been marked by many reversals. Swings between the opposite poles of taxation sometimes wax violent: the largest corporate tax decrease in U.S. history was legislated in 1981. Immediately thereafter, in 1982, many of the 1981 provisions were rescinded with the enactment of the largest peacetime tax increase ever. The Tax Reform Act of 1986 increased corporate taxes even more.

In fact, corporate tax policy has experienced three paradigm shifts in the past quarter-century.[1] A "commercial Keynesian" growth strategy organized economic policy in the 1960s, encouraging capital-intensive mass production with correspondingly high levels of consumption: in modern language, there was a dual focus on supply and demand.[2] A progressive individual income tax was instituted to stimulate demand by shifting the burden off lower-income individuals, the ones most likely to consume marginal income. The supply side was addressed with selective growth incentives, largely in the corporate tax code, to encourage savings and investment. Figure 1 pokes fun at the Keynesian enthusiasm for spending one's way to economic growth.

"Are you so selfish that you can sit there and watch our national economy go to pieces just because you don't happen to _need_ a new car?"

Figure 1. Drawing by Claude; © 1956, 1984. The New Yorker Magazine, Inc.

Twenty years later, the notion that consumption would enhance growth was definitely passé, as shown in figure 2. Keynesian stability had been disrupted by economic crisis in the 1970s: productivity growth rates dropped, and inflation and unemployment persisted simultaneously. At this point the policy-making community began to promulgate a new approach to growth. Critics of Keynes attributed the sharp drop in productivity to lagging investment and insufficient available capital. The new economic philosophy argued that growth could be achieved through an increased emphasis on savings and investment, particularly in steel mills and other capital-intensive sectors of the economy.[3] The new approach, what I call the "hyper-accumulation" strategy, differed from the older one in that it upset the balance between consumption and accumulation which Keynesians had hoped to achieve.[4] The hyper-accumulation strategy peaked in 1981 with the Economic Recovery Tax Act, which created new incentives or expanded old ones to stimulate accumulation.

But expansion of investment incentives in 1978 and 1981 failed to engineer the promised supply-side recovery, and concerns about economic viability continued. America's declining position in the world market suggested a new worry: that many industrial sectors had lost their competitive edge. This made the preferential treatment of capital-intensive sectors seem less fair. At the same time rapid growth in the small business, service, and high-technology sectors of the economy further weakened the bias toward capital-intensive manufacturing.

Figure 2. From Doonesbury. Copyright 1981 G. B. Trudeau. Reprinted with permission of Universal Press Syndicate. All rights reserved.

Figure 3. From *Federation Report,* a publication of the American Retail Federation, vol. 12, no. 48, p. 1.

By 1986 special incentives for savings and investment came to be frowned upon in much the same way that consumption-oriented progressive taxation had been renounced in the earlier period. Figure 3 depicts a member of the business community presenting Ways and Means Committee chair Dan Rostenkowski with a sledgehammer to help him pound tax reform through the House of Representatives. The 1986 Tax Reform Act eliminated most selective growth incentives in an effort to make the tax code neutral toward investment and drew inspiration from an entirely different set of economic beliefs.

This book investigates how sea-changes in U.S. corporate tax policy have occurred. I argue that these shifts have been brought about through the efforts of investment subsystems, coalitions of state and society actors organized around strategies for economic growth. The investment subsystem construct has two key features. First, tax policy is developed according to a general growth strategy. Different strategies of growth are possible; periodically a given approach will capture the public agenda and organize economic policy. Radical shifts which alter the tax distribution reflect changing conceptions about the best way for growth to occur. Thus, ideas and beliefs are part of the motivational structure for policy. By strategy I do not mean a consistent goal or ideology, unambiguously adhered to by its proponents. Rather, the growth strategy acts as a sort of rallying cry which unifies individuals for a variety of ideological and self-interested reasons.

The second feature of the investment subsystem has to do with the mechanisms by which a given growth strategy becomes hegemonic. State actors, pursuing their policy programs, mobilize potential allies in the business community to coalesce around these successive growth strategies. The logic of this coalition strategy rests on several observations.

First, both the state and society in America are extremely fragmented. Deep splits in the business community have prevented a clear class mandate from developing in the tax area. Three groups of sectors (finance and housing, capital-intensive manufacturing, and small business and service) hold vastly different tax preferences as well as distinct visions of how growth should occur. Each new direction in corporate taxation creates a new set of winners and losers. Fragmentation in the private sector is matched by fragmentation in government. An exaggerated separation of powers, federalism, overlapping jurisdictions, and the lack of clear authority hierarchies all contribute to a fragmented system with many competing points of power.

Second, this fragmentation has greatly constrained the presidential power necessary to modern economic policy-making. The Keynesian growth strategy demanded considerable governmental economic activism. Since the earliest years of the republic, such intervention was found only briefly, during the New Deal. Responsibility for this new management of the macroeconomy was vested in the presidency.[5] The Democratic presidents of the 1960s, Kennedy and Johnson, tied their political fortunes to the new activist agenda. Yet presidents received increased responsibility without the power to accomplish the task.[6] Their legislative partners consistently thwarted their ambitious programs. Key congressional committee chairmen, largely southern Democrats, were hostile to the interventionist state and resisted many presidential fiscal initiatives.

Presidents Kennedy and Johnson responded to their dilemma of responsibility without power with a political innovation: state-led public-private coalitions. These growth-oriented presidents and their political entrepreneurs began to cultivate business allies to mobilize support for their economic agenda and to fight their opponents in other branches and parties.[7] Although businessmen have always pressured political figures and presidents have always consulted key leaders of industry, the coalition strategy represented an innovation. The mobilization of business was much more systematic: trade associations representing entire industrial sectors were organized by presidential staff. White House advisers urged business groups to cultivate a political expertise hitherto underdeveloped in these organizations.

The coalition strategy has implications for the relative autonomy of the state. State actors are often portrayed in one of two ways: as autonomous, because they are insulated from private interests, or as captured by these interests. The view presented here differs: state entrepreneurs are seen as increasing their power vis-à-vis political enemies by cultivating and mobilizing private sector allies. Thus, the insulation-capture dichotomy misses the complex, symbiotic relationship often found between factions in state and society.

How do investment subsystems change over time? Economic transformation creates new technical problems to which the state must respond, problems which cannot be accounted for or resolved by the existing paradigm of growth. Alternative growth strategies are introduced into the unstable system as possible new organizing principles. A new strategy is appealing to different groups for different reasons. Economic change disrupts our theoretical understanding of reality. Professional economists are attracted to a new theory if it clarifies those issues which confound the explanatory power of the old. To politicians the threatening economic problems motivate a search for new ideas salable to the public as solutions. Politicians might lack a sophisticated grasp of the idea; but latching onto it, they make it a rallying cry.

Economic transformation assaults interests as well as ideas when it makes the existing set of political institutions and regulations inadequate to the task of promoting economic growth. Business leaders, especially in emerging sectors, may find that governmental policies hinder production or expansion. The changing climate of growth requires a different government infrastructure. Economic transformation alters the distribution of resources within the business community, upsetting the economic balance of power. The perceived political power of declining sectors may also suffer. Business groups which have benefited least from the prior system are the first to endorse an alternative growth strategy.

My explanation for the changes in corporate taxation both shares much with and differs from other models of policy-making. One set of authors have identified paradigm shifts as the cause for tax transitions. Stein argues that fiscal revolutions occur when professional economists radically revise their beliefs about economic functioning.[8] Weatherford agrees that ideology greatly shapes the course of economic policy.[9] My concept of changing growth strategies rests on paradigm shifts. Yet I do not believe that the power of a new idea alone is enough to engineer a transformation. Indeed, when neoclassical thinking regained center stage in corporate taxation in the late 1970s, a new idea did not triumph. Rather, a very old idea again became popular. This resurgence clearly had to do with the preceding paradigm's failure to explain current crisis conditions. But also important was the political attractiveness of the alternative worldview. My approach, then, searches out the political conditions necessary to incubate an alternative paradigm. This enables me to better explain why a set of ideas, such as tax reform, that circulated the Washington community for years suddenly gained in popularity.

A second set of authors have explained tax policy with capitalist state theory. The state is dependent on the economy for revenue; therefore, it is structurally constrained to take action which is in the best interests of the capitalist system and class. Fostering accumulation is at the heart of this task. At the same time the state is relatively autonomous, allowing it to act as a general manager of economic contradictions and the capitalist class.[10] When the state intervenes to manage economic crisis tendencies, it risks becoming the location for capitalist contradictions.[11] Therefore, the state must also work to maintain the legitimacy of the system. O'Connor blames the "fiscal crisis of the state" on the dual needs of accumulation and legitimation.[12] King has analyzed John F. Kennedy's tax policy as a function of state efforts to stimulate both accumulation and consumption.[13]

Capitalist state theory helps one to understand the broader structural context in which policy is developed. Concerns about accumulation do seem to establish the broad outlines of corporate taxation. I agree that tax policy choices are guided by larger strategic aims rather than simply evolving from a hopeless jumble of ad hoc, incremental actions.

I disagree with capitalist state theory, however, on several points. First, this theory implies that functional state action is easily deduced from the logic of economic development. I believe that accumulation can be organized in many different ways and explicitly reject economic determinism. Second, capitalist state theory inadequately theorizes the state and fails to specify who is pursuing functional ends. By identifying the microfoundations of support for an accumulation strategy within both state and society, I avoid this black box characterization of government. Finally, the position that the state acts in the long-term interests of the capitalist class becomes problematic when the state takes action which is dysfunctional. My model accepts that proponents are drawn to growth strategies for other than functional ends.

A third set of authors have explained tax trends, especially the limited success of reform, as a product of bureaucratic politics. Reese uses this type of explanation to discuss why tax reform achieved so little in the late 1960s and early 1970s. Government fragmentation with multiple decision points means that all tax changes must be negotiated. Policymakers often move in incremental steps in order to manage bureaucratic complexity.[14] Witte explains the steady erosion of the tax code as a product of the fragmented system's openness to interest group demands.[15]

These explanations accurately describe a tax code constructed in an incremental fashion and account for why the watersheds in corporate taxation have not been greater. Yet the occasional dramatic shifts in corporate taxation belie the absolute hegemony of bureaucratic norms. My focus is therefore on the broad outlines of corporate tax changes.

Finally, other scholars have used both interest group and state structure explanations to facilitate understanding of the tax universe. My model borrows heavily from each of these traditions. Points of convergence and divergence are presented in great detail in chapter 2.

To what extent does the investment subsystem concept pertain to other policy areas? Policy to some degree creates its own politics.[16] The distinctive characteristic of corporate taxation is its centrality to accumulation, to the state, and to business. This centrality accentuates the participation of and divisions within business, and deemphasizes the salience of labor and public opinion. Corporate taxation is largely a game of elites. Yet the politics of corporate taxation may be applicable to other related policy spheres. Many of the private sector lobbyists who interact with government on tax issues intervene in other realms: budget, trade, science, and monetary policy. The high level of state initiative in building coalitions in this bastion of accumulation, where one might expect the greatest degree of "capture," indicates that the state must intervene in other areas as well. Finally, since accumulation is at the heart of government, decisions made in the tax realm create structural constraints for other political problems.

I have avoided normative judgments about alternative investment strategies. This is not a book about what kind of tax system we should have, but rather about what processes shape the tax system we do have. Yet a practical motivation for this effort is to explore the political openings for effective economic restructuring. With the economic stagnation of the 1970s and the decline of America's competitive position in the world economy, economic renewal has recently been at the center of public attention. Various prescriptions, from targeted industrial policy to the restoration of free-market capitalism, have been suggested as a means of restoring competitiveness and rejuvenating the American economy. In light of this current preoccupation, it makes sense to evaluate the institutional context of government attempts to promote economic growth. Unlike some other advanced industrial economies (e.g., Japan and France), the United States federal government has never had a direct industrial policy to promote growth. Rather, the tax code has been used indirectly to further the economic agenda. Therefore, this book seeks to contribute to future policy efforts by exploring what has motivated past policy experiments.

The following pages tell a story of a series of case studies of corporate tax acts legislated since the early 1960s: the Revenue Acts of 1962 and 1964 (to be considered as a single case), the investment tax credit suspension of 1966 and the Tax Surcharge Act of 1968 (to be considered as a single case), the Economic Recovery Tax Act of 1981, the Tax Equity and Fiscal Responsibility Act of 1982, and the Tax Reform Act of 1986. The tax acts in 1964, 1981, and 1986 radically revised the tax code. Those in 1968 and 1982 were less revolutionary, but interesting in that they revised the fiscal revolution preceding them. The major growth incentives—the investment credit and accelerated depreciation—were at the center of all these discussions.

Data for the cases were drawn from the presidential archives, congressional hearings, trade association documents, and interviews with hundreds of private and public sector participants. To understand the underlying growth strategies, I identify the technical considerations of executive branch policymakers and examine how these assumptions changed over time. To explore business pressure, I reconstruct the pattern of business preferences in each tax case and the efforts of trade association representatives to influence the political process. The stories of how presidents use these coalitions to get their policy agendas passed and the resulting impact on policy make up the bulk of the empirical chapters.

1

Strategies of Growth and Corporate Taxation

Introduction

This chapter argues that shifts in corporate tax policy reflect an exper-
imentation with alternative growth strategies. The postwar tax structure was
developed in accordance with a "commercial Keynesian" growth strategy:
capital-intensive mass production coupled with mass consumption. This growth
strategy and its institutional supports served the economy well, producing
high growth rates in real income and productivity. Despite questions about
the proper balance between investment and consumption and between unemployment and inflation, this approach to growth seemed fairly successful.

The inflationary pressures of the Vietnam War coupled with a productivity
crisis in the 1970s signaled an end to the economic bliss of the post–World
War II period. OPEC machinations threw the economy into a recession from
which it has never quite recovered. The productivity growth rate dropped
abruptly, profits plummeted, and economic truisms such as the Phillips curve
no longer seemed to hold true. Consequently, Keynesian-inspired economic
institutions came under intense scrutiny, attacked as inadequate to guarantee
the continuing health of the economy.

Critics promoted a new growth strategy, what I call "hyper-accumulation,"
which was firmly grounded in neoclassical economics. They argued that
Keynesian policy gave insufficient attention to the investment side of the
growth calculus. Inadequate investment in capital goods had constrained the
expansion and modernization of industry, thereby precipitating the drop
in real income, profits, and productivity growth rates. Prominent business
groups, among the major proponents of the laissez-faire vision, demanded tax
incentives to restore investment and rejuvenate the economy from the supply
side. Tax policy, forged in accordance with these demands, significantly reduced the taxation of capital in the late 1970s and early 1980s.

Yet hyper-accumulation did not achieve enduring predominance. First, the
package of investment-oriented tax incentives and other policy innovations
failed to solve short-term economic problems. In part negated by a deflation-
ary monetary policy, the supply-side innovations of the 1981 tax act were

9

unable to increase investment. The recovery was ultimately led by increased consumer and government demand rather than by supply-side stimulants.

Second, evidence of structural change in the economy suggested that the old logic of accumulation was no longer satisfactory. Capital-intensive industrial sectors had enjoyed preferential treatment by the tax code for twenty-five years. Yet, the new international division of labor was eroding their competitive positions in the world economy. In addition, the economy seemed to be growing in new directions: small business firms as well as service, high technology, and knowledge-based industries provided new jobs and investment opportunities. Unable to share in many of the benefits provided by the existing tax code, emerging sectors called for a radical overhaul of the system. If emerging sectors were the source of future economic health, growth as well as equity concerns required that the tax code be made investment-neutral. Taxation in 1982 and 1986 reflected the shifting economic balance and changing investment strategy.

Trends in Corporate Taxation

Before exploring the growth strategies guiding corporate taxation, let us look more closely at broad tax trends during the postwar years. First, an immediately apparent phenomenon is that corporate taxation as a proportion of total tax revenues has greatly declined. About 30 percent of total tax revenues in the early 1950s, the corporate tax share dropped to 22 percent by the mid-1960s with the creation of the investment tax credit and accelerated depreciation. This trend accelerated in the 1970s, and by 1983 corporate tax's percent of total revenues was down to 6 percent.[1] The decline in corporate taxes has been made up for by an increase in payroll taxes (including items such as social security and unemployment insurance). Payroll taxes were only 4 percent of total tax revenue in 1945 but increased to 32.6 percent in 1982.[2] Parallel to the redistribution of corporate taxes and payroll taxes, the top individual marginal rate has fallen over time (see table 1.1).

This shift in the tax burden is a problem if one supports a progressive tax system: a structure in which higher-income individuals pay greater percentages of their income in taxes. The progressive individual income tax and the corporate tax tend to be disproportionately borne by upper-income individuals. But payroll taxes, calculated as a fixed percentage of income and not applicable above a certain income level, extract a larger relative share from lower-income people. The income tax system becomes even more regressive when effective rather than nominal rates are considered. Effective rates calculate in the many deductions and credits selectively available to high-income taxpayers.[3] The addition of state and local taxes, which tend to be very regressive, further erodes progressivity.[4]

A Western European comparison puts the decline of the corporate tax bur-

Table 1.1. Federal Budget Receipts, by Source, Fiscal Years 1955–82

FY	Individual	Corporate	Payroll
1955	43.9%	27.3%	12.0%
1960	44.0	23.2	15.9
1965	41.8	21.8	19.1
1970	46.9	17.0	23.0
1975	43.9	14.6	30.3
1980	47.2	12.5	30.5
1982	48.2	8.0	32.6
1983	48.1	6.2	34.8
1984	44.8	8.5	35.9
1987	43.2	12.4	35.8

Source: Selected data drawn from table by Joseph Pechman, *Federal Tax Policy* (Washington, DC: Brookings Institution, 1983), appendix table D-4, p. 353. Pechman data drawn from the Office of Management and Budget.

Table 1.2. Tax Revenue's Percent of Gross Domestic Product

Country	1955	1965	1980
United States	24.6	26.5	30.7
Great Britain	29.8	30.8	35.9
West Germany	30.8	31.6	37.2
France	32.9	35	41.2
Sweden	25.5	35.6	49.9

den in a somewhat different light. Total tax revenue as a percentage of gross domestic product is lower in the United States than it is in many other advanced industrialized countries (see table 1.2).[5] But corporate taxation in the United States makes up a larger percentage of the total policy package. Thus, in the United States in 1980 the corporate income tax was 11.1 percent; in Great Britain, 7.6 percent; in West Germany, 6 percent; in France, 4.7 percent; and in Sweden, 3.1 percent. Yet the corporate burden is actually larger in these countries than the figures would indicate: all rely heavily on indirect consumption taxes, part of which are borne by corporations.[6]

A key way in which the U.S. corporate tax system deviates from its counterparts elsewhere is that the erosion of the corporate tax burden has largely taken place with the development of selective tax deductions and credits rather than with across-the-board rate cuts. (A taxpayer subtracts credits from his/her income tax liability, and deductions from the taxable income base.) Although the actual top corporate rate declined only 4 percentage points between 1954 and 1985, the effective tax rates of many sectors decreased dramatically during this period. Steinmo notes many more tax expenditures in the United States than in the other countries in his study.[7]

Most of the corporate deductions and credits were developed as growth incentives to stimulate savings and investment behavior. The largest growth incentives are the investment tax credit and the accelerated depreciation allowance. With the investment tax credit, a corporation could take a tax credit of 10 percent of the cost of a capital investment. The investment tax credit allowed firms to subtract approximately $90 billion from their tax bills between 1962 and 1981. Between 1954 and 1980, the accelerated depreciation allowance added up to almost $30 billion in tax expenditures. Under the 1981 tax act the depreciation allowance was expected to be worth $30 billion a year.[8]

This array of tax expenditures has contributed to the second major trend in corporate taxation: the change in the distribution of the revenue burden. Businesses benefit differentially from the selective growth incentives. Feld found the selective incentives to benefit large corporations disproportionately.[9] Lugar suggested that tax incentives are disproportionately available to firms with capital-intensive production processes, growing markets, large-scale operations, and high profits. Using 1975 data, he found the "receipt of new tax credits per dollar of net income" to be as low as $0.004 in the food and food-processing industry and as high as $0.071 in the lumber and wood products industry.[10]

Because a firm's ability to use these selective tax incentives affects its tax burden, there has been a significant change in the distribution of the corporate income tax. By 1980 capital-intensive manufacturers were paying much lower effective tax rates than labor-intensive manufacturing and service sectors. The Economic Recovery Tax Act of 1981 exacerbated these differences, largely through the accelerated depreciation and safe harbor leasing provisions. *Tax Notes* calculated the tax burdens of major corporations in different industrial sectors and found the rates shown in table 1.3.[11]

A final trend in corporate taxation has been its inconsistency. Within the context of a long-term drop of total tax revenues, corporate taxation has been characterized by the same stop-go quality which has plagued macroeconomic policy generally in the United States. Major tax acts have been passed every few years since 1962, frequently reversing policy. The investment tax credit, to take one example, was created in 1962, suspended in 1966, reinstated in 1967, revoked in 1969, reinstated in 1971, expanded in 1981, contracted in 1982, and revoked in 1986. Corporate taxes were 4.2 percent of the GNP in 1960, dropped to 3.6 percent in 1962 when the investment tax credit was created, and went up to 4.3 percent in 1967 after the credit was suspended. The Economic Recovery Tax Act brought corporate taxes down to 2.1 percent of the GNP in 1981 and 1.6 percent in 1982.[12]

Most dramatic have been the shifts in the 1980s. The Economic Recovery Tax Act of 1981 was scheduled to cut taxes by $748.9 billion during FY1981–86. About 20 percent of the total, or $153.6 billion, was to be in business taxes. Growth was also pursued through the individual income tax with the creation of savings provisions (amounting to a $20.4 billion cut) and a $15.4 billion decrease in estate and gift taxes.[13] But with the passage of the

Table 1.3. Effective Tax Rates by Industrial Sector (%)

Industry	1980	1981
All sectors		20.5
Capital-intensive:		
Mining	14.4	9.4
Paper and wood products	11.1	4
Transportation	11.9	−4.8
Utilities	8.5	11.5
Aerospace	27.4	13.5
Chemicals	18.8	13.6
Labor-intensive:		
Publishing and printing	38.2	36.3
Tobacco	34.2	31.4
Food retailers	31.5	30.8
Nonfood retail	27.2	22
High technology:		
Electronic and appliance	33.5	29.3
Office equipment	23.0	26.7
Financial:		
Commercial banks		−12.6

Tax Equity and Fiscal Responsibility Act (TEFRA) the following year, taxes were scheduled to increase by $205.3 billion during FY1983–87. About one-half of this increase, or $103.4 billion, was in corporate taxation. Among other changes, TEFRA rescinded about one-third of the Accelerated Cost Recovery System (ACRS) benefits which had been legislated the previous year.[14] One corporate lobbyist concluded, "The Lord giveth, the Lord taketh away."[15]

The most recent attack on this long-term trend was the Tax Reform Act of 1986, which returned corporate taxes to 1970s levels.[16] Even more significant than the aggregate figures was the reform effort's treatment of the growth incentives. Accelerated depreciation was scaled back, the investment tax credit was revoked, and a myriad of other savings and investment incentives were repealed.[17]

Convention wisdom suggests that the frequent policy reversals represent a tension between goals of equity and growth. Indeed, it would appear that two very different schools of thought influence the course of tax policy: the progressivity approach and the economic incentive approach. The progressivity school suggests that a tax system is legitimate only if applied equitably. The economic incentive approach holds that tax policy should promote economic growth, thereby maximizing benefits for all by creating a bigger economic pie. Concerns about the allocation of that economic pie should take second place to the efforts to enlarge it.

Specific provisions and concepts of taxation are associated with each approach. The economic incentive or growth school has produced a number of special incentives designed to minimize the tax system's interference with work, savings, investment, and risk taking. The following provisions should be included:

—low marginal rates for the individual income tax, to encourage additional work
—low rates on capital gains, to encourage investment in risky undertakings
—investment tax credit, to encourage investment in capital goods by lowering the cost of this investment
—accelerated depreciation allowances for capital outlays, to generate new funds for corporations and stimulate further investment
—lower corporate rates, to increase the internal funds available to corporations for reinvestment
—savings incentives such as the individual retirement accounts which delay taxing interest on earnings saved for retirement
—depletion allowance, to motivate extractive industries to conduct exploratory drilling
—bad debt deduction, to protect banks against bad loans so they will be willing to finance risky ventures

Provisions associated with the progressivity or equity school tend to emphasize horizontal equity or universality, and vertical equity or progressivity in the tax code. Horizontal equity means that individuals or corporations with equal incomes should pay equal taxes. The tax code should be as universal as possible in its application. Here economic incentives are seen as "loopholes" which distort the equity of the code. Vertical equity or progressivity tailors the tax burden to one's ability to pay. Provisions which reflect the equity school include:

—progressive individual rates
—capital gains taxed as ordinary income
—no special investment incentives
—depreciation allowances based on actual asset lives
—corporate rates commensurate with upper-income individual rates
—no special savings incentives: unearned income should be taxed at least as much if not more than earned income

Tax acts since 1960 have fluctuated between these two approaches. At times acts seem to represent a blend of philosophies. Some of the major reform acts, for example, have reduced tax incentives to achieve horizontal equity. The top rates have been lowered at the same time, in keeping with the economic incentive school (see table 1.4).

One could surmise that the fluctuations in corporate taxation reflect cycles of reform. Yet several problems militate against this simple conclusion. First,

Table 1.4. Goals of Tax Acts: Growth versus Equity

Year	School	Provisions
1962	Growth	Investment tax credit created
		Depreciation schedules speeded up
1964	Mixed	Growth: top individual rate lowered
		Equity: loopholes targeted for reform
1966	Equity	Investment tax credit suspended
1968	Mixed	Surtax—difficult to categorize
1969	Equity	Capital gains tax increased
		Personal exemption increased
		Equity: investment tax credit repealed
1971	Growth	Accelerated depreciation with ADLs
1976	Equity	Increased minimum tax rate
		Added minimum tax preference for intangible drilling costs
		Extended holding period for long-term capital gains from 6 months to 1 year
		Reforms in foreign income taxation
1978	Growth	Major reduction in capital gains tax
		Permanent extension of investment tax credit and expansion to 90 percent
1979	Equity	Windfall profits tax on oil
1981	Growth	Lowered all individual rates
		Lowered top rate on unearned income
		Accelerated cost recovery system (ACRS)
		Safe harbor leasing
		Expanded IRAs, making interest-free savings available to all
1982	Equity	Rescinded ⅓ of the ACRS benefits
		Minimum tax expanded
		Repealed safe harbor leasing
1986	Mixed	Revocation of many selective incentives, producing greater horizontal equity
		Progressivity effectively abandoned, producing less vertical equity

such an explanation demands a theory of the conditions (economic and otherwise) under which equity concerns become important. Second, the mantle of reform is routinely claimed by both sides in tax battles; it is a concept which means many things to many people. Third, ideas have a political and economic context which cannot be ignored.

A Growth-oriented Explanation of Corporate Taxation

Tax analysts have explained the general decline in corporate taxes as an effort to stimulate economic growth. The primary function of taxation is to raise revenue. Yet a capitalist-state analysis suggests that this should be done in a way that promotes economic growth (since the state is dependent on the private economy for revenue) and simultaneously achieves equity (to maintain

the legitimacy of the democratic state.)[18] King argues that growth replaced
equity as the central aim of policymakers when government analysts refor-
mulated taxation in non-zero-sum terms. Determined to augment the total
economic pie and maintain U.S. hegemony in the international political
economy, policymakers recognized that the public good was tied to the interests of capitalists and taxed accordingly.[19] O'Connor posits a tension between
accumulation and legitimation: attempts to address both have produced the
fiscal crisis of the state.[20]

This causal reasoning has an intuitive appeal. Many of the selective tax
incentives which have eroded aggregate corporate tax levels were advanced in
the name of growth. Yet the growth mandate has a deterministic flavor: an
enlightened awakening to the logic of capitalist development inevitably sets
the agenda for corporate taxation. Nor can the concept of a fixed growth
mandate easily accommodate the inconsistencies and reversals in corporate
taxation.

A theoretical construct which emphasizes the centrality of growth to public
policy but rejects the deterministic aspects of this process is the "regime of
accumulation," developed by the French regulation school. A regime of accumulation describes a general strategy to achieve growth and the institutional
arrangements which coordinate production and consumption to this end.[21] The
regime of accumulation specifies the conditions regulating the use of labor,
wage relations, investment, and the monetary system.[22]

The concept of a regime of accumulation is based on three premises. First,
there are a number of ways to combine resources to produce economic
growth, as illustrated by the switch from craft to mass production.[23] Second,
the forces of production are constantly being developed; an economic system
is dynamic rather than static. This means that the constantly changing system
cannot automatically replicate itself through the market law of supply and
demand. Rather, a set of institutional arrangements are necessary to channel
behavior in ways that perpetuate growth and reproduce the system.[24] Third,
different strategies for economic growth favor very different sectors of capital,
creating winners and losers. Therefore, choice of strategy becomes a point of
contention; regimes are developed through political struggle.[25]

A major crisis occurs in a regime of accumulation when the institutions
cannot continue to assure the conditions necessary for growth. This may be
because the regime of accumulation itself has exhausted its potential or because the existing modes of regulation hold back the emergence of a new
regime.[26]

The "regime of accumulation" construct has been criticized on a number
of grounds. One problem has to do with the establishment of the temporal
boundaries of the regime: what has been called the Fordist regime could con-
ceivably be dated from several different points.[27] Disagreements also exist
over the extent to which the Fordist institutional arrangements, such as the
labor-management accord, really represent a strategy. Indeed, Henry Ford

himself never endorsed many of the assumptions about growth associated with the strategy which bears his name.[28] Distinguishing between regimes is difficult. Competing modes of production seem to exist in every period, and mass production itself is not a unitary phenomenon. Conflicting reasons have been given for the decline of the Fordist period.[29]

These criticisms should not be dismissed lightly. Fordism is probably a misnomer: many of the institutional supports were not established until the New Deal and continued to evolve for years thereafter. Boundaries between periods are not easily identified. Policies of each period have often been inconsistent and dysfunctional. Regimes of accumulation should, therefore, be considered ideal types rather than empirical absolutes.

Despite these drawbacks, the tax case demonstrates that general strategies of growth do seem to dominate historical periods. Therefore, I use the concept of "growth strategy" to describe an economy loosely organized around a dominant model of growth and the role played by institutions in channeling economic activity.

The Postwar Fordist/Keynesian Growth Strategy

Components of a Fordist/Keynesian growth strategy began to evolve during the New Deal to organize economic development in the United States.[30] A Fordist regime has two primary identifying features: mass production and the large-scale organization of consumption, with considerable coordination between the two spheres. Fordist mass production breaks down the labor process into narrow tasks, and scientifically organizes and coordinates semiskilled workers into assembly lines to perform these tasks. Special purpose (product-specific or dedicated) machines are introduced into the process to augment worker efforts. Thus, the process is more capital-intensive than other forms of production.[31] This production system leads to much higher levels of output.

Proper functioning of the system depends on a large and stable market, and consistent, high rates of capital investment. First, the rigidity of resources in mass production demands a stable market. Capital-intensive manufacturing entails high fixed costs; dedicated equipment and narrowly trained workers cannot be easily reapplied to other types of products. If the market for a product dries up and makes resources obsolete, economic dislocation results. Mass production also greatly expands output, making a large market necessary.[32] Second, mass production processes require high levels of investment because they are capital-intensive. These costs can be partially offset by productivity increases which expand output for each unit of input. But productivity growth requires a high degree of technological innovation, in itself a costly venture.

The reproduction of the Fordist system depends on the dual tasks of maintaining adequate levels of investment and consumption. The system has been reproduced with a set of institutional arrangements including cooperative labor relations, a stable monetary and credit system, the social welfare state, and macroeconomic policy. The last is central to our concern.

Beginning with the Employment Act of 1946, the federal government undertook to oversee the economy and maintain a stable business climate through macroeconomic stabilization policies that involved the income tax structure among other tools. The paradigmatic basis for these policies was predominantly Keynesian, although neoclassical arguments were also woven into the rationale. Deviating from neoclassical economics, Keynesian theory posited that the self-regulating market suffered from crisis tendencies toward inadequate investment and underconsumption. These tendencies could be offset by government interventions to subsidize investment and stimulate demand. Keynesian policy was thereby tailored to reinforce the pillars of the Fordist order: mass production and mass consumption.

Neoclassical economics portrayed an economy characterized by continuously clearing competitive markets, flexible prices, and an efficient decentralized price system. Since flexible prices continually adjusted to match demand and supply, involuntary unemployment and inadequate demand were not problems and government intervention was unnecessary. To neoclassical economists growth in supply was the avenue to economic prosperity. Supply would grow through saving, investment, and technological innovation.[33]

Keynesian economics deviated sharply from the classical vision of the economy. Inspired by the Great Crash of 1929, Keynes and his followers believed that market regulation alone is insufficient for a healthy economy. Prices are not completely flexible; therefore, the market will not always clear to bring supply and demand into balance. This puts both investment and consumption at risk.

First, capitalist production is plagued by inadequate consumption because output cannot easily be scaled back in response to reduced demand. Output is partially fixed by the production capacity of the machinery, and prices for products are constrained by the wage rigidity of labor. This creates a tendency toward overproduction.[34]

Second, investment is a problem in the Keynesian universe. An external shock could lower interest rates so much that individuals would no longer be willing to hold securities or private debt, reducing the funds necessary for private investment to achieve full employment. Wage rigidity would keep the price of labor from falling as low as its market equilibrium clearing point, thus creating unemployment. The shock could so shake business confidence that even a very large decline in interest rates would not restore confidence, creating an investment gap and high unemployment. The structural characteristics of capitalism also threaten adequate investment. As production becomes more capital-intensive, the productivity growth rate will decline and the rates of return on investment will fall, thus reducing the profitability of investment just when increased resources are needed to sustain full employment.[35]

Although common wisdom characterizes Keynesian intervention as demand-oriented, the postwar regime never entirely abandoned concerns about supply. This was reinforced by the fact that the peculiar brand of Keynesianism which developed in the United States was inherently conservative: what Collins called "commercial Keynesianism." [36] Bosworth writes:

> Yet it is wrong to believe that economic research or economic policy ignored the issue of supply in the postwar period. The reference of Alfred Marshall to supply and demand acting as "two blades of the scissors" became a cliché; economic growth and the determinants of capital formation were among the more active subjects of economic research; and the postwar history of economic policy in the industrial countries is replete with efforts to encourage faster growth of aggregate supply . . . the analytical and prescriptive framework remained highly classical in its view of the determinants of growth of potential output, while adopting a Keynesian perspective on demand. [37]

Tax Policy and the Commercial Keynesian Order

Keynesian economists called for an activist government to address the dual problems of investment and consumption and to generally stabilize the macroeconomy. The federal income tax structure was an important tool to this end. Adequate consumption was achieved primarily by making the personal tax rates nominally progressive. Progressivity stimulated higher demand, transferring a larger proportion of income to lower-income individuals with the greatest marginal propensity to consume. Over time this progressivity was compromised: the marginal top rate on individual income, originally at 91 percent, was lowered to 70 percent in 1964, 50 percent in 1981, and 28 percent in 1986. The top corporate rate dropped to 70 percent in 1964, 46 percent in 1981, and 36 percent in 1986.

The tax code also encouraged demand with a variety of tax subsidies for credit. For example, consumer spending was subsidized with tax deductions for interest on consumer loans. The government encouraged consumer loans with a partial guarantee to banks in the form of the bad debt reserve deduction, which allowed financial institutions to shelter part of their earnings from taxes to protect against bad debts.

The tax system subsidized investment through selective tax incentives which encouraged savings behavior and the rapid replacement of capital plant and equipment. The most important of these incentives were the accelerated depreciation deduction and the investment tax credit. Capital assets (plant and equipment) become obsolete or worn out over time. The tax code recognizes this depreciation as a normal cost of doing business and allows firms to deduct the cost of the asset over its useful life. Accelerated depreciation allows assets to be written off in a shorter period of time, in order to encourage more rapid replacement of capital and the modernization and expansion of production.

Investment incentives were created with the Revenue Code of 1954, the first year in which accelerated depreciation was formally recognized as a device to inspire economic growth.[38] The 1954 tax act allowed an asset to be depreciated in one-half of its useful life. But the Eisenhower years were judicious in the targeted use of the tax code for economic and social ends. Growth incentives were only widely used after the Democrats came into power in the 1960s. A landmark in the use of selective growth incentives was the 1962 development of the investment tax credit, which allowed 7 percent of the cost of a capital asset to be subtracted from taxes in the year of purchase. As with the accelerated depreciation deduction, the function of the investment tax credit was to encourage the rapid replacement of capital assets.

Finally, the tax code was used for macroeconomic stabilization purposes to counteract the highs and lows of the business cycle. The government injected resources into the economy to stimulate private economic activity during periods of slow growth and to pull resources from the economy during booms. This intervention was said to have a multiplier effect: one unit of government intervention sets off successive waves of entrepreneurial activity in the private economy, increasing GNP by a multiple of the initial intervention. The tax system functions to stabilize the economy both in its discretionary application and in its automatic impact.[39]

Despite the ascendancy of the Keynesian paradigm (or its hybrid, commercial Keynesianism), conflict over tax options continued to exist. This primarily concerned the trade-offs between the goals of equity and growth and tensions within each goal.[40] First were conflicts about equity itself: to what extent were the progressive tax system and the selective growth incentives equitable? Some analysts supported progressive rates as necessary to achieve vertical equity. Progressivity is premised on the declining marginal utility of additional income. As income increases and families can devote more resources to luxury items, each dollar means less. So a truly equitable tax system should place higher tax rates on marginal income. According to an "ability to pay" criterion, one is able to pay proportionately more taxes as income increases. Sacrifice theory seeks to ensure that all should make the same sacrifice.[41] Benefits theory suggests that those who get the most benefits from society should pay accordingly.[42] Measuring the rate of the declining utility of money and the value of satisfaction or sacrifice poses problems for the progressivity argument. Critics charge that progressivity distorts fairness, compromises universality, and interferes with the a priori legitimacy of property rights.[43]

Equity disputes about corporate taxation focus on the double taxation of distributed corporate income (as corporate profit and as stockholder dividends). The creation of selective tax incentives also has raised equity questions. Although the myriad of tax incentives were created to promote social and economic goals, the cumulative effect was to distort the horizontal equity of the code and threaten the legitimacy of the tax system. The issue was complicated by a dispute about who actually pays corporate taxes. Undoubtedly some of the corporate tax burden is shifted backward onto labor and forward to the consumer, yet the amount shifted is widely disputed.[44]

A second troubling issue during Lord Keynes's American rule was the right mix between accumulation and consumption, although policymakers believed this to be a matter of fine tuning. A final set of conflicts were technical matters concerning the right mixture of policies to achieve growth. A healthy economy is characterized by both a stable noninflated currency and steady growth. Stagnation or the absence of growth increases unemployment, constrains business profits, and prevents increases in the standard of living. Inflation erodes the income of persons on fixed income, makes it harder for businesses to replace outdated equipment, and devalues assets held in money.

These requisites for growth are not always compatible. Keynesian economists determined that there is a reciprocal relationship between the problems of unemployment and inflation. The Phillips curve was a theoretical construct developed to demonstrate this fact. Gerald Epstein observes: "Both inflation and stagnation create problems. But inflation has become the only way to fight stagnation; and stagnation has become the only way to fight inflation." [45] LeLoup has identified the conflict between inflation and unemployment as a main source of inconsistency in congressional economic policy-making.[46] A related technical issue concerned the blend of fiscal policy and monetary policy.[47]

The domestic trade-offs between unemployment and inflation are complicated by an international component. Domestic inflation has a negative effect on the value of a nation's currency in international monetary markets. As more currency is pumped into the domestic economy and as this inflated money can buy fewer goods, foreign central bankers are more reluctant to hold the overvalued species.

Concern over the dollar's role as reserve currency was exacerbated in the 1960s by increasing balance-of-payment deficits. Balance-of-payment deficits became more politically salient when European bankers began to cash dollars for gold in the mid-1950s. By 1962 the U.S. possession of the "Free World's" monetary stock had decreased from 43 percent to 26 percent.[48] As more dollars were held abroad, there was increasing speculation that the dollar would at some point be devalued; its exchange rate would be lowered to reflect its real value. Should this happen, all the governments and individuals who held assets in dollars would lose money. Central bankers urged the United States to restrict liquidity, maintain low levels of inflation, and use fiscal policy over monetary policy for necessary domestic stimulation.[49]

The attempt to balance these somewhat competing goals of investment and consumption can be seen in the tax innovations of the early 1960s. Kennedy began his foray into the tax field with a supply-side creation: the investment tax credit. The investment tax credit was inspired by the twin economic problems facing the Kennedy administration: stagnation of domestic growth and balance-of-payment deficits. Kennedy advisers argued that an investment-led recovery would be less inflationary than a demand-led one. The investment credit was their supply-side solution.

Despite the stimulus of the investment tax credit, the macroeconomy continued to be sluggish in the early Kennedy years, barely recovering from the 1960–61 recession. Capital investment in 1962 increased only 8 percent instead of the hoped-for 15 percent; unemployment would not budge below 5.5 percent. Advisers worried that another recession was likely, just in time for the 1964 election.[50]

Policymakers now focused on the demand-side of the Keynesian balance, deciding to cut taxes to stimulate consumption. The Council of Economic Advisers wanted the tax reduction to be in the form of lower-income cuts, presented as a macroeconomic stabilization device and free from cuts in spending. The more conservative Treasury and most of the business community wanted the tax cut to be concentrated in upper-income levels, tied to reforms and spending reductions to compensate for the revenue loss, and presented in the neoclassical language of investment. The more conservative version was ultimately chosen, culminating in the 1964 tax cut.

In the late 1960s the issue became balancing monetary considerations with adequate domestic growth. Beginning in 1966 inflation began to build. Investment in 1966 exceeded 1965 levels by 17 percent, unemployment dropped to 1.9 percent in the machinery industry, and the stock market suffered, because of the incredibly high interest rates on bonds. Quarterly demand was increasing by $14 to $16 billion, and capacity was created which could set the economy up for a "post-Vietnam investment slump."[51]

Inadequate funding for the ever-expanding conflict in Vietnam and Johnson's expansive social vision doubtless contributed to inflation. The obvious solution to this dual drain on government coffers was a tax increase; Keynesian stabilization logic also pointed to this solution. The Council of Economic Advisers (CEA) feared that by delaying the tax hike "we could slow the inflation only by throwing the economy into reverse."[52] Advisers were concerned about the international implications of an inflated currency. They also realized that irresponsible fiscal policy could lead to a tightening of monetary policy which would constrain the economy. Gardner Ackley (CEA) wrote that without a tax increase

> the Fed will inevitably be forced to tighten money a great deal more putting further pressure on home building; threatening the solvency of many savings and loan associations; penalizing small businessmen, farmers, and moderate-income home buyers. To alleviate the high interest rates and take pressure off monetary policy a tax increase should be instituted.[53]

Yet increasing taxes seemed easier said than done. For one thing, a strange mix of liberals and conservatives opposed the measure. Liberals thought it would be used to pay for the war in Vietnam; conservatives, for the Great Society. Business support outside the financial community was also limited. But more to our point here, domestic policymakers were reluctant to suffer the consequences of slower growth for the sake of fighting inflation.

The major tax legislation of the period, the tax surcharge, was not enacted until 1968. This legislation applied an 8 percent surtax to individuals and corporations. Accompanying the tax was a $6 billion spending cut package.[54] In 1966, two years before the passage of the surtax, the investment tax credit was suspended as an interim measure. Yet the suspension of the investment credit was short-lived. In March of 1967, nine months before it was due to expire, President Johnson asked Congress to reinstate it.

The main reason why the credit was reinstated prematurely was that it had done its job almost too well. Machinery order backlogs dropped by 7 percent, interest rates on three-month Treasury bills plummeted, and planned investment increases for 1967 went up by only 4 percent. In short, the economy seemed destined for a recession. The investment tax credit was reinstated, and Johnson proposed his surtax five months later.

Thus the commercial Keynesian tax system sought to achieve simultaneously a variety of sometimes conflicting goals, resulting in somewhat contradictory directions in corporate taxation. Taxes would be raised one year to fight inflation or curb the boom in accordance with macroeconomic stabilization. The next year a weakening in the economy would elevate unemployment to the top of the public agenda. Expansion of the growth incentives over time produced a gradual erosion of the corporate tax burden. Yet in the golden age of the 1950s and 1960s the fundamental premises of the tax code seemed to be accepted. With fine tuning of the economy, policy analysts believed that compromise between contradictory goals was possible.

The Economic Crisis and Accompanying Assault on Keynes

An economic crisis upset this policy equilibrium. Although the 1973 oil crisis is often given as the starting point of the crisis, signs of economic weakening in the economy were apparent in the late 1960s.[55] The economic crisis was to call into question many tenets of the commercial Keynesian strategy.

Evidence of the poor performance of the economy took many forms. Most startling was the decline of the productivity growth rate. From 1948 to 1966 U.S. productivity grew at an annual rate of 3.3 percent; from 1966 to 1973, 2.1 percent; and from 1973 to 1978, 1.2 percent.[56] Although the productivity growth rate has declined in other countries as well, many nations have managed to narrow the gap between their levels of productivity and our own. For example, from 1960 to 1983 productivity (or real gross domestic product per employed person) grew only 1.2 percent in the United States. Comparable figures for other countries are 5.3 percent for Korea, 3.7 percent for France,

3.4 percent for Germany, 5.9 percent for Japan, and 2.3 percent for the United Kingdom.[57]

Total factor productivity, a measure of productivity keeping capital constant, also grew more slowly in the United States at only 1.9 percent per year from 1960 to 1973. During the same period, the Japanese rate grew at 6.6 percent; the Italian, at 5.8 percent; the French, at 3.9 percent; and the West German, at 3.2 percent.[58]

Mirroring the productivity problem was a decline of the U.S. competitive position in the world economy. The merchandise trade balance first went into deficit in 1972; by 1984 it was in the red by $140 billion. Even the competitive position of our "sunrise" industries was eroded. The President's Commission on Industrial Competitiveness reported that the United States had lost world market share in seven out of ten of the high-technology sectors.[59]

Also of concern were the high rates of both inflation and unemployment which plagued the economy during the troubled decade, threatening the validity of the Phillips curve relationship. Finally in the late 1970s the new Federal Reserve chair, Paul Volcker, attacked double digit inflation with an extremely stringent course of tight money. But this precipitated a deep recession, so that when Ronald Reagan was elected in 1980 real growth neared zero while inflation remained high.

The worsening economic conditions severely compromised individual prosperity. Businessmen suffered: the average net after-tax rate of profit of domestic nonfinancial corporations dropped from nearly 10 percent in 1965 to less than 6 percent by the second half of the 1970s.[60] The real pretax rate of return on capital (return on total assets in manufacturing) was also affected by the economic crisis: about 12 percent in 1965, it hovered between 4 and 6 percent during the 1970s, and dropped to under 2 percent in 1981.[61]

Workers suffered as well. Inflation-adjusted compensation increased dramatically from the early 1960s to the mid-1970s and then leveled off. Total real wages for the manufacture of durable goods dropped by 17.5 percent between 1973 and 1986; nondurable goods, by 9.7 percent.[62]

The Neoclassical Attack and the Hyper-accumulation Response

The economic crisis prompted a new generation of neoclassical economists to attack Keynesian policies and institutions.[63] As will be discussed later, business groups played a major role in this effort.[64] At the heart of the neoclassical critique of fiscal policy was the assertion that a capital shortage was responsible for the economic decline. Inadequate capital for investment had prevented American companies from expanding and modernizing. This served to curb productivity growth and provide an opening for foreign firms to gain market share. Capital investment contributes to productivity growth by expanding capacity, increasing capital intensity, and updating existing capital goods. Expanded production enables greater economies of scale and better production techniques. Updated capital goods are usually more technologically advanced; innovations enable more output per labor hour.[65]

Critics blamed the shortage of capital on Keynesian macroeconomic policy in general and taxation in particular. Tax policies constrained capital formation by increasing the costs of capital through an adverse treatment of savings and investment. Adversarial taxation, combined with inflation, therefore prevented growth in capital stock and contributed to the decline in productivity growth rates.[66]

Keynesians disagreed with this analysis of the problem, arguing that the productivity slowdown in the 1970s was due to the instability of demand and underutilization of existing capacity. Disruptions in the international commodity markets made demand unstable; this was exacerbated by vacillations in government policy. Lower demand depressed rates of return and profit margins. As Eisner wrote:

> The prime determinant of business investment is demand. Investment in plant and equipment falls off when the economy is sluggish and excess capacity makes additional plant and equipment unnecessary. In such a situation, moderate annual tax benefits to business would appear to have little effect, particularly in the short run. Well-run firms will not be led to invest by tax reductions which increase after-tax earnings but do not make additional equipment profitable in the face of existing idle capacity. Where demand is brisk, firms will invest without special subsidy.[67]

Thus, Keynesians and neoclassical critics had very different explanations for the slowdown. Let us now examine the arguments concerning savings, investment, and capital formation, since they are central to debates about corporate taxation.

Neoclassical economists argue that the tax system has constrained private savings: taxes on capital income consistently reduce the rate of return below the socially desirable amount. The optimal amount of savings is the before-tax or gross return to society from investment. Yet the actual amount is the after-tax or net return to individuals on savings. Historically the inflation-adjusted net return has been about 2 percent.[68] Corporate saving has also been constrained by a depreciation system based on purchase price rather than replacement value. During periods of high inflation, corporations are allowed inadequate deductions to replace assets.

Keynesians retort that the linkage between savings and after-tax rate of return is far from settled. Despite the many changes in the tax code, the private savings rate has remained almost constant, fluctuating around 16–18 percent since 1948.[69] Consistently high rates of gross corporate saving (7.3 percent of the GNP in 1929 and 8.4 percent in 1982) have been stimulated by high individual tax rates, preferential rate on capital gains, and depreciation allowances.[70]

Economists of all stripes are in agreement in worrying about the decline of public savings in the form of budget deficits. Averaging 2 percent of the GNP in the early 1970s, the deficit topped 5 percent in the 1980s. Deficits mean that public financing competes with private investment for a limited money supply, pushing up interest rates and further dampening investment. Former chairman of the Council of Economic Advisers Martin Feldstein argues that on the present track, budget deficits of 5 or 6 percent of the GNP could absorb all net private saving.[71] Paul Volcker puts it succinctly:

> [The] situation poses a strong potential for a clash between the need to finance the deficit and the rising financial requirements for housing and the business investment that is crucial to healthy and sustained recovery. In the end, all those needs have to be met out of saving, and all our experience suggests there isn't likely to be enough to go around.[72]

The relationship between taxes and investment is another point of contention between Keynesians and neoclassical critics. Neoclassical economists charge that taxes have constrained the after-tax rate of return on investment. This contributed to the declining growth of the capital/labor ratio.[73] The capital/labor ratio in the United States increased at an annual 1.6 percent between 1970 and 1980 in the private domestic business economy. Japanese increases for the same period were 8.3 percent per year.[74]

Keynesians disagree, arguing that the growth rate of U.S. investment in capital goods remained at normal levels during the period of decline. Capital investment in the nonfarm business economy increased 3.36 percent per year from 1957 to 1968, 4.17 percent from 1968 to 1973, and 3.25 percent from 1973 to 1979.[75] The decline of the capital/labor ratio was due to the extraordinary number of new workers in the workforce in the 1970s. The total hours of labor input annually increased 0.38 percent in 1948–65, 1.44 percent in 1965–73, and 1.42 percent in 1973–78.[76]

Neoclassical economists charge that tax disincentives to savings and investment reduced capital formation. Constraints on individual saving and investing behavior added up to an aggregate shortage of plant and equipment. In addition, the pool of funds available for investment were diverted to government social goals. Inflation made the replacement of existing capital goods even more expensive. Auerbach and Jorgensen suggest that a "widening gap between economic depreciation and capital consumption allowances for tax purposes" have made it even more difficult for businesses to recover their investments in capital goods.[77] Michael Boskin charged that by 1977 inflation had cost corporations $32.3 billion in an extra tax burden from distortions in inventory and capital cost accounting.[78]

Keynesians denied the existence of a capital shortage. First, if capital shortage were a problem, one should expect to find high rates of utilization of existing plant and equipment. Yet Kendrick found significantly lower patterns of capital utilization after 1973 in most of the nine OECD countries studied.[79]

Second, if the total capital stock is falling, one would think that a shortage of capital stock would drive up the price of capital (or the rate of return on capital). Yet the before-tax rate of return on capital has declined sharply since the mid-1960s: the total business sector rate was 11.2 percent in 1967 but down to 8.2 percent in 1980.[80] Third, Denison found little support for a linkage between inadequate capital and the slowdown of the productivity growth rate.[81]

The capital shortage dispute stems partly from measurement problems. For example, analysts disagree about the extent to which capital declines in efficiency with age.[82] Composition of capital stock also matters: a larger proportion of less durable capital stock makes the total capital stock figures decline. Another disagreement arises from whether to count capital investment in pollution control outlays. High rates of inflation further complicate the calculation of capital stock. Accelerated depreciation permits faster replacement of capital assets but skews the calculation of the value of existing capital goods. These systems of accelerated depreciation tend to be arbitrary and skew investment opportunities.[83]

The Hyper-accumulation Response

The conservative attack on Keynesian economic policy precipitated action in the corporate tax sphere: a cut in the taxes on capital. The new hyper-accumulation strategy was designed to stimulate growth from the supply side: if accumulation potential were assured, consumption would take care of itself. Charls Walker said, "Attention has shifted from the question of how income should be distributed to how it best can be produced."[84]

Tax legislation to expand investment incentives and stimulate the economy from the supply side was enacted on a small scale in 1978 and on a large scale in 1981. The 1978 legislation was initially sponsored by President Carter as a reform initiative. Yet a group of industry representatives, especially from the timber and high-technology sectors, struggled to gain control of the public agenda. They convinced congressional allies to make the lowering of taxation on capital gains the centerpiece of the legislation instead.

The Economic Recovery Tax Act of 1981 (ERTA) cut individual rates across the board by 23 percent, giving the greatest savings to upper brackets in order to encourage saving and investment. Corporate taxes were also greatly reduced through the expansion of investment incentives. A new system of depreciation, the Accelerated Cost Recovery System, abandoned the idea of useful lives altogether. ACRS lumped all assets into only four categories: most vehicles in three years, equipment in five years, and structures in fifteen years (with a few in ten years such as public utilities). The investment tax credit was expanded, and a host of other incentives enlarged or created.

George Kopits of the International Monetary Fund calculated the average "tax subsidy rate" on manufacturing investment for several advanced industrial countries. In 1973 the United States had a tax subsidy rate of 1.3 percent of asset price. Japan and West Germany taxed rather than subsidized capital: their rates were -3.4 percent and -6.7 percent, respectively. France and the United Kingdom had rates of 1.2 percent and 9.8 percent, respectively. After ERTA in 1981, the U.S. rate jumped dramatically to 12.8 percent; Japan had a rate of -3.4 percent; France, of 4.4 percent; Germany, of -5.5 percent; and the United Kingdom, of 13.1 percent.[85]

Post-Fordist Attack on Investment Incentives

The hyper-accumulation strategy's inability to remedy the escalating economic ills precipitated doubts about the efficacy of the selective tax incentives. The expected stimulus from the expanded investment incentives failed to immediately materialize and the economy sank deeper into recession. Investment in plant and equipment for all industry sank from $155.21 billion (1972 dollars) for the first quarter of 1981 to a low point of $138.89 for the first quarter of 1983. Not until the first quarter of 1984, when spending was back up to $161.75 billion (1972 dollars) did investment surpass the 1981 level.[86] When the economic recovery finally came, it was set off by the increased consumer spending that resulted from the huge cuts in individual rates. Therefore, the recovery was led by demand rather than by supply, in keeping with Keynesian analysis. An irony of the act was that, despite its language of accumulation and avowedly anti-Keynesian flavor, the individual tax cuts greatly outshone the investment measures as economic stimulants.

True believers in laissez-faire explained away the outcome. First, the investment incentives were never implemented in their pure form. The fiscal expansion was combined with a tight monetary policy designed to reign-in stampeding inflation. Monetary austerity, by driving up interest rates, deterred industry from investing and largely canceled out the expansionary impetus of the tax act. Second, the Tax Equity and Fiscal Responsibility Act (TEFRA) in 1982 took away many of the benefits of the 1981 bill; otherwise, investment would have been higher. Charles Hulton of the Urban Institute calculated that ERTA would cut the average tax rate on investments in new plant and equipment from 33 percent to 5 percent. TEFRA would increase it again to 16 percent.[87]

Laissez-faire proponents also maintained that the recovery was investment-led. Real GNP grew at an annual rate of 6.4 percent in the first seven quarters of the recovery, as opposed to an average rate of 5.5 percent in the five previous recoveries. Bosworth points out, however, that, although gross investment grew faster, net investment (adjusting for depletion of capital stock) grew at the same rate as it did after previous recoveries.[88]

Another major consequence of the 1981 tax act was the creation of huge budget deficits. The vast cuts in the personal tax rates ballooned an already growing budget deficit. Although the investment incentives cost less, they were implicated by association.

The perceived failure of the investment incentives drew attention to concerns about their distributive consequences and challenged the legitimacy of the measures. Some economists had long been worried about the effect of the investment tax credit and accelerated depreciation on the composition of capital assets in the economy. They feared that the tax incentives favored some kinds of investment over others. Thus the incentives might change the composition of investment rather than increase the total amount of capital.[89] The corporate tax system skewed investment from structures to equipment: income generated by structures is taxed at roughly 30 percent; that of equipment, at approximately 20 percent.[90] Corporate taxation also encouraged the replacement of labor for capital. As was mentioned earlier, these systematic biases produced very different effective tax rates across industrial sectors.

The distortions in the effective burden of corporate taxes paralleled similar distortions in the individual taxes. By the early 1980s the public was increasingly dissatisfied with the uneven application of the income tax. The Advisory Commission on Intergovernmental Relations routinely surveys public opinion on the fairness of the federal income, state income, state sales, and local property taxes. In 1972, 45 percent of those polled considered the local property tax to be least fair; only 19 percent found the federal income tax most offensive. By 1979, 37 percent considered the federal income tax least fair, as opposed to 27 percent who still hated the property tax even more.[91]

Skepticism over the selective tax incentives was reinforced by their failure to reverse the parade of imports into the domestic economy and the erosion of U.S. exporting capacity. Harrison and Bluestone point to the rise of imports as a percentage of the GNP originating in the U.S. manufacturing sector: 13.9 percent in 1969, 37.8 percent in 1979, 44.7 percent in 1986.[92] The investment inducements had disproportionately benefited capital-intensive manufacturing sectors, which were the pride of the American economy during the Keynesian golden age. Selective tax incentives for investment were therefore discredited when these manufacturing sectors continued to lose market share.

Dissatisfaction with the selective incentives was heightened by structural changes in the economy, and by the growing economic and political power of business sectors discriminated against by the old order. In the mid-1960s the profit shares of productive capital and "of circulating capital (financial, trade, ground-rent, petroleum and coal, transport, communications and services)" were about the same. In 1982 productive capital's profit share was 25 percent of the earlier level; circulating capital's share had increased by 60 percent.[93] Between 1979 and 1984 steel companies laid off 45 percent of their workforce. Exports of construction equipment dropped 63 percent from 1981 to 1983; machine tools dropped 60 percent in this period.[94]

Empirical evidence about sectoral change in the economy predicted significant economic restructuring in the coming years. Shifts in the composition of the economy are likely to generate new jobs in rapidly growing, "sunrise" industries; manufacturing sectors will lose jobs. Silvestri and Lukasiewicz project that the wholesale and retail trade and service sector will account for 80 percent of the total rise in employment between 1986 and 2000.[95] Increasing internationalization also works against a prominent role for government regulation of the economy, since national boundaries are becoming increasingly meaningless in the new world order.[96]

A New Investment Strategy: The Human Climate for Growth

The perceived failure of the ERTA stimulants shook faith in the dominant growth strategy. Although capital-intensive investment continued to be important, a growing number of analysts recognized the limits to this use of resources. It was argued that overinvestment can be as disastrous as underinvestment, especially at the cost of inappropriately replacing individuals with capital.[97] Overinnovation or the excessively rapid introduction of new technology also causes problems.[98] Since productivity depends on the human climate in which equipment is introduced, existing technology may not be used to its maximum.[99] Fascination with Japanese manufacturing processes reinforced the emphasis on strategies over pure capital investment.[100] Some analysts came to question the Fordist mass production organization of manufacturing.[101] These insights suggested that investment strategies should be partially redirected into human resources and knowledge-intensive industries and into cutting-edge technologies. These were also areas which offered comparative advantage to the United States in the international division of labor.

Dissatisfaction with the old accumulation strategy thus led to talk of a new post-industrial approach to growth. The post-industrial system would have the following components: Services and knowledge-intensive sectors would be much larger parts of the economy. Production processes would shift from Fordist mass production to "flexible specialization," which produces small-batch specialty products. Investment strategies would therefore also change from an emphasis on capital-intensive investment to an investment in human resources and knowledge-intensive industries. With a larger component of economic activity concentrated in services and more flexibility in manufacturing, it would no longer be necessary to maintain high levels of mass consumption for standardized products. Rather, firms would be more sensitive to fluctuations in consumption patterns. The necessity of government intervention would drop off with the decline in the need to coordinate large-scale mass production and mass consumption. Increasing internationalization would also work against a prominent role for government regulation of the economy, since national boundaries have become increasingly meaningless in the new world order.[102]

Dissatisfaction with the old approach to growth was tentatively demonstrated in the Tax Equity and Fiscal Responsibility Act of 1982 (TEFRA). In spirit and practice TEFRA was a partial repudiation of ERTA. Although the individual tax cuts, the centerpiece of ERTA, were left untouched, the corporate provisions were scaled back considerably. The Accelerated Cost Recovery System deductions were scaled back, the investment tax credit lowered, and some of the other incentives repealed.

TEFRA may be thought of as an effort to address the abuses of ERTA. The 1981 tax act reflected pork barrel politics at its worst, and many provisions found their way into the bill during a bidding war between Democrats and Republicans. Yet, in another sense, 1982 was a precursor of things to come: an assault on the investment incentives which had been the cornerstone of the government's growth strategy.

The Tax Reform Act of 1986 was a more direct attack on the old order. The reform act made profound cuts in the individual rates, continuing a trend of twenty-five years: the top rate was lowered from 50 percent to 28 percent. The act also cut the corporate rate, from 46 percent to 34 percent, but eliminated many of the selective growth incentives which had skewed the tax burdens among sectors. It abolished the investment tax credit, individual retirement accounts, consumer interest payments, and differential taxation of capital gains and cut back accelerated depreciation allowances. The bill transferred a $120 billion tax burden from individuals to corporations.

The tax act was explicitly motivated by a view of growth which differed from the older emphasis on capital investment. First, tax reform sought to achieve neutrality, or a "level playing field," with respect to investment capital. The administration explained that this would allocate investment funds in the most efficient and effective manner. Second, the tax changes aimed to revive investment in human resources. Third, tax reform was expected to improve competitiveness by improving the utilization of resources. Finally, the major remaining selective tax incentive, the research and development credit, was expected to shift investment into new sectors.[103]

The tax reform measure was also inspired by a Republican need to come up with an alternative to the Democratic industrial policy proposals. Industrial policy was designed to redistribute resources toward rapidly growing sectors. Republicans had similar goals but wanted to minimize state intervention. Tax reform offered a mechanism for negating the skews in investment incentives and redistributing resources, while limiting the direct involvement of government. Kenneth McLennan (of the Committee for Economic Development) explained:

> The Democratic Party's need to develop an alternative policy agenda to the Reagan Administration's approach has led to the advocacy of an industrial strategy based on policies which favor the development of specific economic sectors . . . In contrast, the Reagan Administration favors permitting the market system to identify and support

the expansion of promising economic sectors and to permit the automatic and gradual decline of sectors of the economy which have lost their comparative advantage . . . The issue is which of these extremes should play the dominant role in determining the nation's economic strategy for the next decade.[104]

Conclusion

This chapter has explored how the course of corporate taxation followed the waxing and waning of the commercial Keynesian growth strategy. The Kennedy administration revenue acts in 1962 and 1964 sought to stimulate capital-intensive investment and mass consumption, the twin requisites of the Fordist/Keynesian order. But the vitality of this approach was challenged by economic disintegration in the 1970s. When achievement of the Keynesian macroeconomic ambitions faltered, policymakers experimented with alternative growth strategies and taxed to these alternative ends. Neoclassical critics alleged that the Keynesian emphasis on demand actually harmed the economy by deterring saving and investment behavior and creating a capital shortage. The Economic Recovery Tax Act of 1981 sought to correct for inadequate accumulation by expanding tax incentives for investment and saving.

The expanded investment inducements failed to stimulate a supply-side recovery and served to distort economic decisions by making some investments more attractive than others. By the mid-1980s America seemed ready for yet another approach to growth. The Tax Reform Act of 1986 signified a new direction in tax policy.

The experimental, somewhat desultory nature of these probings indicates a certain indeterminacy in the creation of new growth strategies. The logic of capitalist development does not point unwaveringly toward a new paradigm. A strategy of growth differentially benefits groups in state and society, suggesting that political struggle may play a part in its genesis. In the next chapter we develop analytic tools for examining the political struggles which surround corporate taxation in pursuit of growth.

Appendix 1.1

Selected Prominent Growth Incentives

Until 1986 the top marginal rate on corporate income was 46 percent on income over $100,000.[105] Since 1982 a minimum tax of 15 percent has been applied to preference income (that sheltered from taxes by the various deductions) above $10,000.

Very generous depreciation allowance. In the United States we have used accelerated depreciation or declining-balance as opposed to straight-line depreciation. The 1954 tax legislation for the first time explicitly recognized the use of accelerated depreciation; assets depreciated under double declining-balance could be written off at a rate of twice that of straight-line. The 1962 legislation greatly condensed the number of service lives, estimates of the real economic lives of assets for depreciation purposes. In 1971 the Asset Depreciation Range was created, setting up a number of asset categories. In 1981 the Accelerated Cost Recovery System (ACRS) was created. Until then, depreciation had been based on the idea that the cost of equipment should be allocated over its useful life. Over time the length of the useful life was shortened. In 1981 the concept was totally abandoned. ACRS lumped all assets into only four categories: most vehicles could be depreciated in three years; equipment, in five years; structures, in fifteen years; and a few miscellaneous items, such as public utilities, in ten years.

Investment tax credit. A 7 percent credit was created in 1962, suspended in 1967, reinstated in 1968, repealed in 1969, reinstated in 1971, enlarged in 1981, and repealed in 1986.

Research and development incentives. All outlays for R & D are deductible in the first year. A 25 percent tax credit on marginal research and development expenditures was created in 1981.

Capital gains and losses. Until 1969 long-term capital gains (held more than six months) were taxed at no more than 25 percent. In 1969 a 35 percent rate was added to gains of over $50,000. In 1978 the top rate was lowered to 28 percent, and in 1986 the differential taxation of capital gains was repealed. Capital losses can offset capital gains.

U.S. tax on foreign income. Income earned by foreign branches is subject to U.S. tax; a foreign subsidiary's income is taxed when distributed in the United States as dividends. A Domestic International Sales Corporation (DISC) was allowed to defer tax on part of its income until the income was brought back to the United States.

Bad debt reserves. Financial institutions can shelter from taxes part of their earnings in bad debt reserves, created to protect these institutions from unpaid loans.

Mineral depletion allowances. Firms engaged in extracting resources are eligible for allowances to compensate for the exhaustion of the deposit and to offset the cost of exploratory drilling.

2

Business Influence and State Power

Introduction

This chapter explores the political mechanisms which have delivered new directions in corporate taxation. Political analyses coalesce around two theoretical poles: state-centered explanations and society-centered ones. Society-centered analysts argue that policy largely reflects the interests of private sector powers, because the state is *captured* by societal interests. State-centered theorists claim policy to be a product of relatively autonomous politicians and bureaucrats, because policymakers are *insulated* from private pressures.

Neither extreme position in the state autonomy debate seems confirmed by the corporate tax experience. At times the policy *process* seems the quintessence of pork barrel politics; at other times business interests have much less input. The Economic Recovery Tax Act of 1981 was widely perceived as a business orgy in which private interests feasted on the revenue base of the state. By comparison, the Tax Reform Act of 1986, while certainly beneficial to the upper-income contingent, was initiated by state actors and limited handouts to private concerns.

Policy *outcomes* also indicate a varying degree of corporate power. The absolute decline in corporate tax levels during the postwar period has been periodically reversed with reform campaigns. During these periods, loopholes have been closed under the banner of equity. Most spectacular was the 1986 legislation which eliminated many of the selective growth incentives.

This chapter presents an alternative view of state-society relations which accounts for the vacillations in private power. Presidents have organized public/private coalitions to seek enactment of their growth strategies. The inconsistent erosion of the corporate burden can be traced to this institutional development.

State Autonomy and the Structure of Business

The centrality of political struggle to the choice of growth strategies makes a theory of politics necessary. Yet analysts are divided over the relative balance of power between state and society: the issue of state autonomy. Society-centered explanations hold that public policy can be explained as a function

34

of private interests.[1] Organized interests translate into public policy through the self-interests of politicians and bureaucrats. A politician is motivated to satisfy constituent demands in order to realize his own interest in reelection.[2] Iron triangles based on self-interests may develop between players in interest groups, Congress, and the bureaucracy.[3] Within these structures, influence flows from the private to the public sector. Many also argue that this influence has a class bias, since the state is dependent on uninterrupted business investment for its continued health.

Society-based explanations have been used to explain the distribution of the tax burden. Schumpeter suggests that tax patterns provide a sociogram of the power distribution among groups and calls for a new field, fiscal sociology, to study the evolution of the political economy.[4] Bartlett asserts that high nominal progressivity satisfies the demands of middle-class consumers and that targeted loopholes appeal to powerful producer interests.[5] Salamon and Siegfried find lower tax rates among larger corporations; and Jacobs finds that when aggregate concentration among the largest firms went up, taxes on all manufacturing firms were reduced.[6] The increase in Political Action Campaign (PAC) funding has also most certainly enhanced the role of special interests in policy-making. (See appendix 2.1 for a discussion of PAC contributions to the House Ways and Means and Senate Finance committees in 1981.)

The most notable characteristic of the business community in the United States is its high degree of fragmentation. Business demands may generally establish the acceptable range of corporate tax alternatives; however, specific industry demands are often at odds with one another. Fragmentation in the business community means that no unambiguous class mandate for corporate taxation is expressed. This lack of a unified class position is related to the multiplicity of avenues to growth discussed in chapter 1. In the absence of a class consensus or sectoral dominance, state actors have greater autonomy in the decision-making process to determine directions in policy.

Variations in policy preferences among industrial sectors will be found to some extent in any society. However, the points of disagreement between sectoral preferences are exacerbated in the U.S. system for three reasons. First, the connection between finance and manufacturing is very weak. Unlike in other Western countries, banks do not act as owner-managers of industrial firms in the United States. Banks are restricted to lending for short-term purposes; therefore, industrial investment must be funded through equity sales (stock and bond markets) rather than through long-term loans. In West Germany, by comparison, banks have a significant financial interest in firms and are intimately involved with the management and fiscal well-being of their industrial clients. Financial interdependence leads to a convergence between the interests of financial and manufacturing firms.[7] In the United States commercial banks hold only 8 percent of nonfinancial corporate liabilities; in West Germany this figure is 58 percent.[8] Sabel and Piore attribute the separation of banking and manufacturing to the early development of corporations and the late development of banks; the latter had little role in bringing about the former.[9]

These different types of financing systems produce very different types of public policy. A U.S. capital market system which leaves investment and production completely in the hands of management will have only limited capacity for direct state intervention. By comparison a French or Japanese credit-based system with government-administered prices allows the government to guide many industrial decisions.[10]

The role of the dollar as the international currency has heightened the split between banking and manufacturing interests in the postwar period. As large multinational banks increasingly became bankers for the world, they became committed to maintaining a stable currency in order to protect the integrity of the system (and their own profit margins). Bankers exhibited a rabid fear of devaluation and economic problems (such as inflation and budget deficits) which could threaten the currency. In contrast, when faced with a choice between inflation and recession, industrial capital often favored domestic expansion.

The second reason why American business is fragmented is related to the way in which business associations are organized. Since the 1960s, business interests in the United States have been increasingly organized into single-sector trade associations rather than into the umbrella organizations found in many Western European countries. This process of articulation leads to a more narrow definition of policy preference, exacerbating intersectoral conflict.[11] Third, the relative weakness of the labor movement in the United States diminishes class conflict, thus heightening the importance of intraclass divisions.[12]

An industrial sector analysis of business demands illustrates these corporate divisions.[13] This theory assumes that business policy preferences are rooted in industrial structure and policy changes represent the hegemonic ascendancy of one sector of the business community over others.[14]

One of the two primary issues dividing the business community in the tax sphere has to do with a sector's preferences for competing macroeconomic goals: monetary stability or fiscal prosperity. Sectors directly affected by monetary policy worry about the former. The industry's profits or asset holdings may be directly affected by inflation, high interest rates, or balance-of-payment deficits. Housing sales are directly correlated with the level of interest rates; commercial banks, holding assets in long-term government securities, fear inflation. By comparison small business firms, whose profit margins and other resources are meager, fear recessionary dips which they may not survive.

The second issue dividing the business community has to do with the degree of capital intensity of the sector's production process. In capital-intensive sectors, machines rather than workers are used to create much of the value added during production. Most of the selective growth incentives created in the postwar period have aimed at increasing capital investment in fixed plant and equipment. Therefore, capital-intensive sectors have provided the primary political support for these devices (see table 2.1 for a comparison of capital-labor ratios).[15]

Three groups of industrial sectors emerge as major actors in the tax policy debates. A finance/housing group is labor-intensive and worries more about monetary stability than fiscal prosperity. These sectors will be the first to call for a tax increase to curb inflation or balance the budget. A small business/ service group, also labor-intensive, worries more about fiscal prosperity. Since these firms cannot use the selective tax incentives, they tend to pay high effective tax rates and have become increasingly critical of the postwar, capital investment–oriented avenue to growth. The final group of manufacturing concerns, capital-intensive, is most concerned about fiscal prosperity.

Industrial structure makes groups more or less responsive to varying approaches to investment. Not all tax proposals are equally supported by all sectors within a group, since many parochial proposals are designed to meet the interests of one or two sectors. This is also not to say that the preferences of these groups are carved in stone. Here I point out only that groups tend to be divided, in fairly consistent ways, on tax policy alternatives. The reader will note that very little attention is given to either the demands of labor or public opinion. These sources of societal pressure have very little impact in the area of corporate tax policy.

The fragmented structure of the American business community has clear implications for corporate tax outcomes. Deep divisions have discouraged a clear class mandate; conflicting preferences generate contradictory pulls,

Table 2.1. Capital-Labor Ratios (gross book value per man-year, 1957)

	New England	South	Rest of U.S.
Capital-intensive			
Pulp and Paper	$11,225	18,046	11,225
Chemicals	12,226	24,481	13,899
Petroleum	29,835	42,251	43,243
Primary metals	7,447	18,056	13,210
Labor-intensive			
Food and beverages	5,971	6,069	7,293
Tobacco	n.a.	5,656	2,305
Textiles	4,983	5,488	4,156
Apparel	770	826	790
Printing	4,194	4,247	4,269
High technology			
Instruments	3,537	3,642	4,164

making it difficult for the state to build a lasting consensus. The stop-go quality of corporate taxation reflects these pulls. In the early 1960s manufacturing
interests demanded an expansionary fiscal policy, but a few years later inflation and balance-of-payment deficits drove bankers to demand a tax hike. In
the late 1970s, however, the declining competitiveness of industrial capital
led to increased demands by aging manufacturing sectors for state subsidization in the form of investment incentives. The questioning of the old order in
1986 reflected the increased power of the high-technology, small business,
and service sectors—parts of the economy unable to enjoy the benefits of the
investment incentives.

Yet no one sector has been dominant in the postwar United States in the
way that textiles, autos, and steel historically controlled the economies of
Western Europe.[16] These divisions among business have accordingly accentuated the power of the state. To state actors and structure we now turn.

The Structure of Government

A state-centered view contests the presentation of policy as merely a function
of private sector demands and suggests that the origins of policy may be
located in other motivations and interests of state actors. In addition to constituent interests, state actors are motivated by technical goals and institutional interests.[17] This approach does not negate the existence of societal
pressures but points to the causal primacy of other considerations, especially
among nonelected bureaucrats.[18] Levi characterizes rulers as predatory, since
they attempt to maximize revenue collection from subjects.[19]

The separate institutional interests of government players are shaped by
state structure. The institutional structure of the state divides the government
apparatus into a multitude of factions—branches, levels, bureaucratic departments, and partisan groupings. Factions divide along these fault lines, the
opposition drawn differently across political conflicts.[20] Politicians and bureaucrats develop interests according to their institutional affiliation. Institutional interests may be related to the survival or success of the faction, as in
competition between branches or parties, or may concern an individual's goals
for advancement within the organization. That government officials can act
on the basis of their separate political interests presupposed relative autonomy. Because state actors, especially bureaucrats, are relatively insulated
from interest group pressures, they have relative freedom to formulate policy
in accordance with their separate goals and interests.[21] Policy patterns are set
by these general system characteristics.

An institutional analysis has been applied to tax policy in two ways. First,
attention has been given to the ways in which institutional interests supersede
constituent demands, implying greater state autonomy. Manley's study of the
Ways and Means Committee under Wilbur Mills points out institutional mech-

anisms to restrict leakage to special interests and enhance members' freedom to develop good policy.[22]

Second, cross-national comparisons of political institutions have been used to explain variance in policy approaches. Comparing Sweden, Britain, and the United States, Steinmo suggests that the decision-making structures in each country produce very different policy outcomes. The American fragmented political authority has produced a complex and inefficient tax code; Sweden's fairly simple, efficient system is explained by its stable corporatist system of representation.[23] In like manner, Witte suggests that continuous pressure from economic interests on an incremental decision-making process leads to a gradual erosion of the system.[24] Hall searches out the role played by institutions in both state and society in the articulation of interests, dissemination of ideas, construction of market behavior, and determination of economic policy in Germany and France.[25]

The most salient feature of the American state is its fragmented nature. The doctrine of the separation of powers, federalism, overlapping jurisdictions, and the lack of clear authority hierarchies all contribute to a fragmented system with many competing points of power.

At the heart of the problem of political fragmentation is the separation-of-powers doctrine, which divides tasks between the various branches to keep any one of them from usurping power.[26] Authority to legislate rests with Congress; however, the president has the power to recommend measures for legislative consideration.[27] A separation of powers between Congress and the president has institutionalized organizational irrationality in the corporate tax area. Congress has a clearly specified constitutional responsibility to raise revenue, which it carries out through the legislation of tax acts. Responsibility for developing proposals, however, is not spelled out in the Constitution.

The problem of the fragmentation of the American state has been exacerbated with the new economic activism. The federal government was relatively inactive in the nineteenth century, restricting its activities to expressly delegated functions and leaving all else to the states. The complexity of the twentieth century expanded the role of the national government: changes in economic beliefs made the government into economic manager. The Budget and Accounting Act of 1921 made the president into a general manager; the Employment Act of 1946 expanded this role. The balance of power between branches also shifted. Although Congress retained legislative powers, policy formulation and implementation increasingly became a prerogative of the executive branch. This was due partially to the president's expanded capability for gathering information. The Council of Economic Advisers, a body composed of professional economists responsible for forecasting the macroeconomy, was placed within the executive branch. In the twentieth century revenue raising has evolved into a two-stage process with participation from both branches: "The president proposes; Congress disposes."

But increased responsibility for economic policy was given to the executive branch without adequate power to enact the mandate. For example, it was expected that the president would manipulate money aggregates in the macroeconomy in order to curb booms and offset recessions. Although presidents repeatedly requested standby authority to circumvent the legislative process and raise and lower taxes as needed, Congress refused to grant this request. Tax acts typically take at least a year to legislate; therefore, it is nearly impossible for presidents to formulate "optimal" policy. Thus, additional presidential authority without a decrease in Congressional control has greatly limited the success of macroeconomic stabilization.[28]

The pattern of fragmentation and overlapping jurisdictions which characterizes relations among branches is reproduced within the executive branch. Three departments in the executive branch plus the Federal Reserve Board constitute an "economic subpresidency." Each department specializes in a part of the whole: The Bureau of the Budget (now the Office of Management and Budget) has primary responsibility for spending. The Council of Economic Advisers forecasts macroeconomic trends, analyzes general economic issues, and develops the president's annual economic report. The Treasury manages tax collection and currency control. Jurisdictional lines are not firmly drawn, however, so that both the Council of Economic Advisers and the Treasury are very involved in developing tax policy. All three project general economic trends and calculate the fiscal effects of various policy options.[29]

The institutional responsibilities and external constituents of these units are quite different, leading to systematic differences on policy stands. The Council of Economic Advisers has traditionally been more insulated from clientele pressures; its composition of professional economists increases its technocratic flavor. The Treasury, by comparison, has been more explicitly political. Constituent groups who would influence corporate tax policy usually direct their efforts toward the Treasury; heads of this department are often drawn from the business community. The institutional responsibility of the Treasury Department reinforces the need to maintain business confidence.

Treasury has traditionally taken more fiscally conservative stands.[30] In the 1960s the CEA was typically more willing to endure small amounts of inflation for domestic expansion; the Treasury was much less willing to sacrifice stable currency for growth. The Federal Reserve Board has traditionally joined the Treasury in the chorus against inflation and sensitivity to the effect of fiscal policy on balance-of-payment deficits. A proliferation of units for making economic policy has further complicated matters. Porter identifies 132 bodies now responsible for developing taxing and spending proposals, thus eroding the knowledge monopoly once enjoyed by the Council of Economic Advisers.[31]

Presidents have attempted to coordinate disparate groups involved in economic issues through special policy forums. John F. Kennedy initiated the "Troika" consisting of the Council of Economic Advisers, the Bureau of the Budget, and the Treasury. Lyndon Johnson expanded this to the "Quadriad" with the addition of the Federal Reserve Board. Richard Nixon contributed the Cabinet Committee on Economic Policy and the subsequent Economic Policy Board; Jimmy Carter, the Economic Policy Group. Yet none of these efforts achieved the coordinating importance that the National Security Council did in defense policy.[32]

After the president has developed his tax initiative, he must convince Congress to legislate it. First, the bill is considered by the Ways and Means Committee. The committee holds hearings on the measure: at this point the interested public is officially brought into the process. Then the committee "marks up" the bill, debating each measure's inclusion and drafting the legislation. The bill is then debated under "modified closed rule" on the House floor, which limits amendments. If the bill is passed, it is sent to the Senate, where the Senate Finance Committee carries out a similar process. Ultimately, the two versions of the bill are made consistent in the conference committee.

There is evidence that Congress, like the executive branch, has suffered from a gradual fragmentation of authority. In the early years of the postwar period committee chairmen enjoyed enormous power in their substantive areas. The negative side to this was that a hostile chair could simply refuse to report a piece of legislation out of committee. Since the committee chair were disproportionately conservative southern Democrats, liberal legislators bemoaned their considerable power. The positive side to this arrangement, however, was that a chairman could discipline committee members and limit their vulnerability to outside pressures.

The problem of fragmentation has been worsened by the decline of the political party. Parties in the nineteenth century functioned to elect candidates and construct policy, helping to overcome the institutional fragmentation of the American state. The twentieth century has witnessed a decline in parties at precisely the point when integration is most needed.[33]

Reforms to democratize Congress and the party structure have increased the fragmentation and permeability of the system and decreased state capacity.[34] These institutional reforms have altered the individual politician's incentive structure and made it harder for him to act on the basis of things other than constituent demands. Thus, institutional changes have restricted Congress's capacity for rational decision making.[35] Open hearings have downgraded the influence of the Treasury and the Joint Committee on Taxation staffs.[36] Since these reforms, the making of tax policy has been more susceptible to private pressure. Strahan points out, however, that tax legislation since 1984 has been marked by somewhat greater stability due to a different policy context and increased leadership in Congress.[37]

The Public/Private Coalition

Which type of explanation has greater relevance for corporate taxation? The extreme version of neither the state-centered nor the society-centered model can adequately account for the vacillations in policy outcomes and the differential influence of business interests. There are two reasons for this. First, the high degree of fragmentation in both state and society partially negates the dominance and autonomy of both spheres.

Second, neither explanation allows for the mutuality of interests which develops between actors in the public and private spheres. Society-based views recognize a congruence of interests between state actors and society; however, this congruence is narrowly defined. Politicians and bureaucrats have limited concerns beyond their own economic self-interests. Because these limited interests are satisfied by meeting constituent demands, state actors are *captured* by society-based groups.

State-centered views correctly point out that politicians' interests transcend an economistic reading. Bureaucrats and politicians have institutional interests that are unrelated to the interests of their society-based constituents. However, these views generally assume that, in order to maximize the other policy concerns, state actors must *insulate* themselves from private pressures. In fact, public and private sector actors can join forces on the basis of shared interests. Also, key decision makers within the state have worldviews which have been shaped by their societal origins. Politicians with backgrounds in industry have difficulty escaping this perspective, even when they are not directly "captured."

An understanding of politics which emphasizes the linkage between state and society seems appropriate. There are three central points to the public/private coalition model. The first derives from an institutional analysis of the American state. U.S. institutions are characterized by fragmentation. The existence of this fragmentation means that *factions* exist within the state apparatus. These factions or small groups vie with one another for political power and for control of the public agenda. This fragmentation is a dynamic variable, manifested to greater or lesser degrees at various points in time. For example, fragmentation may be lessened by partisan unity, when the same party controls both branches of government. Electoral competition generally tends to exacerbate fragmentation. The fluidity of this fragmentation opens possibilities for various combinations or coalitions among players in both the public and private spheres.

Second, the *interests* of factions within the state may *converge* with those of groups in society. Public and private factions share a mutual interest in the success of a particular investment strategy or policy solution. Interests converge in the technical issues which preoccupy policy networks of individuals in both the public and private sectors.[38] The organizational intersection of political and economic systems ties the interests of capitalists to the institutional responsibilities of state actors.[39] Political necessity also ties state actors to business allies: politicians develop a policy agenda and approach like-minded business groups to help achieve that agenda.

The final point, then, is that the balance of power in this intrastate political infighting may be altered by *coalitions* with private sector groups. This convergence of interests motivates groups to form alliances in order to maximize their interests and power vis-à-vis their political and economic opponents. Political entrepreneurs take the initiative in pulling together these coalitions and draw upon factions within both the state and society. Political actors' successes in manipulating and mobilizing private pressures are the source of their strength.

The joint participation of private and public sector factions is reflected in policy outcomes. State actors define the broad outlines of the initiatives in accordance with the economic strategy endorsed and take the lead putting together the coalitions. Politicians' choices of agenda, thus, greatly influence policy directions as well as the chances for success of individual business groups. Yet business allies' demands comprise the details. Business groups use their "privileged position" to set the range of acceptable alternatives.[40] Thus, there are a whole range of tax options relegated to the nondecision sphere, or options which are never really considered.

The coalition approach presents a distinct view of state-society relations. Since state actors turn to private sector groups for assistance in achieving their policy agenda, political players are neither passively captured by special interests nor autonomous from them. For example, the model differs from an iron triangle view of state-society interactions in that (1) state actors initiate the political alliance and (2) the coalition represents a strategy rather than an enduring arrangement.

This approach suggests that the interests of actors in each realm converge; therefore, the boundaries between state and society are not rigidly defined. In this vein Katzenstein writes, "The distinction between state and society connotes a gap between the public and the private sector which exists in no advanced industrial state." Rather, governing coalitions "find their institutional expression in the distinct policy networks which link the public and the private sector in the implementation of foreign economic policy."[41]

Recognition of this link between private and public has emerged in the American literature in the work on presidential strategies. Before congressional reforms, presidents relied on party and congressional leadership to tie them to voters and legislators. However, the reforms of the 1960s and 1970s compromised traditional channels of authority and consequently the presidential capacity to lead. With the decline in authority of go-between leaders, the president has turned increasingly to interest groups as a means of building policy coalitions. By involving supportive business groups in legislative lobbying, presidents enlarged or found alternatives to the electoral coalitions that had sent them to office.[42] Heclo asserts that "each president during the last twenty years has felt increasingly compelled to mobilize the White House to build the equivalent of a presidential party for governing." McQuaid links presidential mobilization of business power to the emergence of the activist state.[43]

Public/Private Coalitions in Corporate Taxation

The corporate tax cases discussed in the following chapters reveal considerable use of the public/private coalition. To secure political advantage and manage economic policy-making, executives organized public/private coalitions around a growth strategy. These coalitions were of enormous import in bringing about passage of the acts. In the process the interests of both state actors and business allies influenced policy outcomes. Although the direction of policy initiatives was often set by state actors' political interests, policy outcomes were limited to the range of alternatives acceptable to their business allies.

In the early 1960s President Kennedy was attracted to the "commercial Keynesian" growth strategy as a way to differentiate himself from years of Eisenhower nonintervention. Kennedy had campaigned on a promise to "get the country moving again"; his vision of America as empire mandated a strong economic base. This made economics a key issue for the administration and one on which it was willing to make considerable concessions. In 1962 the administration concentrated on the supply side with the development of the investment tax credit. The 1964 tax cut focused on the demand side.

Although the president's resulting fiscal policy was far from revolutionary, economic intervention by the government was rejected by Republicans and southern Democrats alike. Even the 1962 investment tax credit, clearly a pro-capitalist measure, was opposed on the grounds that it would give the government excessive influence over private investment decisions. Unfortunately for the president, southern Democrats controlled many key committee chairs in the legislative bodies.

Large parts of the business community responded more favorably to the new economic activism compared with the Republican legislators who generally represented them. Export-oriented manufacturing interests had generally felt frustrated with the slow growth rates of the Eisenhower years, resulting from macroeconomic timidity. The Chamber of Commerce publicly accepted the expansionary deficits; only the banking community seemed adamant that an expansionary tax cut be accompanied by revenue-raising reforms.

To augment its power against fiscal conservatives in Congress, the administration pulled together a core group of private sector supporters in a business-based lobbying group.[44] The "Business Committee for Tax Reduction in 1963" differed from the usual business groups which lobby for legislative concessions. Unlike other lobbying groups, it was organized by the administration, made up of many business sectors, and oriented toward a larger policy vision.

The Business Committee for Tax Reduction helped the administration by expressing widespread support for the tax bill and convincing hesitant Congressmen to vote for it. Business Committee members sent out mass mailings asking their members to support the measure and educated other business groups to the president's way of thinking. Treasury Undersecretary Henry Fowler wrote that the Business Committee "has been of immeasurable assistance in marshaling support among the various established trade organizations and avoiding the 'knee jerk' type of opposition that normally characterizes response to any initiative from a Democratic President."[45]

As the public/private coalition model predicts, state actors took the lead in the direction and content of the legislation, so that the institutional interests of executive branch actors greatly influenced decisions made about the timing, content, and ideological orientation of the bill. For example, Kennedy was originally persuaded to package the 1964 tax cuts as a long-term growth stimulus rather than a short-term macroeconomic stimulation. Then a dip in the economy in the spring of 1963 quickly generated criticism of the administration from without and panic within. Kennedy backed away from the neoclassical position and billed the measure in recession-fighting terms. With an upturn in the economy, the president returned to the long-term growth perspective. The timing of the intervention was also influenced by state-centered concerns. Henry Fowler persuasively argued: "Your Administration should be inextricably associated with 'good times' in the minds of the people . . . Can that rare political asset—Kennedy prosperity—be preserved until November 1964?"[46]

But as allies to the administration, business groups enjoyed considerable influence. The administration routinely polled business to evaluate political support for competing measures and tried to stay within the range of alternatives acceptable to the business community. Items in which finance and manufacturing were in agreement were usually passed; measures which split the business community were frequently dropped. Fowler argued that the Business Committee for Tax Reduction should not be "divided or paralyzed in their movement by the lack of a definite target."[47]

Again working within a Keynesian paradigm, Johnson used a public/private coalition to muster support for a 1968 surtax, in order to curb inflationary trends in the economy. Although initially Johnson seemed indifferent to the inflation, a revenue hike increasingly seemed necessary to pay for domestic peace and foreign war—the Great Society and Vietnam. Ultimately passage of the surtax became a symbol of the administration's efficacy. Joseph Califano advised the president, "I have a strong instinct that what happens in the current tax fight may be a critical turning point in your presidency, not only vis-à-vis the Congress, but perhaps on a much larger scale." [48]

Passage of the surtax was resisted energetically by both conservatives and liberals in Congress. Liberals saw it as a war tax; conservatives, as a way to pay for the detested Great Society. Emerging as the leader of the opposition, Wilbur Mills fought a fundamental battle to keep revenues low and government restrained.

The administration turned to business groups to circumvent the bill's enemies. The multisector tax group forged in 1968 was reminiscent of the 1963 Business Committee for Tax Reduction. At the core of the coalition were the housing and real estate groups that were most concerned about inflation. [49] Again, the timing of the major decisions reflected the president's own institutional interests and auxiliary policy agendas. Yet business groups also were instrumental in shaping the bill. David Rockefeller, one of its strongest supporters, first called for a tax hike in 1966 as part of a broad policy agenda to curb inflation. The administration polled prominent businessmen at regular intervals during the decision-making process to try to gauge support for the measure. During legislation, concessions were made to attract business: manufacturers were allowed to deduct their investment tax credits before calculating the 8 percent measure, and the surtax was tied to spending cuts.

In the late 1970s Ronald Reagan campaigned to rid the nation of Keynesian activist economic policy and return it to a laissez-faire state. The "hyperaccumulation" strategy endorsed lower, less progressive rates and expanded incentives to save and invest. In 1981 Reagan saw his dream come true with the largest tax decrease in the history of the United States: individual rates were cut by 23 percent and investment incentives were greatly expanded. The 1981 act thus fulfilled a major campaign promise and represented a key element in the president's supply-side ideology.

Reagan encountered considerable resistance to his legislative agenda from Democrats for both ideological and political reasons. The supply-side personal cuts were rejected as unfair and unsound; Democrats were reluctant to relinquish demand-oriented progressivity. The losing party also had felt repudiated by Reagan's recent budget battle and were determined to use taxes to recover their status and partisan pride. Jimmy Carter reportedly called Rostenkowski and said, "Do what you have to do, but win!" [50]

The corporate provisions were not greatly disputed. The Democrats calculated that the best chance for victory would be to fight the Republicans on the personal cuts and make concessions on the corporate tax structure. In this vein Rostenkowski put forward to business groups a roster of policies left out of the Republican alternative. The president responded by launching a highly sophisticated business lobbying effort. A core of corporate supporters was put together, in part from the three hundred business groups that had participated in the administration's budget battle. This core group, called the "Bomber Squad," helped to engineer the final passage of the act. When the president appeared on television to request support for the tax cut, business supporters tied up the telephone lines of key congressional offices for the next forty-eight hours.

Corporate tax benefits thus became the medium of exchange for buying legislative support. Because of the symbolic significance of the act, the near desperation of the political players, and the choice of corporate taxation as the unit of bargaining, special interests played an extremely prominent role and more concessions were made than usual.

Ronald Reagan's ideological program and political interests in securing its enactment were the guiding force behind the tax act. Yet, as a result of their key role in the political fight, business groups had considerable input into the bill. Many of the corporate provisions were hammered out by the business community ahead of time. Although cutting corporate rates, speeding up depreciation, and lowering capital gains were all on the corporate wish list, private sector groups had negotiated a compromise. The Reagan team chose accelerated cost recovery as its core corporate proposal because it calculated that the adoption of ACRS would bring in 80 percent of the business community.[51] Charls Walker, a powerful Washington corporate lobbyist and architect of the provision, was the chairman of President Reagan's tax transition team.

Almost immediately after the 1981 tax act was signed into law, pressure began mounting to reverse the monumental tax cut. The pressure for a tax increase that began in August of 1981 ultimately resulted in the Tax Equity and Fiscal Responsibility Act of 1982, the largest peacetime tax increase in the postwar period.[52] In spirit and practice TEFRA was a partial repudiation of the Economic Recovery Tax Act legislated only eleven months before. Although the individual tax cuts, the centerpiece of ERTA, were left untouched, the corporate provisions were scaled back considerably.

Why did the president abruptly reverse his commitment to the investment incentives? Conflicting economic problems—slow growth and the budget deficit—were ultimately resolved in favor of political damage control. Only a month after ERTA was legislated the stock market fell dramatically, accompanied by a drop of the dollar on the international currency exchange. This development riveted public attention on the budget deficit and greatly alarmed the administration. For months the president deliberated over an appropriate course of action. He finally decided that the budget deficit presented a more damaging political problem than breaking his promise not to raise taxes and pushed ahead with the TEFRA alternative.

In 1982 the coalition strategy was extended to members of the other party: Reagan turned to the House Democrats as a source of support. The puzzle is why the Democrats went along. The Democrats had suffered a major humiliation in 1981, and most on Ways and Means refused to mark up a tax bill in 1982. Breaking with tradition, the 1982 legislation was initiated in the Senate. But the Republicans offered the Democrats a chance for input on the act in a secret forum called the "Gang of Seventeen," a bipartisan group of legislators and executive branch officials. The broad outlines of TEFRA were hammered out in secret before the public policy process began. Since both parties felt that it was to their mutual advantage to remain united, they cooperated to an amazing extent with very little interparty competition. Legislation in 1982 thus set the stage for partisan cooperation on taxation.

In 1982 political unity made extensive concessions to business unnecessary; however, the executive branch still tried to mobilize private support to pressure opposing legislators and recalcitrant trade associations. A sophisticated lobbying project called the "Boiler Room Operation" kept files on all congressmen and senators, tallied votes, and lobbied legislators.

Although direct concessions to business were limited in 1982, business groups intervened at key points to influence policy formulation. In December of 1981 President Reagan was on the verge of proposing a massive excise tax increase but the Chamber of Commerce persuaded him to abandon this plan. Shortly thereafter the Business Roundtable and financial sectors convinced the president to move away from his original commitment not to raise taxes.

In 1986 a public/private coalition constructed around a very different approach to growth was successful in gaining passage of the Tax Reform Act. The "reform" claims have been questioned: the act abandoned progressivity and ignored the budget deficit.[53] But the act was revolutionary in greatly increasing the corporate share of total tax revenue and eliminating many of the special growth incentives which had been a prominent part of the tax code for many years.[54]

Partisan leadership on both sides endorsed tax reform and investment neutrality as an antidote to economic decline. Tax reform was also fueled by the institutional interests of its major proponents. The Republicans saw tax reform as an alternative to the Democratic proposals for industrial policy to shift resources to emerging high-technology sectors. They also feared that the Democrats would make it a major campaign issue and wanted to claim "fairness" for the Republican party. Reagan had long wanted to lower the individual rates.[55]

The Democrats thought that tax reform was going to be a big issue in the 1984 election and wanted to be included. In the past, cooperation with the president on fiscal issues had produced better results than competition. As the *New York Times* put it, the bill was a "political standoff." Guy Vander Jagt (R–MI) explained, "There's enough glory and gain to go around for Republicans and Democrats."[56] Reagan and Rostenkowski went on television together making a bipartisan plea for tax reform. The two men agreed to a contract of silence; Reagan would not criticize the House effort until the markup was completed. Although the administration's support wavered at points, the commitment held.

Enormous impetus for the corporate side of reform came from the business community: from high-technology, small business, and service groups, who had benefited least from the previous capital-intensive investment approach to growth. The increasing disparity between effective tax rates in the corporate community made "equity" an issue in corporate taxation. As early as 1982 several tax groups had formed to protest high effective corporate tax rates. At the core of the business group—what eventually became the 15/27/33 Coalition—were the companies left out of the 1981 tax cuts oriented toward capital-intensive manufacturers.[57] The greatest opponents of reform were predictably the capital-intensive manufacturers.

The business supporters were organized into a cross-sector group called the Tax Reform Action Coalition (TRAC). TRAC performed the usual tasks of lobbying and vote counting, and also staged a variety of media events to draw public attention to tax reform. When the rates were dramatically lowered in the Senate bill, many more business groups were lured to join the reform effort.

President Reagan and Chairman Rostenkowski staked their reputations on tax reform; its success was due largely to this bipartisan endorsement. Yet business allies were highly influential in building support for reform during the prelegislative period and in carrying out day-to-day lobbying. Many details of the president's reform measure (called Treasury II) were constructed to include the core supporters.

Conclusion

This chapter has critiqued the extreme poles of the state autonomy debate. First, neither the state- nor the society-centered model explicitly accounts for the considerable fragmentation within the business community and within the American state. Yet this fragmentation creates factions on both sides of the state-society boundary, which vie for political power and economic benefits. Second, neither explanation allows for the mutuality of interests which can develop between factions in the public and private spheres. Third, neither model recognizes that state actors can gain advantage over political enemies by forming alliances with private sector groups. Thus, success in manipulating and mobilizing private pressures may be the source of political strength.

Presented instead has been the coalition strategy, a technique in which presidents actively mobilize private sector interests for political support. This strategy lies outside the capture-insulation trade-off and suggests a more interactive view of state-society relations. The following chapters describe a series of cases in which desperate presidents turned to the public/private coalition to enhance their influence over policy.

Appendix 2.1

	Senate Finance Committee		
Member	Total Contributions 1979–80	PAC % of Total	Business % of PAC
William Armstrong (R–CO)	$15,392	48.1	100
Max Baucas (D–MT)	51,675	92.4	68.6
Lloyd Bentsen (D–TX)	510,337	4.8	100
David Boren (D–OK)	13,743	0.0	0.0
Bill Bradley (D–NJ)	383,074	23.5	97.1
Harry Byrd, Jr. (Ind–VA)	975	76.9	100
John Chafee (R–RI)	103,084	10.6	91.4
John Danforth (R–MO)	46,478	1.4	100
Robert Dole (R–KS)	1,255,105	33.8	88.3
Dave Durenberger (R–MN)	281,603	17.3	89.5
Charles Grassley (R–IA)	2,074,922	37.3	76.1
John Heinz (R–PA)	404,540	1.4	60.0
Russell Long (D–LA)	1,653,332	26.9	91.5
Spark Matsunaga (D–HI)	175,820	11.9	85.5
George Mitchell (D–ME)	—	—	—
Daniel Moynihan (D–NY)	580,776	39.9	63.7
Bob Packwood (R–OR)	1,521,344	23.6	67.4
William Roth (R–DE)	1,110	4.5	100
Steven Symms (R–ID)	1,873,018	35.3	81.5
Malcolm Wallop (R–WY)	23,307	13.1	100

House Ways and Means Committee

Member	Total Contributions 1979–80	PAC % of Total	Business % of PAC
William Archer (R–TX)	$248,297	0.0	0.0
L. A. Bafalis (R–FL)	110,200	7.4	47.7
William Brodhead (D–MI)	33,284	55	42.6
Barber Conable (R–NY)	37,249	28.2	33.6
William Cotter (D–CT)	135,387	47.2	85.6
Philip Crane (R–IL)	221,070	6.1	56.2
Thomas Downey (D–NY)	183,973	49.2	33
John Duncan (R–TN)	157,435	56.0	83.6
Harold Ford (D–GA)	115,660	47.6	64.3
Wynche Fowler (D–GA)	139,939	37	69.9
Bill Frenzel (R–ME)	129,929	44.6	94.1
Richard Gephardt (D–MO)	173,281	54.2	85.2
Sam Gibbons (D–FL)	93,791	53.4	93.1
Willis Gradison (R–OH)	130,405	6.1	62.9
Frank Guarini (D–NJ)	186,977	38.2	48.1
Kent Hance (R–TX)	49,677	24.7	89.8
Cecil Heftel (D–HI)	333,798	38.9	76.6
Kenneth Holland (D–SC)	123,930	76.1	86.9
Andrew Jacobs (D–IN)	36,666	0.0	—
Edgar Jenkins (D–GA)	112,974	63.9	94.6
James Jones (D–OK)	291,431	50.1	97.6
Raymond Lederer (D–PA)	139,972	58.9	39.9
James Martin (R–NC)	562,786	53.5	84.2
Robert Matsui (R–CA)	245,694	33.5	68.9
Henson Moore (R–LA)	166,747	45.3	77
Donald Pease (D–OH)	62,910	48.2	21.1
J. J. Pickle (D–TX)	373,601	25.3	94.5
Charles Rangel (D–NY)	104,070	53.3	80
Dan Rostenkowski (D–IL)	275,930	65.6	84.6
John Rousselot (R–CA)	156,119	60.7	83.7
Martin Russo (D–IL)	182,757	47.3	55
Richard Schulze (R–PA)	163,376	46.7	81.3
James Shannon (D–MA)	329,861	37.9	33
Pete Stark (D–CA)	39,086	70.5	37.5
Guy Vander Jagt (R–MI)	121,969	7.6	13.6

3

The Revenue Acts of 1962 and 1964

Introduction

Herbert Hoover recommended a big tax increase in 1931 when unemployment was extremely high and a large budget deficit was in
prospect.

John F. Kennedy recommended a big tax reduction in 1962 when
unemployment was again a problem, although a much less serious
one, and a large budget deficit was again in prospect.

The contrast between these two Presidential decisions symbolizes
the revolution in fiscal policy that occurred in the intervening thirty-
one years. This revolution was the main ingredient in the transition
to the "new economics," the installation of which was widely hailed
in the early 1960's as the basis for confidence that full employment
and steady growth would be maintained in the future.[1]

In the above quotation, Herbert Stein takes note of a conceptual transformation that shifted economic practice from a laissez-faire approach to the
Keynesian "new economics." This new growth strategy entailed high levels
of capital investment, maintenance of high levels of demand to guarantee
markets for expanded productive output, and macroeconomic stabilization of
the economy. Keynesian economic concepts had circulated around Washington since the New Deal; however, these ideas came to fruition only in the
1960s and then only in the hybrid form called "commercial Keynesianism."[2]
In what Stein has called a "fiscal revolution," Kennedy and his men radically
altered the meaning of "fiscal responsibility" by openly defending budgets
out of balance, as well as government intrusion into private investment decisions.[3] That this sharp divergence from the status quo occurred in a noncrisis,
peacetime economy was especially surprising.

This chapter explores how corporate taxation developed into a vehicle for
commercial Keynesian growth. I argue that the ultimate breakthrough of the
new economics was facilitated by the political ambitions of the new Democratic rulers, the interests of an important part of the business community, and
the political alliance between the two.

To understand the Keynesian revolution, one must begin with what came before it. President Eisenhower had shown himself to be a fiscal conservative. This

position in retrospect seems a mixed blessing.[4] The U.S. economy suffered through minor recessions, which our Western European allies avoided with Keynesian macroeconomic stabilization programs. Yet the strategy worked to keep inflation nearly nonexistent.[5] From the vantage point of three troubled decades, the 1950s inspire nostalgic reminiscence. At the time, however, a sense of unfulfilled possibility hung in the air like smoke from a summer barbecue. For the country over which he presided, Eisenhower, the all-American hero, seemed to stop just short of greatness.

John F. Kennedy recognized a political opening and seized it. Kennedy was no ardent economist. Only five years before his election he had been a relatively obscure senatorial underachiever, his record for absenteeism among his greatest claims to fame. In large part, Kennedy's initial endorsement by the Democrats seemed related to the vagaries of party competition: the message of unfulfilled potential was a way to differentiate the Democratic challengers from the incumbent Republicans. Yet, like Hegel's world historical actor, Kennedy adopted the vision of the new economic activism for political purposes but ultimately made his campaign theme a key organizing principle of his administration.

Kennedy's message of new economic activism found a receptive audience in internationally oriented manufacturing and banking interests, the initial skepticism of business notwithstanding. Manufacturers envied Western European growth rates and dreamed of similar achievements at home. Bankers saw growth as a solution to balance-of-payment deficits and gold outflows: trade surpluses would help to offset dollar outflows. Although businessmen remained dubious about the monetary consequences of the unbalanced budget, they supported the concept of government-orchestrated growth.

Less taken with Kennedy's economic charms were fiscal conservatives from both parties in Congress, who dominated many legislative positions of power. In the face of this considerable political opposition, Kennedy's people put together a broad-based group, the "Business Committee for Tax Reduction in 1963." The coalition lobbied Congress vigorously, interceded on behalf of the administration with other business groups, and in return sought to influence the content and ideological orientation of the Revenue Act of 1964.

Macroeconomic Context

The economy was at a standstill when Kennedy took office in 1961: 5.5 million people were unemployed, capital utilization was about 80 percent, and FY62 unemployment was anticipated to be 6 to 7 percent.[6] Conditions improved only marginally during Kennedy's first year in office. The Council of Economic Advisers had optimistically forecast that the 1962 gross national product would total $570 billion but were "shaken" when the Commerce Department pronounced the second-quarter GNP to be only $555 billion.[7]

Plant and equipment expenditures increased only 8 percent as opposed to the desired 15 percent; unemployment bottomed at 5.5 percent. Economic advisers Paul Samuelson and Robert Solow wrote that for the first time a Kennedy recession was a strong possibility and would lead by the time of the 1964 election to the highest average unemployment rate of any postwar administration.[8]

Paralleling the stagnation of domestic growth were yearly increases in the balance-of-payment deficits and decreases in the United States' gold hoard. Balance-of-payment deficits averaged $1.5 billion annually during 1950–56 and $3.9 billion during 1958–59. Europeans suddenly began to make claims on America's gold supply, using dollars accumulated from payment deficits. Treasury gold outflow, averaging $0.4 billion in 1950–56, increased to $1.7 billion in 1958–59.[9] The United States' share of the "Free World's" monetary stock declined from 43 percent to 26 percent by 1962.[10] The payment deficits had to be curbed, or at least the United States had to find a way to convince European bankers not to cash in their dollars for gold.

State Factions: Political and Economic Agendas

Two models framed the debate over economic policy: the neoclassical framework and the Keynesian approach. The two differed on three fundamental issues: the appropriate role of government in the economy, the engine of economic growth (investment or consumption), and the legitimacy of budget deficits. The neoclassical view rejected government intervention, posited investment as the source of growth, and renounced budget deficits. Keynesian economics viewed government intervention as necessary and proper, identified both consumption and investment as necessary to growth, and portrayed budget deficits as an appropriate tool for macroeconomic intervention. Keynesian thinking has been described as not merely an economic model but a paradigm of state-society relations. Krieger writes:

> "Keynesian" refers *not* to an economic doctrine, but to a vision of society which involved state efforts to harmonize interests through diverse economic and social policies, to politically regulate the market economy, and to take a tutelary role in securing business and trade union approval for central economic policies.[11]

Eisenhower's economic policy provided a most recent example of neoclassical thinking. A reluctance to meddle with the economy made the Eisenhower administration reject both demand-oriented expansionary policy and supply-side investment initiatives.

Keynesian macroeconomic stabilization surfaced in the form of public works projects during the New Deal, but the experimental radicalism of the

1930s was ultimately rejected. The Employment Act of 1946 explicitly made the government responsible for managing the macroeconomy; yet the United States only slowly made use of this potential.

Kennedy responded to his inherited macroeconomic ills with a policy package that borrowed from each of these traditions, commercial Keynesianism.[12] This approach had two basic components: Keynesian countercyclical fiscal policy to expand or contract consumption, and investment incentives to spur growth from the supply side. The Kennedy initiatives differed from European Keynesian policies in that they relied to a great extent on taxation instead of spending, emphasized investment as well as demand, and directed a large percentage of government transfers to upper-income persons and to business.

The two prongs of the commercial Keynesian growth strategy were represented in Kennedy's two major tax initiatives. The Revenue Act of 1962 was signed into law on October 16 of that year. The 1962 act created the investment tax credit and changed the rules concerning the taxation of income from U.S. foreign subsidiaries, reporting requirements on interest and dividend income, and the taxation of savings and loan institutions. Accompanying this tax legislation was an administrative shortening and consolidating of depreciation asset lives (see table 3.1).

Table 3.1. Selected Provisions of the Revenue Act of 1962 (HR 10650)

The 7 percent investment tax credit. The credit was created to allow a purchaser of capital goods to receive up to 7 percent of the cost as a credit on his tax liability.

Taxation of foreign subsidiary income. Two primary provisions were involved here. First, the gross-up provision stipulated that foreign subsidiaries no longer could deduct foreign taxes from their profits before the base for U.S. taxes was established. Rather, credit for foreign taxes paid could be taken as a credit against the domestic tax liability.

Second, the anti–tax haven provision established that income from nonmanufacturing U.S. foreign subsidiaries was subject to immediate U.S. taxation unless the subsidiaries were located in and the income was reinvested in an underdeveloped country. Previously, taxation could be delayed until the income was repatriated.

A third provision in the president's original proposal was rejected by Congress. This provision required that all income from manufacturing U.S. foreign subsidiaries be subject to U.S. income tax immediately instead of when the income was repatriated.

Taxation of thrift institutions. Thrift institutions had been able to set aside tax-free 12 percent of their yearly profits as a bad debt reserve. The adminstration had proposed lowering this to 3 percent. However, Congress legislated three possibilities for calculating the reserve. Savings institutions could limit taxation to 40 percent of their taxable income, setting the other 60 percent aside as a reserve, or set aside no more than 3 percent of the value on real estate loans outstanding or themselves calculate an amount necessary to bring the reserve up to a reasonable amount.

A reporting requirement on interest and dividend income. The president had proposed a 16.5 percent withholding on interest and dividend income; Congress rejected this and substituted more stringent reporting of this income by banks and corporations.

Entertainment and travel deductions were restricted.

Source: *Congressional Quarterly Almanac*, 1962, p. 478.

The second Kennedy tax act, the Revenue Act of 1964, was actually signed into law on February 26, 1964, after Kennedy's death. The president's original proposal featured across-the-board rate cuts to stimulate expansion and to reduce so-called fiscal drag caused by excessively high taxation. Also part of his proposal were reform measures to satisfy liberal loophole-closing as well as revenue-raising purposes. These included repealing the 4 percent dividend credit, speeding up corporate tax payments, and changing the rules for stock options. The most important reform items in the president's original proposal were dropped during the legislative process (see table 3.2).

The choice of the commercial Keynesian economic program partly reflected the political ambitions of the new president. Kennedy's need to differentiate himself from Eisenhower, a large labor constituency, and the importance of growth to the Democratic platform pointed to more active government intervention in the economy. Kennedy was elected in the middle of the 1960–61 recession, partly on his campaign promise to "get the country moving again."

The commercial Keynesian nature of the new governmental activism was influenced by the composition of the Kennedy administration. Policy positions were divided between two power poles. At one pole, Walter Heller and the Council of Economic Advisers endorsed a more explicitly Keynesian policy package. At the other, Douglas Dillon and the Treasury worked from

Table 3.2. Selected Provisions of the Revenue Act of 1964 (HR 8363)

Individual income tax rate reductions. Rates were changed from a range of 20–91 percent to 14–70 percent. Individual taxes were thus reduced by $9.1 billion a year.

Corporate income tax rate reduction. Rates were reduced from 52 percent to 48 percent, a $2.4 billion savings. Special reductions were made for small businesses. Corporate tax payments were speeded up so that all the tax liability would be paid in the year in which it was incurred.

Interest and dividend income credit and exclusion. The 4 percent credit was repealed. The president had asked that the $50 exclusion be repealed as well, but Congress doubled it instead.

Capital loss carryover. Capital losses could be carried over for an indefinite number of years to be offset against all capital gains and an annual $1,000 of ordinary income. The president had proposed several other major changes in the treatment of capital gains which were rejected by Congress. These included the taxation of capital gains accrued at death, the extension of the capital gains holding period from 6 months to 1 year, and the lowering of the capital gains rate. Before, individuals could apply 50 percent of the gain to ordinary tax rates or pay a 25 percent rate on the entire gain; the president wished to change these figures to 40 percent and 21 percent ratio, respectively.

Oil and gas provisions. The bill rescinded the privilege of grouping oil and gas properties in order to get extra benefits from the depletion allowance. The president proposed and Congress rejected structural changes which would have effectively reduced the depletion allowance.

Also rejected was the proposal to limit itemized deductions to totals greater than 5 percent of a taxpayer's income.

Source: *Congressional Quarterly Almanac,* 1964, p. 518.

a somewhat revised neoclassical worldview, accepting government intervention if it was directed toward investment.

Heller's Keynesian plan for action included an avid endorsement of budget deficits and a central role for demand management. To stimulate demand, Heller advocated tax cuts (and public works) from the earliest days of the administration. He believed that budget deficits were necessary to close the gap between actual and potential GNP. This gap could be filled only when the production capacity of the economy was increased to full employment (defined as 4 percent unemployment). Balanced budgets exerted a drag on the economy and contributed to the GNP gap. This was due to the peculiarities of accounting: a balanced federal budget operating at full employment actually ran yearly surpluses.[13] Heller and the CEA attended to investment as well. They believed the administration should pursue growth strategies aimed at modernization and expansion of industry that would "advance productivity and competitiveness in world markets . . . and take measures to protect the dollar during the transition period."[14]

Douglas Dillon and the Treasury Department based their policy prescriptions on neoclassical economics. Although Dillon shared Heller's desire to cut taxes, his rationale differed. Dillon attacked progressive taxation on the neoclassical grounds that it interfered with savings, risk, and investment.[15] Dillon resisted budget deficits both because they had no honorable place in the neoclassical scheme of things and because he feared they would trigger a run on the U.S. gold stock. Consequently, Dillon urged that any tax reductions be balanced by cuts in government spending.

Thus, Dillon was primarily concerned with balance-of-payment deficits and urged that solutions to domestic stagnation not interfere with this goal. Heller worried that the domestic economy would be sacrificed to international monetary concerns, and argued that a growing domestic economy was the best long-term solution to balance-of-payment problems. The policy prescriptions for the problems of domestic growth and payment deficits were unfortunately quite different. Tax cuts to stimulate demand can cause inflation and exacerbate currency problems. Balance-of-payment deficits dictate high interest rates to keep investment at home and to curb the trend in foreign portfolio investment. High interest rates, however, hurt domestic expansion. Walter Heller described the mutually exclusive goals as a "cruel dilemma of economic policy":

> Economic expansion at home will, temporarily at least, worsen our balance of payments . . . Measures for quickly improving the balance of payments and reversing the gold flow will check domestic economic recovery, prolonging and increasing unemployment. Tightening of credit to keep funds from flowing abroad will also keep them from flowing to U.S. businesses and home builders . . . We

believe that it would be short-sighted folly to sacrifice the domestic economy for quick improvement in the balance of payments.[16]

How can one explain these very different approaches by the two presidential advisers? Significantly, the two had very different backgrounds. As a professional economist, Walter Heller's reputation lay in developing and defending policy according to his Keynesian training. Dillon's background in the financial community sensitized him to balance-of-payment concerns. The differing tasks of their two departments also influenced the presidential advisers. Treasury's jurisdiction over balance-of-payment deficits and the national debt made it obviously reluctant to pursue deficit spending. The Council of Economic Advisers likewise had to confront unemployment and domestic growth directly.

A third major source of influence in the policy debate was Wilbur Mills (D–AR) and other key congressional fiscal conservatives. Mills's orientation was neoclassical: he sought lower, less progressive tax rates but resisted budget deficits and manipulation of tax levels for short-term stabilization purposes. As head of the House Ways and Means Committee, Mills could choose how and when to report bills out of committee and thereby control fiscal legislation.

The Pattern of Business Demands

The dawning of the 1960s found a business community that was in transition. A more activist economic policy gained support from those who were both frustrated with the seemingly unnecessary recessions under Eisenhower and willing to believe that the business cycle could be tamed. In 1958 a committee set up by the Rockefeller Brothers Fund recommended a variety of growth stimulants including a 5 percent across-the-board tax reduction.[17] As a measure to counter the business cycle, the Commission on Money and Credit (CMC) suggested that flexible standby authority be given to the president to increase or decrease individual income taxes by as much as 5 percent for up to six months. Walter Heller noted, "It's doubtful that we will again get such blue-blooded launching facilities as the CMC Report."[18]

Clear differences existed within the broad willingness to countenance an activist state. Financial interests wanted all domestic economic policy to be tailored to management of the balance of payments.[19] Within this constraint private bankers were eager that the government take a more active part in formulating economic policy, one that was targeted toward investment and carried out within a balanced budget. Canterbury calculated that the large New York banks stood to lose "$2 billion of foreign official deposits" if the dollar's role as reserve currency were lost.[20] Some felt that bankers were using the balance of payments as a weapon to oppose other policies:

The balance of payments question seems to have certain rather explosive political implications. I got the distinct impression that the commercial bankers felt that balance of payments furnished them with a weapon to attack budgetary deficits and the labor movement. On the other hand, the labor people obviously fear that the solutions to this problem might "come out of their hides." Several members of the academic community expressed fears that many of the social programs they have advocated might be deferred or cut back because of the balance of payments situation.[21]

Walter Heller reported in June of 1962 that President Blessing of the Deutsche Bundesbank, the West German central bank, had been urged by U.S. bankers to put pressure on the administration. The bankers reportedly said, "Why don't you convert some of your dollars into gold to put pressure on the Kennedy Administration to pursue more conservative policies?" Blessing "rejected such suggestions out of hand."[22] Similar warnings from European bankers during the first year of the Kennedy administration were also thought to have been inspired by New York bankers:

> In the past few days, we have been warned of the bad international economic and political consequences of an excessively defensive or even apologetic attitude toward our Federal budgetary and financial policies . . . The immediate source of these warnings are Per Jacobsson of the IMF and E. van Lennep, the high Dutch Treasury official who chairs both OECD's financial working party and OECD's monetary committee. Traveling New York bankers have been telling European listeners that the dollar is in for trouble because of the loose inflationary fiscal and monetary policies of the Kennedy Administration. After thus undermining European confidence in the dollar, the New York bankers tell U.S. via the financial press that Europeans will lose confidence in the dollar unless we are good boys, i.e., cut spending, balance the budget, restrict credit, raise interest rates. The fact is that European bankers and financiers, who don't worry about balanced budgets in their own countries, worry about U.S. budget balance only because their New York counterparts tell them they should. The governor of the Belgian central bank has told U.S. that Swiss—and other—bankers get their views about the U.S. economy in packaged form from their New York correspondents.[23]

The macrolevel concern about balance-of-payment deficits and monetary integrity in general was reflected in microlevel positions of the banking community on tax policy issues. In 1962 banking supported the investment tax credit (as less inflationary than demand stimulation) and changes in foreign taxation to curb the dollar outflow. In 1964 they wanted rate cuts to be conditional on spending reductions and reform, and concentrated in the top brackets (to stimulate investment rather than demand).

Manufacturing sectors were increasingly supportive of the commercial Keynesian growth strategy. Where the financial community worried about balance-of-payment deficits, manufacturing interests longed for the expansion of the domestic economy. Manufacturers accepted a government role in stimulating both supply and demand, and were more tolerant of budget deficits.[24] Walter Heller found in a November 1962 meeting with forty business economists that 80 percent of the group favored a substantial tax cut, even with a large deficit and increased expenditures.[25] Manufacturing sectors supported tax reduction earlier and demanded fewer qualifications, such as revenue-raising reforms. Manufacturing and finance agreed, however, that, if possible, spending cuts should accompany tax reduction, and both wanted the tax cuts concentrated in the upper income brackets.

The level of political organization among small business was relatively low in the 1960s.[26] The Chamber of Commerce (representing both large and small concerns) supported tax reduction regardless of reform, a position similar to that of other manufacturing groups.[27] The Chamber of Commerce consistently opposed the investment tax credit, fearing that the incentive would give preferential treatment to some businesses and discriminate against "small or money-losing companies that have no money for expansion."[28] The following *Fortune* commentary reflects these equity concerns: " 'For the boys that are in, they are in more,' writes an apparently tired small businessman, discussing the 7 percent credit in the *Wall Street Journal*. 'But for the boys that are out, they are out further. What a discouraging prospect!' "[29]

The Revenue Act of 1962

Although Kennedy is best known in the fiscal realm for his 1964 tax cut, his first major revenue initiative was passed in 1962. This effort is of interest for two reasons. First, the act created the investment tax credit, one of the major corporate growth incentives. Second, the initiative was met with considerable suspicion by the business community and was passed only with great difficulty. The lessons of 1962 motivated the administration to develop the coalition strategy in 1964.

The Revenue Act of 1962 was first proposed in 1961 and included the investment tax credit plus reform measures to offset revenue losses. The original investment incentive was a 15 percent credit on capital outlays *exceeding* a firm's depreciation allowance.[30] This approach was designed to motivate *additional* investment. To offset these losses the president proposed a change in the treatment of capital gains on depreciable property, a withholding provision on interest and dividend income, repeal of the $50 exclusion and 4 percent credit on dividend income, changes in business entertainment deductions, changes in the tax preferences of mutual savings and loans, and changes in the treatment of U.S. foreign subsidiary income.[31]

Despite their concerns about growth, many businessmen were initially quite skeptical about the investment tax credit. They preferred accelerated depreciation as a policy vehicle for state subsidization of capital investment, worrying that the investment credit allowed the government excessive control over private investment decisions.

Leaders of industry testified in full force against the investment credit: the Chamber of Commerce, the Committee for Economic Development, American Telephone & Telegraph, and about fifty others from the business community. George Tervorgh (Machinery & Allied Products Institute) pronounced the credit "as complicated as it is novel." After five weeks of Ways and Means hearings, the outcome looked dubious.[32] The *New York Times* commented:

> Seldom has such a measure caused a deeper split among its friends. And seldom have designated beneficiaries of tax legislation joined in opposition with those whose taxes were to be raised . . .
>
> The concept of the Administration was that industry, and perhaps labor, would largely unite in favor of a measure which would grant a tax credit of 8 percent for expenditures incurred in modernizing plants through the installation of new machinery and equipment. But it developed that, while industry is eager for tax remission as a stimulation, it wants this in the form of larger annual allowances for plant depreciation—leaving to management the choice of what to do with the revenue thus retained.[33]

In the face of general business opposition the administration set about to lobby Wilbur Mills (Ways and Means chair), urging that the credit would serve the "broad interests of the Nation" and offering material benefits.[34] Mills told George Ellison (AFL-CIO, Arkansas) that he would report out the bill if the AFL-CIO would "promise to cease stirring up grass roots complaints in his district." Ellison asked Kennedy's staff if they could arrange this.[35] Mills also requested a Titan II missile base for Arkansas and asked the president to dedicate a combination watershed and recreation project, saying that "no one else will be acceptable."[36]

The administration returned in January 1962 with a new, more palatable proposal: an across-the-board 8 percent tax credit. They estimated that the new credit would add $1.8 billion to 1962 corporate profits (about 6 percent of their total).[37] A still skeptical Donald J. Hardenbrook (National Association of Manufacturers president) labeled the investment credit a "subsidy" for some businesses that would place heavier burdens on all business.[38] H. Ladd Plumley (U.S. Chamber of Commerce president) called the provision a "gimmick" and a regrettable "instance of the Administration's failure to give credence to responsible business opinion when it is sincerely offered to it."[39] The National Oil Jobbers Council feared that the new credit's impact would be limited: "This tax credit will not be enough to induce a single jobber to buy one item more than what he would otherwise have purchased." [40] Large manufacturing concerns with substantial foreign operations objected to the credit's exclusive applicability to domestic plant and equipment.

Many financial groups, by comparison, supported the measure as a means of stimulating growth and offsetting the balance-of-payment deficits. Charls Walker (American Bankers Association vice-president) believed the investment incentive would increase American productivity and curb the dollar outflow. [41] A Chase Manhattan Bank study explained that "a rate of growth in durables is essential for full prosperity . . . As durables go, so goes prosperity." [42]

In the Senate an unusual coalition of conservatives (led by Harry Byrd, D–VA) and liberals (led by Albert Gore, D–TN) formed to oppose the capital spending incentive. [43] But by this time the president's office was able to mobilize more manufacturing support. [44] In August a Research Institute of America survey of six thousand executives found 65 percent in favor of the credit. [45] Ironically, the president's battle with the steel industry in April 1962 actually increased support for the investment credit, even while decreasing support for Kennedy in general. U.S. Steel's price hike focused attention on industries' difficulty in affording capital goods expenditures. [46]

After the steel crisis and stock market crash, the administration began to court business more fervently. Meetings were held with business to discuss the tax bill and the economy in general. At a May Business Council meeting, the Committee on Taxation produced a report criticizing the current legislation. [47] Fowler made an "extemporaneous rebuttal," pointing out the virtues of the investment tax credit. On July 12 the president staged a major luncheon with leaders of industry to smooth relations and solicit advice on a range of economic issues. [48] A commitment to depreciation reform, announced immediately after the steel battle at the Business Council meeting, also seemed to help the investment credit. [49] Fowler observed, "In the press conference that followed, Mr. Blough went out of his way to exude goodwill and approbation of this announcement as an important step toward the restoration of business confidence and the betterment of government-business relations." [50]

Support also increased when the Ways and Means Committee added a carryback provision. If a firm could not use the entire credit in one year, it could apply the credit to taxes paid during the three previous years. [51] The investment tax credit finally adopted by the Senate also differed from the administration's original version in that the depreciation basis of an asset would be decreased by the amount of investment credit taken. [52]

The opposition to the investment tax credit was augmented by hostility to the reform measures designed to offset its revenue losses. A number of interest group lobbying campaigns were carried out to scuttle the various reforms. One major reform was a 16.7 percent withholding rate on interest and dividends, estimated to recoup $600 million of the $850 million lost. [53] The House

Ways and Means Committee increased the rate to 20 percent and passed it with minimum discussion in January 1962.

The reform measure, however, generated intense controversy in the Senate proceedings. The Association of Stock Exchange Firms and the Investment Company Institute charged the provision with serious administrative problems and feared that it would drive savings from banks to other investment opportunities.[54] Most financial associations recommended better reporting systems, such as the American Bankers Association's automatic data processing system with taxpayer account numbers.[55] Perhaps the most virulent attack on the provision was made by William Jackson, president of the Investor's League:

> Withholding of tax on dividends and interest is equivalent to the federal Government ordering the millions of shareowners in the American economy and even greater numbers of people with savings in savings and loan associations and banks to lend it money without even one red cent of interest.
>
> Dressed up in any fancy language you like, this proposal smacks of police state methods . . . It is in a sense burning down the house to catch the mouse.[56]

The administration countered that withholding was not a new tax but simply collected what was owed. Excessive withholding was not really a problem since children and nontaxable institutions would be exempt and refunds would be made each quarter. The cost of compliance would be small.[57] Only one financial person, John Sadlik (vice-president of the Franklin National Bank of Long Island), testified in support of the withholding provision. Sadlik believed a data processing system to be more burdensome than the proposed withholding. At the close of this testimony, Senator Kerr joked, "If you feel you need police protection to get out of the building safely we will provide it."[58] The banking industry, led by the U.S. Savings and Loan League, engineered a massive letter-writing campaign against this "hottest tax issue in nearly two decades."[59] Savings institutions urged shareholders to contact their legislators and protest the provision. One letter asserted that about 60 percent of all individuals would lose one-fifth of their receipts of dividends and interest.[60]

The letter-writing campaign initially had an effect opposite to the one intended. The letters revealed "an incredible amount of misunderstanding and distortion." One-third to one-half of the thirty thousand letters to Paul Douglas (D–IL) were from individuals who believed that dividends and interest were not taxable.[61] As the campaign mounted, many came to believe that the savings institutions were deliberately lying to their constituents.[62]

At a May 9 press conference, the president attacked the savings institutions for "misinforming many millions of people" in the campaign.[63] Shortly thereafter the U.S. Savings and Loan League, motivated by fear that political action against withholding might endanger the Ways and Means compromise for the taxing of mutual savings institutions, agreed to call off the letter-writing campaign.[64] The administration made concessions to the industry to simplify paperwork for withholding, extend exemptions to tax-exempt organizations, and liberalize the quarterly refund procedure.[65] Yet the mail campaign had already succeeded. In mid-July the Senate Finance Committee voted ten to five against withholding and substituted a reporting requirement: banks must notify the Treasury of all payments of interest exceeding $10.[66]

The "hurricane of controversy" was stirred up in the House over a second reform proposal, the taxation of savings and loan institutions.[67] Kennedy proposed reducing the bad debt deduction from 12 to 3.5 percent, making savings institutions comparable to commercial banks.[68] The high bad debt ratio for mutual savings institutions was created in 1951 to prevent the high rate of mortgage foreclosures experienced during the Great Depression. Commercial banks vigorously opposed this disparity, pointing out that in 1960 mutuals paid effective tax rates of less than 1 percent while banks paid 35 percent. Sam Flemming of the American Bankers Association charged that savings and loans

> try to identify a 125-billion-dollar industry, which pays income taxes of less than 1 percent of income after dividends and interest, with the small saver. This identification escapes me. The fact is that the average account balance in savings and loan associations is $2,100. This is more than twice as large as the average savings balance in commercial banks.[69]

Savings and loan representatives retorted that their investments in fifteen- to twenty-five-year housing mortgages made them susceptible to heavy losses during recessions. Banks which issue short-term business and consumer loans do not face such economic threats.[70] At a press conference in early February Norman Strunk (U.S. Savings and Loan League vice-president) called Treasury's argument "penny wise and pound foolish," and warned that tax revenues would be decreased by diminished building activity.[71] The industry threatened to wage an "all-out battle" to defeat the measure.[72] Ways and Means ultimately caved in to the industry's demands, and savings and loan companies continued to enjoy a much lower rate of taxation.[73]

The final set of reform provisions were designed to increase taxes on the foreign income of U.S. corporations in order to "neutralize the impact of the tax system on the choice of investment" in the United States and Western Europe.[74] The administration thereby hoped to curb tax havens, decrease capital outflows by 10 percent, and alleviate the balance-of-payment problems.[75] The proposals to curb tax-oriented foreign investment included three major changes: revocation of the right to defer taxation of foreign income until it was repatriated, measures to reduce tax havens, and a "gross-up" provision.

Deferral of U.S. taxation of foreign income until it was repatriated had been a right enjoyed by American foreign subsidiaries for forty-four years. The administration was concerned that this gave an extra tax-based motivation for direct foreign investment, since profits could be reinvested abroad tax-free.

The tax haven problem had grown enormously: for example, fifty-nine U.S. subsidiaries were established in just seventeen months in a small Swiss canton with an 8 percent corporate tax rate.[76] The anti–tax haven provision tried to curb investment in nonmanufacturing concerns for the purposes of sheltering funds.

The "gross-up" proposal gave American business the most concern. Previously, foreign subsidiaries had been allowed to subtract foreign taxes paid from their income base before calculating U.S. taxes owed. According to the new proposal, when dividends were returned to the United States from foreign subsidiaries, taxes would be based on the total earnings. Allowances for foreign taxes paid would be made in the form of tax credits after the tax had been calculated.[77]

Industry argued that the administration misunderstood the impact of direct foreign investment on the balance of payments. According to the Manufacturing Chemists Association, direct foreign investment actually has a positive impact on balance-of-payment deficits and repatriates more dollars than it exports. The problem lies with portfolio investment: buying foreign securities and shifting bank accounts.[78] The Industry Committee on Foreign Investment (organized by H. J. Heinz within the International Chamber of Commerce) provided data on nineteen multinational companies to refute the administration's balance-of-payment arguments.[79] Senator Gore wondered whether the claims of this group were really representative, arguing that "if one assumes these 19 companies are typical, then the best way to solve our balance-of-payments problem, the best way to solve our unemployment problem, is to move all of our factories and our industry and our business abroad."[80]

Opponents charged that, by lowering profits, the provisions countered the Alliance for Progress goal of encouraging risky Third World investment in areas of political unrest.[81] The provisions ran contrary to the reciprocal trade legislation under consideration by Congress. Albert Gore responded that industry representatives were trying to "blackmail" Congress by threatening to defeat the trade bill if the tax provisions were passed.[82] Industry representatives doubted that direct foreign investment had really decreased domestic employment.[83] Finally, industry questioned the equity of the tax changes.[84]

Opposing industry groups again carried out a fairly traditional lobbying campaign against the provisions. A group made up of Sinclair Oil, General Telephone and Electronics, McGraw-Hill, Pfizer International and others organized to testify jointly before the committee.[85] The final provisions were considerably less stringent than the administration's proposals.[86]

By the time the Ways and Means Committee finished marking up the bill, the reform provisions had been greatly scaled back and the bill was no longer in balance. The investment tax credit would cost $1.8 billion, but the reform measures would only yield $1,295,000 annually. Concerns about revenue losses caused southern Democrats (led by Howard Smith, D–VA) and Republicans to oppose the package.[87] Many fiscal conservatives were reluctant to vote against withholding if the investment credit created major revenue losses, so they decided to kill both measures.[88] To this end John Byrnes (R–WI) charged that "the Administration-backed tax reform bill would give a 'tax bonanza' to owners of gambling casinos, bars and race horses while imposing hardships on millions of people with savings accounts."[89] The Ways and Means Committee cut the investment credit from 8 to 7 percent, reducing lost revenue to $1.175 billion.[90] The bill passed on March 29, 1962, by 219 to 196, with only 1 Republican in favor.[91]

The administration hoped to recoup some of its losses in the Senate, especially the provisions concerning the taxation of overseas business earnings and the repeal of the dividend credit and deduction.[92] Yet opposition to the bill in the Senate seemed stiff and broad-based. Manufacturing opposed the investment tax credit and the foreign income tax changes; banking, the withholding provisions; and labor, the failure to repeal the dividend credit and what it saw as the general pro-business tone of the bill. One labor leader remarked, "We couldn't kill the bill by ourselves, but we figured that together with the National Association of Manufacturers, the Chamber of Commerce, and other opponents, we might do it."

Despite efforts to kill it, the Senate passed the bill by fifty-nine to twenty-four on September 6, 1962, after eight days of debates.[93] It took many deals to make the bill a reality, prompting Gore to conclude in disgust that "a constant string of compromises and accommodations with respect to one special interest after another can lead to no good end." Douglas added, "The leadership on both sides of the aisle have tried to protect the wealthy and powerful, have opposed the Administration in connection with many crucial features, and have opposed provisions designed to protect the general tax payers and the Treasury."[94]

The Revenue Act of 1964: Proposal Development

During the tax battles in 1962, the administration began working on the proposal which would become the Revenue Act of 1964. The precipitating event for serious consideration of the measure was the stock market crash on June 4, in which $11 million was lost. Dillon was to address the New York Financial Writers Association on the balance-of-payment deficits but presented the plans for tax reduction instead.[95]

Although the tax cuts have been retrospectively hailed as a great Keynesian accomplishment, in reality the rate reductions meant many things to many people. The first issue to be resolved was the timing of the tax reduction. Although the cuts were first proposed in January of 1963, the administration considered enacting a "quickie" tax cut in the summer of 1962. The summer tax reduction was a temporary, 3 percent, across-the-board individual tax cut effective July 1 or September 1, 1962, to last until July 1, 1963. The revenue cost would be $3.7 billion calculated as a $4.8 billion tax reduction in FY63 minus $1.1 billion in revenue feedback. The corporate rate would be permanently reduced from 54 to 49 percent.[96]

The Council of Economic Advisers vigorously lobbied for an early cut to ward off the threatening recession.[97] Arthur Okun argued that an early small tax cut could prevent a later larger one.[98] Samuelson and Solow explained:

> A stitch in time doesn't save nine, but each extra billion of government stimulus designed to keep the recovery's momentum going may be worth a couple of billions spent later to stem a downward slide . . . I've thought much about anti-business sentiments, and feel that more can be done for confidence by expansionary policies—early tax cuts—than by any feasible alternatives.[99]

To Arthur Schlesinger the early cut was necessary to protect the image of the Democrats as a party of recession fighters.

> The great historic reason for the popular appeal of the Democratic party over the last generation has been that the American people regard it as the party which can be relied on to take action against recession . . . There is also need to balance the July 11 announcement on tax depreciation. Standing by itself, this announcement might lead some to think that we are abandoning the ancient Democratic faith in the support of demand and are instead trying to fight the stagnation on the trickle-down theory.[100]

Fearing inflation, Treasury wanted to announce plans for the cut but delay implementation until 1963 as planned.[101] Treasury wanted to tie tax reduction to later revenue-raising reforms and to package reduction as a long-term measure rather than as a short-term, macroeconomic stabilization tool.

Both sides used political business cycle arguments to support their claims: how to avoid a recession before the 1964 election. Treasury suggested that the administration engineer a medium-length recovery, then a short downturn, followed by a brisk recovery immediately before the election. This scenario precluded an early tax cut. Henry Fowler argued: "Your Administration should be inextricably associated with 'good times' in the minds of the people . . . Can that rare political asset—Kennedy prosperity—be preserved until November 1964?"[102]

The CEA favored a long expansion and "bold action now." Okun suggested that Fowler's short recession would be hard to control, could entail unemployment surpassing that during Eisenhower's administration, and would have a much lower rate of growth in the GNP than the 4.5 percent target. Plus, a strong recovery would be hard to achieve "after another abortive expansion." [103]

The administration actively solicited private sector views on early tax reduction. The financial community opposed the immediate cuts. G. Keith Funston, president of the New York Stock Exchange, went on television to caution against hasty tax reduction without spending control. [104] Douglas Dillon's canvass of the Treasury's Advisory Committee (drawn from the American Bankers Association and the Investment Bankers Association) produced only one investment banker in favor of the measure. [105]

By comparison, many in the manufacturing and the small business community wanted earlier tax cuts. The U.S. Chamber of Commerce, calling for a budget deficit for the first time in its history, urged that immediate cuts be legislated irrespective of their budgetary impact. "The best hope and prospect for future balanced budgets and fiscal sanity lies in removing immediately the tax rate deterrents to economic growth." [106] Murray Shields, head of a Wall Street consulting firm, canvassed forty executives in twenty different industries and found widespread panic over the economy and stock market slide. Heller cited Shields:

> In a curious twist that we hear more and more often, the anti-government business community is looking to the President to exercise his powers under the mandate of the Employment Act of 1946. He says that the impression of "indecision and impotence" coming out of Washington is more damaging than any of the alleged anti-business moves . . . His recommendation is an across-the-board reduction in taxes of 4 points in the individual and 4 points on the corporation tax . . . and he urged "whirlwind speed" . . . This is strong stuff from a mild-mannered man like Shields. [107]

Labor leaders and the liberal Americans for Democratic Action also supported the cut, charging that the administration's "conservative economic policies have already gone too far toward appeasing business complaints by tax concessions." [108] George Meany proposed a $5 billion cut in the lowest income bracket, to begin on September 1, 1962, and last through July 30, 1963. [109]

Conservatives in Congress (Wilbur Mills and Harry Byrd) resisted early action on tax reduction. [110] On August 6, Mills warned Kennedy that congressional cooperation was unlikely: the country was not currently in a recession, and there was no consensus as to whether the reduction should be concentrated in higher or lower brackets. Mills also expressed skepticism about economic forecasts, citing the FY62 GNP prediction as an example of their unreliability. He urged Kennedy to freeze spending at the current level and lower taxes within a balanced budget. [111] Senate Finance chairman Harry Byrd so vehemently opposed the quickie tax reduction that he wrote a letter to Ladd

Plumley charging the Chamber of Commerce with "fiscal irresponsibility." [112] Hubert Humphrey, however, reported that a majority of Senate Democrats would support the measure. [113]

After a summer of hesitation, an early tax cut was ultimately rejected for economic and political reasons. The economy promised some marginal improvement: despite low business investment, consumer and government spending was increasing. [114] Ways and Means hearings on the subject produced no consensus among expert witnesses. [115] Public opinion polls revealed ambiguous support for the measure. In early July the *New York Times* observed "amazing unity" in support for the measure. [116] Yet by August *Business Week* noted that, of 150 "high-ranking executives," 6 to 4 were against the measure. [117] Finally, inside advisers feared that a divisive legislative debate could be damaging to the president's overall economic policy plans. [118] On August 13, Kennedy rejected the early cut for lack of "clear and present danger"; Mills promised tax reform in 1963. [119]

A second question concerning tax reduction was whether to concentrate the cuts in the upper or lower brackets. Not surprisingly, the business community wanted cuts in the upper brackets. Donald Hardenbrook (National Association of Manufacturers president) supported the Herlong-Baker tax bill sponsored by Sydney Herlong, D–FL, and Howard Baker, R–TN. This would reduce personal taxes over 5 years by at least 25 percent. The bill would lower the maximum individual rate from 91 to 40 percent, and the corporate rate from 52 to 47 percent. [120] The Chamber of Commerce's proposal would reduce the top rate from 91 to 65 percent, divide the lowest bracket in half, and decrease all other rates. [121]

Conversely, labor and liberal Democrats wanted cuts in the lower brackets. The AFL-CIO proposed a $9 billion cut in the lowest income bracket immediately, followed by a $5.5 billion cut in higher brackets and corporate taxes coupled with reform at a later date. [122]

A third dilemma was whether the tax cut should be presented as a Keynesian instrument to stimulate consumption or a neoclassical economic strategy to maximize growth. In the consumption camp were the CEA, labor leaders, and liberals. Labor groups were angry at the administration for its excessive concern with "stimulating investment directly instead of stimulating it by beefing up consumer markets." In an ironic vein, a labor leader called the administration one of "compassion, but not full employment." [123] The CEA reported the following about a meeting with AFL-CIO staff:

> The AFL-CIO staff people have long been unhappy with both the actions and the inactions of the Administration . . . With the unemployment rate stuck at 5–6 percent they regard the spectacle of the Administration's economic troops marching off to fight the problems of the balance of payments, inflation, and economic growth with undisguised dismay . . . Their main gripe these days centers around

the scuttlebutt, concerning Federal tax policy. They think they will wind up next year, like this year, with the dirty end of the stick—big cuts for the fat cats, some crumbs for the little folk, and no reform. They wonder if they wouldn't do better if this so-called "anti-business" administration reversed itself and became violently "anti-labor." [124]

Conversely, Dillon, Mills, and the entire business community wanted to frame the tax cut as a supply-side stimulant. Dillon reported a meeting with the heads of all the larger New York banks:

The entire group favored a revision of the tax structure which would promote incentives to work and to invest. All of them felt that this should be coupled with clear-cut and strong efforts to curb expenditures . . . None of the bankers present thought there was any need for a tax cut at this time designed to increase purchasing power and so ward off a recession. All of them would strongly oppose such action. [125]

Douglas Dillon also argued against the macroeconomic stabilization rationale on the basis of the president's self-interests: "Use of the cyclical argument pointing toward 1964 indicates a major political interest on your part in the bill, which stresses the very reason for which many Republicans secretly oppose any bill at all." [126]

A fourth consideration was the extent to which the administration should embrace deficits as appropriate policy tools and acknowledge them as likely side effects of the cuts. Walter Heller campaigned for budget deficits to come out of the closet, arguing that deficits were not an evil in and of themselves. By 1963 parts of the business community found deficits tolerable, many believing that lost revenue would be made up through increased entrepreneurial activity. The Council of Economic Development was an early convert, the Chamber of Commerce changed course in the summer of 1962, and in November the Advisory Committee on Labor Management endorsed tax reduction even with a budget deficit. [127]

Opposing the budget deficit were fiscal conservatives and financial interests who worried about the impact of deficits on the dollar. Charls Walker, vice-president of the American Bankers Association, urged that the purpose of the cuts should be to create a climate for high rates of growth rather than deficit spending. "The stakes are these: the continued prosperity and success of our free enterprise economy; our leadership in the free world; and as a consequence, the prospects for the free world itself." [128] The European central bankers agreed that the "deficit should be presented as a cost of essential tax reform" and should be financed out of current savings. [129]

The administration's posture regarding the budget deficit was somewhat inconsistent. During his famous Yale speech, the president publicly rejected the idea that deficits cause inflation or that a balanced budget is automatically a good thing.[130] Yet on other occasions the administration tried to avoid saying that the tax cuts were geared to produce growth-stimulating budget deficits. Dillon convinced the president to soft-pedal the deficit before fiscal conservatives in Congress: "The line we walk is a very narrow one. What seems most important is the motivation behind our actions. In other words, any suspicion that the Administration considers that a deficit is good per se tremendously increases the pressures in Congress favoring drastic expenditure reductions."[131]

A fifth issue was whether to make tax reduction contingent on reform. Tax reformers included both liberals and conservatives. Fiscal conservatives, Douglas Dillon and Wilbur Mills both considered reform vital to offset revenue losses. Liberal tax reformers within the administration, such as Stanley Surrey (Assistant Secretary of the Treasury), joined them. Liberal senators Albert Gore and Paul Douglas led the pro-reform forces in Congress. Douglas criticized the administration's lack of commitment: "by not having a virile stance in favor of tax reform, you have permitted the reform provisions to be gutted. When you throw the tax reform overboard, you just permit the pirates to take over the ship."[132]

The antireform position also drew individuals from many political leanings. Some liberals feared that tax reduction might be delayed by reforms. The AFL-CIO economic policy committee observed that, "once the tax reform issue is introduced, every pressure group will insert its oar and the wrangling will go on forever."[133] Heller reflected:

> I opposed cluttering up the 1963 tax cut by inclusion of tax reforms—and I never bought the argument that vested interests, just because we feed them a high-protein diet of tax cuts, would be any less venal or voracious when we kick them in their private parts.[134]

Most of the business community with the exclusion of financial interests opposed reform. The Advisory Committee on Labor Management warned that tax reform should not be allowed to delay the cuts.[135] The Business Committee for Tax Reduction argued that tax reduction should take place first and foremost; reforms could follow later.[136] Some business interests were against tax reform for the same reason that liberal reformers supported it—they had a lot to lose.

Spending cuts were a final problem for tax reduction, demanded by fiscal conservatives in both parties as well as by businessmen. Ways and Means ranking minority member John Byrnes offered spending cuts as the price for Republican support of the bill.[137] Resisting expenditure limitations, Heller got carried away during congressional testimony and blamed the "basic puritan ethic of the American people" for the misunderstanding of budgetary matters. For months afterward, the remark surfaced in hostile settings.[138]

The Tax Program Is Announced

President Kennedy presented the broad outlines of his tax program in his State of the Union message on January 14, 1963. Taxes were to be cut by $13.6 billion: $11 billion in individual and $2.6 billion in corporate taxes. Revenue-raising reforms would total $3.4 billion, producing a net tax cut of $10.2 billion.[139] The individual rate structure (20 to 91 percent) was to be changed to 14 to 65 percent. The tax cuts were to be accompanied by revenue-raising reforms including changes in the dividend credit and exclusion, capital gains taxation, and oil provisions.

The president announced in his January 1963 budget message that 1964 spending would be $98 billion with a deficit of $11.9 billion. Spending would thus increase $4.5 billion over spending for FY63, which was itself $6.5 billion above the figure for FY62. The administration immediately came under attack from Republicans and conservative Democrats, who charged "fiscal irresponsibility" and vowed that tax cuts would be contingent on spending reductions.[140]

Considerable consensus seemed to exist for the cuts in the fall of 1962 and winter of 1963. In one public opinion survey, only 5 percent of the population wanted no tax reduction at all; 45 percent wanted tax reduction with reforms and spending cuts; 36 percent, tax reduction with spending cuts but no reforms; 5 percent, tax reduction with reforms but no spending cuts; and 6 percent, immediate tax reduction with no strings attached.[141] Richard Mooney observed: "It is a rare moment when a Democratic President, a Republican ex-President and leaders of the business community and the trade union movement agree on a major issue of economic policy. This is such a movement."[142]

Yet initial consensus disappeared as soon as the actual details of the program were announced, since different groups held vastly dissimilar views of the tax cut's form and purpose. The *New York Times* commented that "there is not now, never has been, and probably never will be a consensus on what the problem is, so neither is there a consensual answer."[143] *Business Week* noted the business response: "Cautious from the first, their reaction became even sourer as time went on." Some felt that the president's proposal was "a fake by comparison with what he had seemed to promise."[144]

The administration's initial portrayal of the cuts took neoclassical form. This was due partially to the failure of the recession-fighting quickie tax cut.[145] Kennedy told the Economic Club of New York that this was not "a mere shot in the arm to ease some temporary complaint" but an effort to increase "the financial incentives for personal effort, investment and risk-taking."[146] John Kenneth Galbraith called it the most Republican speech since Hoover.

The neoclassical cast was also aimed at appeasing Wilbur Mills. Mills told Fowler that, although he believed "the present tax rate structure is a drag on the economy," tax reduction necessitated both reform and expenditure control, and suggested a ratio of $11 billion of revenue loss to $5 billion of reform. The president should portray the bill as a mechanism for long-term growth in his State of the Union address.[147] To accommodate Mills, President Kennedy drastically revised his tax proposal, abandoning the two-stage concept and giving it a retroactive date of January 1, 1963.[148]

In the early spring of 1963 the economy showed signs of weakening, and opposition to the reforms eroded support for the bill. The administration began to present the tax cuts as a recession-fighting measure and to indicate ambivalence about reform.[149] In a February speech to the American Bankers Association Kennedy said: "If we cannot get the reform, then quite obviously you are going to have to rewrite the package . . . What we need is the bill this year, and nothing should stand in its way."[150]

As concerns about the economy subsided, the administration returned to the neoclassical portrayal and tax reform.[151] Kennedy had been criticized by his business allies for straying into Keynesian territory. Gabriel Hauge (vice-chairman of Manufacturers Hanover Trust Company) commented:

> Your tax program was initially presented, and rightly in my view, as a long range growth-stimulating measure, but later it came to be defended as a prospective anti-recession device. This latter characterization, however carefully it may have been designed to broaden Congressional support, now appears to be boomeranging as the likelihood of near-term weakening in the economy recedes.[152]

Taxation in the Ways and Means

The Ways and Means Committee, chaired by Wilbur Mills, began hearings on the proposal on February 6 but only finished drafting the bill on September 10.[153] The committee's delay was due in part to Mills's care to construct a bill that would pass in the House. In 1958 newly appointed chairman Mills lost his first major bill on the House floor and had moved slowly since. His extreme care and frequent tardiness earned the body the nickname the "No-Ways and By-No-Means Committee."[154]

The committee essentially gutted the president's major reform proposals in its months of deliberation: the capital gains changes, dividend exclusion, and oil provisions. The administration had proposed that the long-term capital gains holding period be increased from six months to one year and that accumulated capital gains no longer be forgiven at death. Accompanying this proposal had been a rate cut. Capital gains had been taxed with a formula of 50 percent of the gain at normal rates or the entire gain at 25 percent. This was to be changed to 30 percent at normal rates or the entire gain at 19.5 percent. The financial community (especially stockbrokers and investment bankers) immediately mobilized to oppose the increases. G. Keith Funston (New York

Stock Exchange president) led an attack on the extension of the capital gain holding period and the plan to tax capital gains at death.[155]

Instead of increasing the capital gains holding period, the committee created two new categories: gains for assets held from 6 months to 2 years would be taxed at current rates; for assets held over 2 years, 21 percent of the gain would be taxed at ordinary rates or all the gain would be taxed at 40 percent.[156] The committee rejected the proposal to tax capital gains at death, a proposal which the administration considered vital and would have generated $750 million a year in revenue. In addition, the committee allowed capital losses to be carried forward and offset annually against all capital gains and up to $1,000 in ordinary income for an infinite number of years.[157]

Another reform repealed a provision allowing individuals to escape taxes on a proportion of dividend and interest income: the first $50 and 4 percent thereafter. Again, the financial community, major proponents of the *general* concept of reform, objected to the *specifics*. Republican members of the committee transmitted these objections by heavily lobbying Mills to abandon the proposal.[158] Ways and Means finally decided to accept a compromise offered by Hale Boggs (D–LA) and John C. Watts (D–KY). The 4 percent dividend credit would be repealed, but the $50 exclusion would be doubled. It was estimated that the compromise could cost $300 million.[159]

The gas and oil changes were the last major business-oriented reforms in the president's package. Currently no more than 50 percent of a firm's net income after deductions for development, operations, and other business expenses could be offset by the depletion allowance. To narrow the offsetting capability of the depletion allowance, the administration narrowed the scope of profits considered "net income." It proposed taxing profits from the sale of mineral property as ordinary income instead of capital gain if tax deductions for capital investment had already been taken. Changes were to be made in the taxation of extraction industries operating abroad.[160]

The administration used these indirect means of altering the depletion allowance because it was reluctant to attack the provision directly. The Democratic party represented powerful oil interests; many southern Democrats were committed to protecting those interests. At the same time the depletion allowance was a popular target for the president's liberal constituency. The structural changes to lower the allowance without attacking it directly represented a compromise.[161]

This strategy did not work, however, and the oil industry waged war on Ways and Means. An American Petroleum Institute representative testified that producers would have preferred a direct cut in the depletion allowance to the complex changes in the proposal.[162] The American Gas Association claimed that the provisions would cost the industry an additional $280 million in taxes a year.[163]

Some considered the industry's lobbying a case of overkill. One industry lobbyist concluded that it was a mistake to have demonstrated such political and economic power. Cecil King called the hearings a waste of time: "Our whole hearing process has tended to be thrown into disrepute." [164] The Ways and Means Committee, however, was sufficiently impressed to reject all but one relatively minor provision, generating $40 million in tax revenues.[165]

As the House committee scaled back the president's reform proposals, the deficit projections grew proportionately larger. On August 12 the executive branch proposed a revision in the rate structure to keep the revenue loss within the $10 to $11 billion range.[166] The rate range, 14 to 65 percent under the original proposal, was changed to 14 to 70 percent. Reforms were expected to yield only $690 million in new revenues instead of the hoped-for $3.3 billion.[167] The Ways and Means Committee reported the bill out of committee on September 10. Disagreeing with the concept of tax reduction without spending cuts, nine of the ten Republican members of the committee wrote a minority report; the bill was "fiscally wrong—a time bomb for inflation." [168] On September 25 the bill passed the House 271 to 155.[169]

Senate Finance Takes Action

The Senate Finance Committee began hearings on the bill on October 15, 1963, and finished December 10. The administration expected difficulty getting the bill through Senate Finance. Senator Harry Byrd, chairman of the committee, opposed the bill on budget deficit grounds. Henry Fowler suggested to the president that the opposition would fight the measure using strategies of delay and expenditure controls. He feared that the liberals Gore and Williams would join Byrd in opposing the bill. The Republicans meanwhile would try to "put a Republican trade-mark on this tax bill in the form of specific expenditure limits." [170] Fowler recommended that the president preempt congressional action on expenditure controls by ordering the FY65 budget to be kept below $100 billion. He warned that opponents "will wish to divide the Administration from its allies in the business and financial community and ride the acknowledged thrust of public and editorial opinion for expenditure control as an accompaniment to a tax cut." [171]

When Congress reconvened in January, the Senate Finance Committee marked up the bill in two weeks, an amazingly short period of time. Although Chairman Byrd continued to oppose the bill personally, he made a commitment to move it through the committee as quickly as possible. Undoubtedly this was due largely to the support generated for the bill by the death of President Kennedy. Also important was a bargain agreed to by President Johnson and Harry Byrd: expenditure reductions for fast action on the tax bill. Johnson followed Fowler's advice. In January he proposed an expenditure level actually below that of 1964.[172] Finally, the broad-based support enjoyed by the legislation in the business community paved the way for rapid passage. The bill passed the Senate on February 7, 1964, seventy-seven to twenty-one. The Senate essentially passed the House version, except that the capital gains rate reductions were eliminated.[173] Since the Ways and Means Committee had failed to tax gains at death, the administration felt that the rate reductions were unjustified and urged that they be dropped from the bill.[174]

Business Support for Tax Policy

Despite the initial hostility of the corporate community, the administration's 1964 tax reduction effort was greatly assisted by business support. After the struggle over the 1962 tax legislation, the administration set out to systematically cultivate and utilize potential corporate allies. Fowler suggested organizing "a private, independent, non-partisan organization" to support the tax bill and submitted a list of candidates to form the core. A Temporary Executive Committee should convene the larger Organizing Group in order to discuss recruitment strategies and adopt a Statement of Principles. President Kennedy should attend this meeting, review the background of the bill, and urge that the group membership be as broad and representative as possible. Fowler suggested an agenda for the meeting: approval of the Statement of Principles, discussion of organizing methods, and choice of techniques.[175]

Fowler suggested that the group should strive for a May meeting with a membership in the hundreds, recruited through mailings and personal telephone calls. The administration (Treasury, Commerce, and the presidential office) could put together a list of five hundred names and addresses of potential members. The list should include leaders from industrial sectors, representatives of the various geographical areas, and individuals having knowledge in tax policy through participation in prior policy-making forums. After the May meeting the committee would be totally autonomous; Fowler and Larry O'Brien would serve as liaison persons.[176]

The president met with thirty-five business leaders on April 25 and formed the committee according to Fowler's plan. The group, the previously mentioned "Business Committee for Tax Reduction in 1963," set a target of recruiting three hundred leaders of industry by June 1.[177] The co-chairmen of the group were Henry Ford II (Ford Motor Company) and Stuart Saunders (Norfolk and Western Railway). Vice-chairmen were Mark Cresap, Jr. (Westinghouse), Sam Flemming (Third National Bank of Nashville), and Frazar Wilde (Connecticut General Life Insurance Company). Other Executive Committee members were Frederick Kappel (AT&T), David Rockefeller (Chase Manhattan Bank), and J. Harris Ward (Commonwealth Edison of Chicago) among others.[178] Despite the administration's key role in its origins, the committee denied being organized by the executive branch. At the committee's national conference, held in September of 1963, Frazar Wilde asserted:

> The Business Committee for Tax Reduction is an informal organization unique in many ways. The idea was endorsed by Treasury and

by the President. But the organization itself and its program were developed by a bipartisan group of businessmen who wrote their own ticket.

Contrary to some reports, the Committee is not the servant of the Administration. The Administration has in no way tried to direct it. The policies, the statements, and the judgments guiding the activities of the Business Committee were written and carried out by its Executive Committee.[179]

The Business Committee endorsed a $10 billion tax cut taking effect as early as possible in 1963, called for tax reduction separated from tax reform and expenditure control, and avoided taking stands on specific reform proposals.[180] The group proved extremely useful to the administration during the legislative process, conveying widespread support for the tax bill and convincing hesitant congressmen. Fowler explained:

> With the final decisions of the Ways and Means Committee in the closing weeks in August and the reporting out of a definite bill on September 10, the way has opened, for the first time, for tangible concrete declarations of organizational support of a specific bill and the opportunity to initiate a beginning of a "grass roots" campaign.[181]

The goals of the grass roots movement were twofold: "approval of the House bill and a call for its early enactment by the Senate." In order to maintain the momentum of this movement, the administration decided not to push the Senate to consider the reform measures dropped by the House. Fowler felt that attempting to start up some of the reform measures again would be divisive for passage of the act. Rather, Dillon should state clearly to the press that the president was willing to forgo further consideration of those reforms. Fowler wrote:

> This statement should enable most of the organizations who favor the House bill to concentrate their efforts in the Senate on securing early enactment, thus unifying the forces for tax reduction this year rather than having them divided or paralyzed in their movement by the lack of a definite target.[182]

The Business Committee was also helpful in bringing other business groups around to the president's way of thinking. Fowler was able to persuade a number of trade associations to formally support the bill.[183] He credits the Business Committee for this:

> I should add that the assistance of The Business Committee, and the affiliation with it of many of the principal executive officers of many of the leading industrial companies and financial institutions of the country, has been of immeasurable assistance in marshalling support among the various established trade organizations and avoiding the "knee jerk" type of opposition that normally characterizes response to any initiative from a Democratic President. In short, the influence

of The Business Committee, plus some very timely infiltrating initiatives by some of the leading members and staff of the committee in established organizations, has been most helpful. With that assistance, so far as we can tell, all of the established organizations that have entered the fray have come in clearly in support of the bill on final passage. Some organizations have remained neutral, such as the NAM, and only one organized lobby seems to be in open opposition, namely, the American Farm Bureau Federation.[184]

The administration encouraged organizations favoring the bill to "bring home to their members the need for a concrete expression of sentiment of constituents to individual Congressmen and Senators in favor of the enactment by Congress this year of the House bill or something substantially resembling it." [185] In response business groups sent out mass mailings supporting the measure. The Chamber of Commerce's *Tax Alert Bulletin* was one such response. Fowler found these activities especially helpful in persuading Republican and southern Democratic legislators to vote for the bill. Fourteen out of fifteen southern governors supported the bill, largely as a result of the efforts of the business groups.

The Business Committee for Tax Reduction in 1963 was thus extremely useful to the administration in mobilizing support for the tax bill. A Democratic president, elected with a narrow margin and reputed to be antibusiness, was undoubtedly in need of additional support. Yet one must ask what the price of such support was in policy terms. In the case of the 1964 tax cuts the administration was forced to endorse expenditure limitations and abandon many of its reform efforts.

Conclusion

Because President Kennedy had campaigned on a promise to "get the country moving again," his political fortune was tied to the successful implementation of an activist economic agenda. Yet his desire to move beyond the noninterventionist policies of Eisenhower enjoyed questionable support. Fundamental trade-offs in the economy mirrored by deep divisions in state and society prevented a clear consensus on the appropriate course of action.

Macroeconomic conflict centered around two issues. First, should the state intervene in the economy? This was a question which elicited a resounding no from Eisenhower's noninterventionist Republican constituency. Second, given intervention, should the primary economic goal be to protect the gold supply by curbing balance-of-payment deficits or to stimulate domestic growth?

These three policy positions—nonintervention, deficit reduction, and domestic stimulation—had their supporters within state and society. The business community had begun to be sympathetic to a new activist program; however, industries worried about different economic goals. Thus, financial groups worried about balance-of-payment deficits: they opposed deficit-fueled expansionary fiscal policy but thought that selective growth incentives could help the economy grow out of imbalance. Manufacturing groups worried about growth and were more amenable to commercial Keynesianism. Small business, to the extent that we have information, was the last to leave the noninterventionist stance, expressing skepticism about the growth scenario.

Factions within government were also divided on the appropriate course of action. Within the executive branch, state actors were divided as to the best means for achieving prosperity. The balance-of-payment deficits were of primary concern to Douglas Dillon and the Treasury. Walter Heller in the CEA described himself as a Keynesian "growthist." The nonintervention stance was assumed by many congressional Republicans and southern Democrats. Therefore, the president had to contend with the partisan opposition of the GOP and the skepticism of members of his own party in legislating his activist agenda. The divisions in state, society, and economy are shown in table 3.3.

Given this pattern of divided goals and elite support, no obvious policy presented itself to satisfy either the functional requisites of macroeconomics or the mandates of the capitalist class. Nor were key actors in agreement on what the final outcome should be. Therefore, the making of tax policy was far from deterministic.

In the face of competing goals and political conflict, the administration embraced a coalition strategy, although not until well into the president's term. Business groups were largely antagonistic during the legislation of the Revenue Act of 1962; lobbying efforts centered on opposing reform provisions which threatened each sector's self-interests. But after the struggle over the 1962 legislation, the administration pulled together a core group of private sector supporters to develop a business-based lobbying group. The Business Committee for Tax Reduction in 1963 was a very different kind of business lobbying group. Organized by the administration and oriented toward a larger policy vision, the movement was of political benefit to both the executive branch activists and their business allies. The coalition strategy helped the president gain the acquiescence of his political enemies and legislate this activist agenda.

This alliance between factions in state and society can be seen in their dual

Table 3.3. Divisions in State and Society over Tax Options

Goals	Business	State	Policy
Domestic stimulation	Manufacturing	Heller/CEA	Keynesian tax cuts
Balance of payment	Finance/housing	Dillon/ Treasury	Lower rates/ reforms
No state intervention	Small business	Mills/House conservatives	No tax cuts without budget cuts

influence on policy outcomes. On the one hand, state-centered conflicts and interests were extremely influential. Kennedy's electoral victory over Richard Nixon set the stage for an activist economic policy. The packaging and timing of policy initiatives were calculated to satisfy the president's institutional interests. When the economy dipped in the spring of 1963, justification for the tax cuts suddenly shifted. Kennedy abandoned the rhetoric of long-term growth and took on the language of macroeconomic stimulation. Political business cycle dynamics were responsible for the timing of the tax acts: the rejection of the quickie tax cut in 1962 and the implementation of tax reduction in 1964. The Kennedy administration also wanted business-oriented tax reduction to bear a distinctly Democratic stamp. For this reason the investment tax credit rather than the more popular accelerated depreciation was the vehicle for capital-investment stimulation.

On the other hand, business interests had a considerable impact on the course of corporate taxation during these years. The administration routinely polled industry allies before taking action. The Kennedy people made an effort to satisfy both manufacturing and financial interests. Therefore, items on which the two groups agreed were included in the 1964 act. The cuts were concentrated in the top bracket and were tied to spending reductions. Reforms which threatened to divide business and prolong the process were dropped from the Senate proposals. In the final analysis, the dependence on business allies in the partisan competition for political power greatly limited the degree of freedom the administration had in determining tax policy outcomes.

4
The Tax Surcharge of 1968

Introduction

In the early 1960s President Kennedy tied his political fortunes to a new economic activism and redirected tax policy toward a "commercial Keynesian" growth strategy. Yet the heyday of the commercial Keynesian hegemony was short-lived, already unraveling by the end of the decade. Responsibility lay with an economy out of control, unhinged by a number of economic and political stresses. Booming growth in capital investment and demand generated inflationary pressures; spending for both guns (Vietnam) and butter (the Great Society) strained government coffers. Inflation combined with rising balance-of-payment deficits threatened the viability of the dollar's reserve currency status.

The proper Keynesian intervention for the economic quandary was to increase taxes: this would ease the pressure of the boom and subdue the manic phase of the unruly business cycle. In addition to the macroeconomic rationale, a tax increase was necessary to pay for the Great Society and the Vietnam War. The administration began to consider this option in 1966. As an interim measure, the investment tax credit was suspended in September of 1966 but was subsequently reinstated in March of 1967 with a softening in the economy. Congress finally passed the 8 percent tax surcharge on individual and corporate rates in the summer of 1968, over two years after initial consideration of the measure. Accompanying the tax increase was a spending cut package eliminating $6 billion in expenditures, $6 billion in appropriations, and $14 billion in budget obligational authority or future spending.

Why did the surtax legislation take two years of struggle and delay? The question is important since failure to restrain the economy during this period has been generally considered a cause of economic troubles during the 1970s. Difficulty of enactment was related partially to the nature of the policy requirement: it's politically easier to cut taxes than to raise them. In addition, the 1964 tax cut unified true believers in Keynesian macroeconomic stabilization with those inspired by the neoclassical rationale. The former sought tax cuts to offset dips in the business cycle; the latter wanted to reduce rates permanently to inspire savings and investment. When increasing taxes became the task at hand, these diverse elements could not easily be brought together; fiscal conservatives fought to defend the lower rates. Politics also

81

worked against easy enactment of the surtax. Congressional liberals feared the tax increase would be used to escalate military intervention in Asia; conservatives suspected that increased tax revenues would be diverted to antipoverty programs.

The tax increase divided the business community. Bankers and those with housing interests were early and committed supporters of the measure: inflation and balance-of-payment problems could only be controlled with a program of fiscal restraint. Small business violently opposed the measure, sharing the concerns of conservative congressmen. Manufacturers were skeptical but ultimately persuaded. As in 1964 the administration turned to business allies, drawing support from first financial and later manufacturing interests to cope with a recalcitrant Congress. Again, the coalition strategy gave tax intervention a commercial Keynesian caste.

Macroeconomic Context

When the Johnson administration began to consider a tax increase in 1966, the economy was booming: quarterly demand was increasing by $14 to $16 billion, yet the economy could only maintain price integrity with quarterly increases of $11 billion. The president and his advisers were worried about the inflationary implications of the expansion. For example, in the machinery industry unemployment had dropped to 1.9 percent in the second quarter of 1966; under such conditions wage demands were not easily restrained. Machine orders were backlogged by an average of ten months, a 29 percent increase over the year before.

Although in the short term excessive demand would compete for resources and drive prices up, in the long term it could create an oversupply of capital goods. A Commerce Department–Securities and Exchange Commission (SEC) plant and equipment survey found that planned investment outlays for 1966 were 17 percent above the 1965 level, half a billion dollars higher than the plans reported in February, and were especially heavy in railroads, nonelectrical machinery manufacturing, aircraft, and petroleum.[1] Heller worried that excess capacity was being created, setting the economy up for a "post-Vietnam investment slump."[2]

This investment boom put pressure on the credit markets. Bank loans to business increased 22 percent from January through July of 1966, limiting funds for home mortgages. The unsatisfied demand for capital goods increased machinery imports by 44 percent in the first half of 1966, thus exacerbating the balance-of-payments crisis.[3] The expansion was fueled in part by government deficits, which were much larger than projected. The war in Vietnam was costing $122 billion a year; the war's uncertain future complicated predictions about government borrowing.[4]

The boom put upward pressure on interest rates. To curb the inflationary trends, the Federal Reserve had adopted a tight monetary policy using high interest rates to try to cool off the economy and alleviate the outflow of dollars and gold by attracting investors to American accounts. This created a credit crunch in selected industries such as construction. The Fed then tried and failed to reduce rates with easier monetary policy.[5] Chairman William Martin explained, "While higher interest rates have been due partly to heavy business credit demands, they also reflect market expectations of strong economic revival and the need to finance a huge Federal deficit."[6]

Most alarming was the behavior of the stock market. By the end of August the Dow Jones industrial average had dropped 21.6 percent from what it had been on February 9. Analysts attributed the drop to the incredibly high rates on bonds. Since interest rates were eventually expected to go back to their normal levels, investors could buy long-term bonds and realize capital gains of up to 20 percent. Stock investors also worried that the Federal Reserve's tight monetary policy to curb the boom would create a recession.

State Factions: Economic and Political Agendas

Keynesian logic dictated a tax increase to counter the boom. President Johnson's economic advisers began to recommend a tax increase to reduce the then 3 percent inflation rate in 1966; Gardner Ackley (CEA) warned that, should the tax increase be delayed for one year, "we could slow the inflation only by throwing the economy into reverse."[7] The international implications of an inflated currency also motivated a tax hike; an inflated currency could threaten the balance-of-payment deficits and gold supply.

Domestic policymakers worried about the low rates of unemployment. Unemployment, 3.7 percent in the first quarter of 1966, was expected to drop to 3 percent by the end of the year. The tight labor market coupled with two years of accelerating prices could produce 6 to 7 percent wage increases in 1967.[8] Referring to the proposed tax increase, Secretary of Labor Wirtz suggested that "American business is for it because they think it will restore enough unemployment to be a buffer against extreme wage demands and labor shortages."[9]

Policymakers considered a tax increase to ease monetary policy. For example, during the downturn in 1966, Walter Heller recognized that additional net fiscal restraint was unnecessary, yet a package of "tighter taxes and easier money" would "*put our lopsided economy back on an even keel by loosening the tight money tourniquet that has squeezed housing and small business.*"[10] Yet William Martin (chairman of the Federal Reserve) pointed out that lowering interest rates was constrained by balance-of-payment considerations.

> Somewhat easier money would seem to me desirable if fiscal action is taken to enable it, even though the extent to which money can be

eased will be limited by balance of payments considerations, since too much or too rapid an easing could produce an outflow of funds to Europe and a drain on our gold supply that could quickly become serious.[11]

A tax increase was also considered for the purpose of decreasing budget deficits. Members of the Council of Economic Advisers, Keynesians all, continued to campaign against balanced budget idolatry: a deficit "consistent with a sound and noninflationary economy" they found perfectly acceptable.[12] But others feared that the 1968 deficit projections would leave the administration open to charges of fiscal irresponsibility. William Martin argued that such charges could have negative political consequences both domestically and internationally:

> In my considered judgment, it would be a mistake to come out with prospective budget deficits of virtually unprecedented size without coming out for an increase in taxes . . . I would be far more concerned about the effects at home and abroad of a failure to propose an increase in taxes than I would be about the effects of proposing one.[13]

The major economic factor working against the tax increase was the prospect of recession, considered a greater risk than the boom.[14] In 1966 Califano argued that "there are too many signs of softening to risk a definite tax boost decision now."[15] Yet Ackley thought that the vigorous easing of monetary policy and liberal social security increases would stimulate the economy enough to offset the restraint.[16] Henry Fowler argued that increases in defense expenditures would prevent any economic softening.[17]

Not to be minimized was the role of the Vietnam War in the tax debate. As the Johnson administration became increasingly committed to escalation in Vietnam, paying for the war was an obvious concern. Already in 1966 advisers realized that Vietnam expenditures would probably increase by $4 billion more than had been calculated for the FY67 budget. The tax increase would pay for increased defense spending; timely revocation of the surtax could prevent a postwar recession.[18]

The president's political interests (as well as economic concerns) became linked to the surtax: the administration felt that successful legislation of the tax would reassure the public and demonstrate that the president was in charge. In this vein Fowler suggested that the tax increase would "psychologically restore confidence at home and abroad that the United States would not tolerate a serious inflation."[19] Ackley also saw "desirable psychological effects":

—it will make people feel they are *sharing in the sacrifices required by Vietnam;*
—it will make labor and business more willing to accept *voluntary*

restraint because they will realize *that we are serious about fight-ing inflation;*

—it will make *European central bankers more confident* about holding dollars.[20]

As the surtax became a major point of contention in Congress, it became a symbol of the entire Johnson presidency. Joseph Califano advised the president:

> I have a strong instinct that what happens in the current tax fight may be a critical turning point in your Presidency, not only vis-à-vis the Congress, but perhaps on a much larger scale . . . Like it or not, the White House and the Presidency are identified with the Mahon pack-age. If that package loses and if you get stuck either with no tax bill or with provisions of the kind Mills is now peddling, I think the ball game may well be over on the Hill for the rest of the year. Indeed, you may have an increasingly difficult time running the Executive Branch of the Government and leading the country.[21]

Congressional liberals (mainly Democrats) were of two minds about the tax increase. Most of them accepted the Keynesian macroeconomic rationale for increasing taxes during a boom and perceived the measure as mandatory for the continuation of the Great Society program. Thus, Louis Martin (Deputy Chairman for Minorities of the Democratic National Committee) wrote to Califano:

> The demonstration we had this morning led by fifty children and their leaders from Mississippi is just the beginning of mass demon-strations from all across the country—including white Appalachia—all protesting cutbacks in funding for various poverty-antipoverty programs . . . We should direct the public outcry in a direction which can result in more money for the Great Society programs and other needs of the country . . . We should make it clear to the people why there is not enough money. BECAUSE WE CANNOT GET A TAX INCREASE.[22]

Later, during the legislation of the surtax, conservatives tied spending cuts to the tax hike. Liberals were then put in a double bind, since the spending reductions would scale back many programs. Yet many continued to be con-vinced by the administration's logic that "without a tax increase, the pressure on the antipoverty programs will be tremendous. Thus, the best chance of protecting social progress is to get the tax bill enacted."[23]

Liberals were also uneasy about the tax bill as a means of paying for the Vietnam War: the surtax came to be called "the war tax." Representative Patsy Mink (D–HI) withheld support, believing that the money would not be "available for increased social purposes . . . The war is killing the Great Society." Barefoot Sanders (legislative liaison) reported: "On Vietnam, people in the district [James Burke, D–MA] want to 'win or get out.' The proposed tax increase has led some people in the district to feel that this would be an appropriate time to end the war—that is, it is not worth increased taxes."[24]

In addition, liberals were reluctant to endorse an across-the-board tax, to avoid further burdening their working class constituents. Therefore, liberals preferred tax reform. The administration responded that tax reform required a lengthy and difficult political process; the surtax legislation was needed immediately in order to generate revenue. Ultimately, however, one condition for passage of the surtax was that a major tax reform act would be legislated the following year.

Congressional conservatives (Republicans and southern Democrats) had precisely the opposite concerns. They had supported the 1964 tax cuts for neoclassical reasons, wanted to keep rates low, and renounced government macroeconomic stabilization policy. They believed that the budget deficits could be remedied with spending cuts. Conservatives also feared the surtax would enable expansion of the Great Society. Representative H. R. Gross (R–IA) said, "Until President Johnson gives a clear demonstration that he has stopped playing politics with the nation's fiscal affairs, and until he lays before Congress a hard and fast program for drastic reductions in his spending programs, I have no intention of succumbing to blandishment and voting for a tax increase."[25] Yet conservatives were willing to tolerate these indignities for the sake of the Vietnam War. Senator Richard Russell (D–GA) remarked, "I favor providing the funds for fighting this war, but I do not accept the theory that we can have butter and guns over an indefinite period of time."[26]

Wilbur Mills (D–AR) played a major role in the opposition to the surtax. Initially, the administration surmised that Mills was holding out for larger, more specific expenditure cuts. Schultze believed that Mills and the Ways and Means Committee were ultimately in favor of the tax increase but were "playing 'chicken', in an 'eyeball-to-eyeball' confrontation. I can't be positive—and obviously I'm not the world's greatest expert on what moves the Congress—but I think that if we are willing to take a strong and unyielding stand, they will blink first."[27] Later it appeared that the congressman from Arkansas was fighting a fundamental battle to keep revenues low. Sanders recounted:

> Mills told Eastland that he is not going to have any hearings on the Tax bill this year and that he is not going to report a Tax bill this year. He said the only hearings his committee will have will be on expenditure reductions. He told Eastland that it took 13 years to remove the taxes that were put on during the Korean War and that he did not want to be a party to developing a similar situation out of the Vietnam conflict.[28]

Mills's unwillingness to go with the program was strengthened by a growing animosity with Johnson. Mills thought the administration had misled him on the investment tax credit suspension and felt "hurt" that LBJ had not visited him to discuss the tax bill.[29] Rostenkowski warned, "The way Mills has been acting, I'm telling you that the tax bill is in very, very bad shape."[30]

The tax act became a valence test of people's positions on the new economics, the Great Society, and the Vietnam War. The administration therefore packaged the measure in different ways to different groups. With liberals the administration emphasized the tax measure's role in enabling the Great Society and minimized its role in furthering the Vietnam War. Barefoot Sanders prepared Johnson to meet with Democratic congressmen: "This group will be receptive to maximum cuts in non-Vietnam defense expenditures."[31] To deal with conservatives, administration staff advised emphasizing the war and deemphasizing increased revenue's role in expansion of the Great Society.

Pattern of Business Interests

Although financial interests had been reluctant to embrace Keynesian tax cuts to offset recessionary tendencies in the early 1960s, they enthusiastically endorsed tax increases to counter the boom of the late 1960s. Inflationary pressures would worsen balance-of-payment deficits, increasing pressure for deflation, threatening the gold supply, and possibly affecting the dollar's status as reserve currency. The housing industry joined the financial community in recommending anti-inflationary fiscal policy. They found the alternative solution to inflation, high interest rates, to have a direct and disastrous effect on the housing industry and therefore to be unacceptable. New residential housing starts fell by 34 percent from January to July of 1966. In 1962 these housing starts represented 3.3 percent of the GNP; by 1966 they were down to 2.8 percent.[32] The National Association of Real Estate Boards asserted that there had not been such a crisis in the mortgage market since the 1930s.[33] Hervey Machen informed the president about a conference he had had on inflation and "tight money" with businessmen from his district:

> Perhaps the most important point generally agreed upon is that the current tight money–inflation situation has hit almost all facets of the building industry more severely than most persons have realized . . .
>
> Some present described the effect as hitting them "like a ton of bricks." The builders, the savings and loan and mortgage banking institutions feel that they have been caught in a pinch . . . All called for a general tax increase: "the time has come to spread responsibility for fighting inflation across the broad economic spectrum instead of maintaining it in the banking and building sector."[34]

Financial concerns favored the tax surcharge much earlier.[35] Bankers and housing representatives supported the surtax unconditionally, unlike their manufacturing peers.[36] In an administration survey of business economists in

October 1966, employees of financial institutions clearly favored tax increases more than industrial economists did:

> *Most economists from banks and financial institutions want a tax increase.* They are convinced that, if you don't propose a tax increase in January, the bond market will absolutely go to pieces and interest rates will climb to new peaks.
>
> On the other hand, *most of the industrial economists are not ready to volunteer* to have their companies' profits sliced by a tax hike. Some are genuinely concerned that a tighter fiscal policy—with continued tight money—would add up to excessive restraint on the economy.[37]

In the early 1960s President Kennedy mobilized considerable support among manufacturers for the deficit-generating tax cuts to counter economic recession. By the late 1960s manufacturers faltered in their enthusiasm for the new economics when Keynesian logic mandated a tax increase. Manufacturing interests were especially repelled by proposals to suspend the investment tax credit and accelerated depreciation in order to reduce capital spending. Manufacturing interests also initially opposed a corporate rate increase, although many came to support the surtax when the administration finally began pursuing this option in earnest.[38] Compared to financial capital, manufacturers favored a tax hike later. Manufacturers also differed from their banking peers in the conditions they placed on support for the surtax, most notably that nondefense spending be cut.[39]

Small business trade associations generally opposed any tax increase. They joined manufacturers in opposing the investment credit suspension, explaining that the investment tax credit facilitated cash flow for those small firms which experience difficulty securing loans.[40] Small business largely opposed the surtax: retail groups were the president's only supporter in this group.[41]

Voluntary Controls on Capital Expenditures

The administration first started contemplating a tax increase in the spring of 1966. In May the president canvassed his closest advisers to establish what economic justification existed for a tax increase and what strategies should be pursued.[42] Although inflation, high interest rates, excessive capital spending, balance-of-payment deficits, and the revenue needs of the Vietnam War and the Great Society all pointed to a tax increase, the surtax was not passed for two more years. Because of limited business support, the administration decided to forgo a tax increase in favor of voluntary controls on capital outlays. Although financial and housing interests wanted a tax increase, manufacturing groups favored voluntary controls by business and spending cuts by government. Henry Fowler reported the Business Council Treasury Consultant Group's position: "There is less fear of inflation on the part of this group than on the part of the financial community," and "they see no need for a tax increase at this point in time." The group was also "strongly opposed to the elimination of the investment credit," arguing that such a strategy was likely to affect long-term investment projects which were necessary and have no bearing on short-term capital outlays.[43]

Manufacturers' reluctance to support a tax increase was expressed at a March 30 White House dinner. Invitations were issued to members of the Business Council, a number of "graduate Business Council members," "plus enough others to make sure the 100 largest companies in the U.S. are represented."[44] Much of the discussion at the dinner was devoted to how private industry could do their part in curbing capital investment. The president presented the voluntary spending restraint program as an alternative to stronger intervention and received praise for his indirect approach. Remarked one participant,

> I feel that all these great efforts of the President to counsel with the private sector to try to work by guidelines and voluntary programs are invaluable. I can't help but feel that if stronger medicine is later found necessary, it will be accepted more readily because of earlier involvements in measures which might have avoided it.[45]

Industry enthusiasm dissipated, however, when the president raised the specter of a tax increase. At 11:00 P.M., when the president finally asked who might support a tax increase, not one person present raised his hand. When pushed, participants acknowledged their preference for a modest income tax increase over the repeal of the investment tax credit.[46] One guest later expressed the belief that the total animosity to tax intervention that greeted the president's request for support was due to the discomfort the guests felt at volunteering an answer in such a setting.[47] And in a poll a few days later, John Connor (Secretary of Commerce) found that the current antitax sentiment did not rule out future support.

> Some say that the tides of inflation are running swift now and that by next month they probably will favor tax increases, corporate and personal, in such a form that they can be easily taken off later. Others say that the inflationary trends have begun to turn, although the evidence won't be available until late summer or early fall, and that a tax increase could have harmful effects then in a declining economy.[48]

Although the reported unanimity against the tax increase was perhaps overstated, it drew a sharp response from members of the financial community. Harvard's Department of Economics Overseers Committee was flabbergasted by the industrialists' lack of support for a tax increase. Within the committee there was general agreement by both the financial leaders and the economists on "the need to raise taxes" and the fact that "there is no solid evidence of any sort that this year's boom is about to slow down to a safe speed." The group concluded that the businessmen at the dinner were tongue-tied, reluctant "to sign a blank check on the nature of the increase," and preferred that the first move come from the administration.[49] David Rockefeller wrote to the president:

> Along with the rest of the business and financial community I have been following your recent comments on questions of economic policy, and particularly on the possibility of a tax increase and expenditure reductions, with a great deal of interest. The impending decisions on fiscal policy strike me as critically important. For that reason, I am impelled to write you of my own views on the matter—the more so since they are, at least in one respect, apparently at odds with the prevailing view at your dinner last week for business leaders.
>
> I was frankly surprised to read that none of those present raised their hand in support of a tax increase now. I personally have come to the conclusion that such action—on a carefully limited and temporary basis and combined with a renewed effort to prune back and postpone non-essential spending—should be delayed no longer.[50]

After the dinner many businessmen wrote to tell the president that they planned to implement his voluntary expenditure controls approach. In an informal survey, NAM found 100 percent cooperation in the seventy-three firms interviewed.[51] The U.S. Chamber of Commerce sent telegrams to top CEOs soliciting plans on capital spending projects and found many of the plans to be in compliance with the president's recommendations.[52] John Connor (Secretary of Commerce) reported that "many hundreds of business and financial leaders are responding to your appeal for voluntary action to moderate inflationary pressures and ensure the continued orderly expansion of the Nation's economy."[53]

Suspension of the Investment Tax Credit

By the fall of 1966 it became apparent that, despite the enthusiastic reception to the voluntary spending curbs, the investment boom had not abated. An informal group of top-level presidential advisers called meetings to determine whether the president should propose a fiscal package to address the economic malaise. Joseph Califano reported to Johnson that the advisers

> are unanimously agreed on the desirability of an immediate and comprehensive new economic program to insure stable prosperity. They believe such a program should be submitted early in September—if possible, this week. They believe the program outlined below would *clear the atmosphere of many uncertainties and anxieties, would let*

the president appear to "take charge" of what seems to many a disintegrating situation, and would *steer the economy onto a sound course.*[54]

The presidential advisers agreed about the need for and timing of a tax increase; however, they diverged on the kind and distribution of the measure. Arguing that the crucible of inflation was a surge in plant and equipment investment, Gardner Ackley wanted to suspend both the investment tax credit and accelerated depreciation on buildings. A tax on corporations also seemed appropriate, since corporate profits had increased faster than individual wages and labor's cooperation would be secured.[55] Arthur Okun (CEA) added that accelerated depreciation on buildings, in essence a subsidy to the construction industry, was inappropriate during periods of rapid growth and competition for credit. Newly negotiated construction wage agreements were providing unacceptable annual increases of 6 to 8 percent.[56]

Fowler opposed the suspension of the investment credit and of accelerated depreciation, sensing overwhelming opposition among manufacturers. Fowler's position was ticklish, having assured business in 1962 that the credit would not be revoked and reinstated as a tool of macroeconomic stabilization. The suspension proposal prompted industrial leaders to complain of a breach of faith. Fowler argued the manufacturing line: The credit suspension would damage the balance of payments and growth. The investment credit had been created to match the investment bias in our major competitors' tax codes; suspension would return the United States to a disadvantage.[57]

> In summary suspension of the investment credit is a measure that is inconsistent with the long-run needs of the economy, is fraught with uncertainties as to its actual effects in the short run, and is of doubtful appropriateness in relation to the likely nature of prospective inflationary pressures. Therefore against a limited and somewhat dubious gain must be placed the cost of proposing suspension at this time: namely that suspension of the credit now may be a measure that will seriously jeopardize and not fit in with a properly balanced type of tax increase program that the situation in January will actually warrant.[58]

Fowler recommended as an alternative a 5 percent surtax on corporate profits for 1966 and a 10 percent surtax for 1967. A surtax would take effect immediately and would be compatible with the more ambitious tax increase on individuals and corporations that the president was considering announcing in January if the economic situation did not improve. It would also lower high corporate profits and could be used to negotiate more moderate wage increases with labor.[59]

The administration finally decided to suspend the investment tax credit and accelerated depreciation on buildings, but include FY67 budget cuts of $1.5

billion to soften resistance. The proposal generated conflicting responses from the business community. Bankers wanted immediate fiscal intervention to take pressure off monetary policy. Robert Roosa sent the president a telegram on August 31: "Strongly urge you confirm administration determination use fiscal measures to reduce need for additional federal reserve restraint stop this only effective way check rising interest rates and avoid financial panic." [60] The CEA reported: "We and the Treasury have been in touch with financial types over the weekend. We find considerable fears and get universal calls for 'action.' All want the Fed to ease up. But most of all they want you to act and to 'take charge' of the situation." [61]

Most housing and finance groups supported the suspension of the investment tax credit: these sectors were the president's only support in the September 1966 Ways and Means hearings. Real Estate Board representative John Williamson explained:

> As responsible citizens and members of the business community, we are fully prepared to share the burdens necessary to reverse the inflationary trends which plague the country today . . . Since the building sector of the economy has already been hard hit by the restraints imposed by tight money and high interest rates, the Government should not increase the severity of the recession in this industry by imposing tax penalties. [62]

Others in banking and housing foresaw the political objections to the investment credit suspension and argued for an across-the-board tax increase instead. The surtax could take effect immediately whereas the investment credit suspension would have a fairly lengthy start-up period. William Biggs (Bank of New York) explained, "If they are not fair in suspending it, it will have quite a damaging effect on confidence, which would be most unfortunate at this time." [63]

Manufacturers were also concerned about the effect of monetary trends on their stocks, blaming the stock market drop on high interest rates. Yet their first concern was to protect themselves from increased taxation and to preserve the growth incentives: the investment tax credit and accelerated depreciation. They considered limits on capital spending an inappropriate mechanism for fighting inflation. The Manufacturing Chemists reckoned that inflation is demand pull not cost push; therefore, the country needed increased plant capacity to decrease prices. Charles Stewart (Machinery and Allied Products Institute) argued that the suspension would compromise the long-range goal "of achieving and maintaining a modern industrial base." Imported steel's inroads into the domestic market were contributing $1 billion a year to the U.S. balance-of-payment deficits; cutting the investment tax credit would only exacerbate this. [64]

Manufacturers also argued that suspending the tax credit would not succeed in curbing capital spending. A Douglas Airlines executive testified that capital projects have a much longer lead time than the sixteen-month suspension period specified. The American Paper Institute calculated this lead time to be about two to three years.[65] Therefore, the suspension was not a good device for short-term stabilization.

Industry predicted many negative side effects from the suspension. According to the National Association of Manufacturers, the suspension would actually aggravate tight money instead of taking the pressure off monetary policy. "There is no certainty that the bill would substantially reduce business requirements for funds for financing capital expansion. It is, however, certain that by increasing current tax liability it would reduce the ability of corporations to finance expansion through internal funds, without recourse to credit markets." The Railway Progress Institute argued that the suspension would aggravate already serious shortages like those in freight cars and locomotives. Expansion in Vietnam was sure to require additional capital spending.[66]

Finally, it was predicted that the suspension would negatively affect the partnership which had so far characterized the Johnson administration's relationship with the business community. Ward Keener (B. F. Goodrich) feared a loss of confidence "because the depreciation and investment credit moves were originally sold as permanent legislation."[67] William Verity (president of Armco Steel) warned the president:

> Suspension of the credit will act as a selective and discriminatory tax increase, with the heaviest penalty falling on those companies who are trying hardest to create new job opportunities and to make American industry more competitive with overseas producers. Perhaps the hardest hit will be companies like Armco in the basic industries . . .
>
> Even more serious, in my opinion, is the impact that any action to suspend the investment credit will have on the productive partnership which your administration has developed with industry. Such action must be considered a breach of faith with industry, and ultimately, with the American working man. The mutual confidence which has resulted in an almost unprecedented period of growth and prosperity will be seriously weakened, if not destroyed.[68]

Persuading Congress of the advantages of the measure was also difficult. Mills thought the Federal Reserve's tight monetary policy was already slowing the boom. Additional fiscal restraint under those circumstances would plunge the economy into recession. Mills also wanted more information: "I can pass a tax bill, but I don't have the information I need. The Administration won't level with me on the budget. When they do, I will go to work."[69]

The Arkansas congressman pushed for a formal quantitative economic forecast and asked Fowler to bring Ackley to the hearing to "assure the Committee that in supporting the suspension of the investment credit they would not be triggering a recession in 1967." Fowler finessed Mills request, explaining that no such forecast was possible until the 1967 spending levels had been established. To assure Mills yet protect Ackley from the potential "purely mischievous questioning in the Executive Session" by Republican opponents, Fowler proposed a preliminary session between Ackley and Mills.[70] The administration agreed to provide Mills with an anonymous forecast written by Ackley and based on alternative expenditure projections. Mills was to present the material as "coming from an unidentified expert."[71]

With Mills's support, one other major problem remained: how to get the suspension through the legislative process without amendment. Manufacturing interests set out in full force to oppose suspension of the credit. Trade associations and firms of railroads, machine tools, paper, aircraft, chemicals, mining, steel, autos, and electronics among others testified against the provision. Only three individuals from manufacturing concerns supported the suspension: William Murphy (Campbell Soup), Frederick Kappel (AT&T), and Stuart Saunders (Pennsylvania Railroad). All three were quite close to the administration, involved in the Business Council, and on the Treasury consultant committee.[72]

The administration anticipated many requests for exemptions and exclusions. A number of industries (railroads, steel, airlines, and farmers) lobbied for outright exemptions. The administration feared that "if any one industry is exempted other exemptions will naturally follow." Mills and Ullman were able to convince most of the House Democratic Ways and Means Committee members to uphold this position. In the Senate Finance Committee, Smathers and Long favored exemptions for farmers and railroads.[73] A compromise was made to pacify small businessmen and farmers but avoid industry-specific breaks: a $15,000 exemption.[74]

The other major amendment was a concession to the airline industry: an effective date of September 8, 1966, instead of the president's date of September 1. TWA placed an order for $40 million on September 2 and wanted to receive the benefits of the credit. Fowler explained, "Permitting this order to obtain the investment credit is one of the factors that may make it possible to reach a solution of the problems of the airline industry without going to an outright exemption for that industry."[75]

The investment credit suspension was short-lived. In March of 1967 the president asked Congress to reinstate the credit, nine months early. The credit was reinstated prematurely because the suspension worked almost too well. Interest rates dropped dramatically: three-month Treasury bills declined 22.2 percent; new municipal bonds, 15.1 percent. Machinery order backlogs were reduced by 7 percent; the utilization rate of capital goods declined, and the supply of skilled labor increased. Planned investment increases for 1967 were only 4 percent; by comparison, investment had gone up by 16 percent in 1965 and 17 percent in 1966. Signs of a weakening economy prompted restoration of the credit to avoid a recession. The action had never been popular to begin with; changes in economic signals reinforced the political pressure against suspension.

The precipitating event triggering reinstatement was the release of the Commerce Department–SEC survey on the state of the economy mentioned above. Administration strategists worried that, when the survey was released, speculation about reinstatement would begin and investment would further decline. Ackley recommended that the president propose reinstating the credit the same day the survey was released.

> If we make the announcement immediately after the release of the investment data (now scheduled for Friday), we will not have to face the barrage of questions about the meaning of the data, and what we expect to do about restoring the incentives—the answers to which could raise more doubts and slow down investment plans still further. Likewise, it will not appear that we have been bludgeoned into the action by the inevitable editorial and by Congressional demands that we do it.[76]

Johnson's actions were well received by Congress and the manufacturing community.[77] Republicans immediately mobilized to nullify most of the effect of the six months of suspension. Ways and Means Republicans wanted to make the reinstatement retroactive to October 10, thus retroactively applying the credit to all but one month's worth of contracts. Mills and most Democrats opposed these measures.[78] Henry Fowler wrote an open letter to George Smathers (distributed to Senate Finance) urging "fiscal responsibility"; Congress largely acquiesced.[79]

Surtax Proposal Development

Although the administration chose suspension of the investment credit as an initial intervention, it seriously considered proposing a surtax in January 1967 in order to take the pressure off monetary policy and offset the projected budget deficits. Yet signs of an economic downturn had already appeared by the end of 1966, inspiring fears of a recession. Gardner Ackley described the fundamental dilemma as "Potentially very large budget deficits in an economy that now seems to need no new restraint."[80]

Finally, it was decided that the president would call for a 6 percent tax increase in his State of the Union message but would wait until later in the year to push legislation. Fowler recalled:

> It seemed wise for both the President and the Congress to take this final decision when the course of economic developments accompanying the inventory readjustment and the leveling-out of demand in various sectors of the private economy indicated that these drags

could be absorbed. During this period it seemed to be the wise course for both fiscal and monetary policy to remain stimulative.[81]

The administration's plan to get the surtax on the books but not press for it was almost foiled by the Joint Economic Committee. During committee hearings in February few outside witnesses and no testifying legislators supported the tax proposal, and all agreed that economic stabilization was the only rationale for a tax increase.[82] A February 20 press release predicting no tax hike pushed the administration into action. Fowler and Ackley urged committee chairman William Proxmire to remain flexible. Treasury staff asked Representatives Boggs, Martha Griffiths (D–MI), and Senators J. W. Fulbright (D–AR), and Abraham Ribicoff (D–CT) to delay decision until more information was available, and not get "locked in to a fixed position now."[83] The Joint Economic Committee's March 17 bipartisan report urged flexibility. Although the administration was ultimately correct in predicting an upturn, the wait-and-see game continued. Ackley noted:

> Taking account of these favorable factors on the horizon, nearly all economic forecasters are reaching the objective technical verdict that *we are building up steam for a new surge.*
> Still, the surge has not yet started . . . Thus, *we could not make an airtight case today to the Congress* that fiscal restraint will be needed.[84]

As evidence of the downturn evaporated, finance and housing again began to push hard for a tax increase.[85] Individuals from key banks and trade associations publicly supported the measure: Chase Manhattan Bank, Prudential Insurance Company, Morgan Guaranty, Bank of America, American Bankers Association, and the Irving Trust Company.[86] In July, Fowler and Martin dined with the heads of the nine major New York banks. Only one opposed a tax increase and one preferred expenditure cuts first. The rest vigorously supported it, and most felt that the surtax should be higher than 6 percent.[87] The U.S. Savings and Loan League urged that a tax increase be considered independent of spending cuts.[88] The National League of Insured Savings Associations and the Life Insurance Association of America wrote a joint letter to the president:

> In the consideration of this legislation, we must clearly recognize that we are faced with a condition, not a theory. The Federal Government is confronted with the prospect of a deficit of unconscionable proportion. Estimates of this fiscal year's deficit range around $29 billion. Even in an economy as dynamic and diverse as ours, a deficit of this size cannot be tolerated.[89]

Manufacturers were also more favorable to the idea of a tax increase, although they remained less enthusiastic than financial concerns. In July 1967 after the economy dipped briefly into recession the administration solicited the view of ninety-four businessmen on the tax increase: eighty-four favored the tax but forty wanted to wait until an upturn was certain.[90] In an August survey the National Association of Business Economists found that 69 percent of the manufacturing economists and 83 percent of the commercial bank and nonbank finance employees supported the increase.[91] Charles Stewart (president, Machinery and Allied Products Institute) testified:

> The surcharge recommendations to a large extent are based upon an economic forecast of the Administration. That forecast does not seem to take into full consideration the fact that the economy is giving off mixed signals at the present time as to its strength and movement. Congress should certainly await clearer economic evidence before granting final approval to such substantial tax action as that proposed.[92]

In the July survey thirty-five of the ninety-four businessmen made their support conditional on nondefense spending cuts and 50 percent wanted a surtax of only 6 percent.[93] Only one of the leading New York bankers surveyed in the same month who favored a surtax mentioned spending reductions and most thought a higher tax necessary.[94]

In contrast to the administration's proposal, manufacturing interests wanted the surtax to be applied *after* subtracting the investment credit.[95] Henry Ford II wrote to the president that applying the surtax before the credit would impose more than a 10 percent addition to tax liabilities for "corporations that are engaged in plant modernization and expansion in this country as well as those firms that have significant investments overseas." Ford and others sent wires to Wilbur Mills demanding that the proposal be modified. Their demands were ultimately met.[96]

The National Federation of Independent Business found 90 percent of their members opposed to the tax. Small business was especially hard hit by the rising interest rates since it typically pays a percentage or two above the prime rate. Yet drastic cuts in nondefense spending were the fiscal intervention of choice for this sector of the economy.[97] The U.S. Chamber of Commerce also opposed the surtax and continued to do so until very late in the spring of 1968, when the tax was made contingent on spending cuts.[98] The Chamber argued the following:

> The economic evidence presently available does not indicate that the business resurgence which the administration foresees will occur so soon, nor in the magnitude suggested by the tax surcharge proposal . . . The national Chamber favors deferring a tax increase until it is substantially more certain than now that there will be a major upturn in the economy and inflationary pressures are more apparent. We believe it would be ill-advised to attempt to raise revenues by a tax increase when such a rate increase might well result in an actual reduction of revenues.[99]

The administration was finally persuaded to move forward, and in August 1967 Johnson announced a new fiscal initiative. Several events convinced the president's advisers: First, a much larger troop commitment in Vietnam appeared necessary; costs were already running $122 billion a year.[100] Second, even without additional troops in Asia, the FY68 deficits promised to be much larger than projected: January's forecast was $8 billion, July's was $19 to $20 billion. Deficits of this magnitude were 50 percent larger than the highest previous peacetime deficit, that of 1959.[101] Third, recession had ceased to be of concern. A decline in inventory investment (rather than a drop in final sales) was responsible for the earlier sluggishness; trends were now reversing. Schultze wrote, "The mere fact that inventory investment will not be declining so rapidly from now on will give the U.S. a sharp boost in the growth of the GNP—the decline in inventory investment will no longer be offsetting the steady rise in final sales." [102] Residential construction was also increasing.[103]

The impending surge was reflected in financial markets: investors were reluctant to buy long-term securities. Despite the Fed's easy-money policy, long-term interest rates stayed high.[104] Finally, prices and wages were again climbing; Fowler predicted a 3 percent price increase in the absence of successful tax legislation.[105] Johnson's announcement of new surtax legislation briefly rallied the Treasury bond market and depressed the stock market. But bonds fell again and stocks rebounded when rumors circulated that Congress probably would not pass the legislation very quickly.[106]

The Legislative Process

When the president introduced the new fiscal package in August of 1967, he was convinced that all chance of recession had disappeared and hoped to sign the tax surcharge quickly into law. Yet ambivalence about the tax hike and idiosyncratic political competition delayed passage for another ten months.

The greatest problem was that of getting the support of Wilbur Mills. Responsible for reporting the measure out of the Ways and Means Committee, Mills's cooperation was pivotal. At one point the administration explored (and rejected) ways to sidestep the normal procedure, such as reporting out through the Rules Committee.[107] Hale Boggs (D–LA) argued against these measures, since many members would not support the surtax unless it was sanctioned by Mills: "With Mills you can get it out of Committee and without Mills you can't. I'm not sure you will get a bill out as a package as we now have, but you'll get it out in some form and you'll pick up some Republicans such as Conable if you get Mills' vote." [108]

Mills offered a practical explanation for his reticence: the leadership lacked votes for passage, and he would not report the bill out of committee until passage was assured. Passage depended on Republican support and spending reductions. Thus, Stanley Surrey (Treasury) reported a discussion with Al Ullman (D–OR):

> Mr. Ullman very strongly emphasized that at the present moment we do not have the votes for the tax bill either in the Committee or in the Congress; that we need Republican votes to get the bill out of the Committee, and that a number of Republicans are thinking along the same line. Mr. Ullman stated that he and most of the others on the Committee recognized the need for a tax increase but believe that it cannot be accomplished without direct leadership by the President . . . which . . . will make it possible for the Committee and the Congress to vote for the tax bill despite the very heavy public sentiment.[109]

On October 3, Mills adjourned the Ways and Means tax bill hearings until some accommodation could be reached on the expenditure problem. Mills's insistence on spending cuts presented numerous problems for the administration. Since spending cuts were in the Appropriation Committee's jurisdiction, chairman George Mahon considered Mills's intervention to be a gross violation of protocol. Mills and Mahon also had very different priorities. Mahon, responsible for allocating the cuts, had to deal with the constituency groups, which wanted to protect their programs. His maximum reduction limits were based on an assessment of the ease with which budget cuts in various areas could be made and a desire to protect the programs to which he had previously appropriated funds. Mills conceptualized spending cuts in the aggregate. As a means to reduce excessive government spending, they were an abstract technique for solving the problem of an expanding government.

The administration spent the fall contemplating how to cut spending without sacrificing the Great Society programs, alienating George Mahon and the liberal Democrats, and losing the support of constituents. Without the tax increase, even more spending cuts would be made and economic problems would escalate.[110] The tax increase was necessary to preserve what Fowler later called the "record performance of 93 months of uninterrupted prosperity."[111] Fowler was most anxious to get a tax cut and most willing to cut expenditures to get it. Larry O'Brien and Barefoot Sanders were the most pessimistic about the chances for success and the most concerned about offending the liberal vote. Schultze thought up a way to protect Mahon's jurisdiction: Mahon should introduce "his own 'line item' controllable expenditure bill" proposing cuts in nondefense spending of $2 to $2.5 billion. This would be joined by a $2 billion cut in non-Vietnam defense spending and, to please Mills, the establishment of an evaluation commission to review federal programs.[112]

Fowler and Schultze met with Mills and Mahon to develop a new three-part bill: the tax measures submitted on August 3, a 2–10 percent expenditure reduction formula, and the commission to review federal programs (dubbed the "Mills Commission").[113] Convinced of the administration's sincerity, Mills reopened the Ways and Means hearings but focused on expenditure reductions rather than tax increases.[114]

Mahon reportedly "blew sky high" when he heard that further cuts were to be made and that they were to be decided on by Mills.[115] Mahon felt that his committee had already cut as much as possible from the appropriations budget. But even more unacceptable was the idea that Ways and Means would exercise jurisdiction over the appropriations process. Califano explained: "Mahon thought that any slim chance of passage of the expenditure reduction portion of the bill would be completely eliminated if Schultze and Fowler presented it to the Congress through the Ways and Means Committee."[116]

The administration tried to make its case again in the first weeks of 1968. However, after two days of testimony, Wilbur Mills delivered his opinion: "The Administration had come up with a better case of 'the existing dangers without a tax bill' than it had last year; but Congress simply was not going to enact a tax increase on the basis of economic forecasts, particularly when federal spending was still on the upswing."[117] Privately, Mills told the administration that they needed to come up with 175 Democratic votes before he would consider reporting it out of committee; yet, even with the votes, Mills would make no assurances that he would report it. The administration did a massive canvass at the beginning of February and found at best 150 to 155 votes.[118]

Then, in March 1968, a run on gold gave new life to the dying surtax. *Business Week* reported, "The gold-rush attack on the dollar has made Congress take new notice of the economy—and the impact of Capitol Hill fiscal action at home and abroad." At the same time Johnson announced a need for more troops in Vietnam. The gold crisis and the war buildup gave the president grounds to demand a new "program of national austerity to assure that our economy will prosper and that our fiscal position will be sound." The president also indicated increased willingness to tie spending cuts to a tax increase.[119]

Barefoot Sanders calculated that it was time to push for the surtax: "I suppose it is stating the obvious to say that major progress toward enactment of the surtax bill would have a very beneficial effect on the gold rush panic. My judgment is that there is enough concern in the House right now that if a Tax bill were on the floor we could pass it."[120] The legislative effort was helped by Johnson's decision not to run again. *Business Week* commented, "By removing himself from politics, Johnson probably succeeded in moving the tax bill a step back from politics."[121]

The administration and congressional leadership saw two alternative routes to the tax act. The first was to pressure Mills to report it out of committee immediately. Fowler had earlier extracted a promise from Mills that the bill could be reported whenever the administration wanted it. Sanders recommended that they could even convene a special meeting of the Ways and Means Committee to vote the bill out. Such a move, he argued, would "have a major effect on the present near panic." The second course was to offer spending cuts to the Republicans and attach the proposal to a Senate measure, violating the Ways and Means Committee's jurisdiction.[122]

Ultimately, the second course of action was chosen. John Williams (D–DE) joined by George Smathers (D–FL) offered the surtax in an amendment to an excise tax bill. There was some partisan conflict over the amount that current expenditures should be cut: $4 or $6 billion. Ultimately the administration conceded the $6 billion figure, believing that the level could be lowered in conference. A few days later, the Senate passed the surtax legislation in an "Easter Basket" bill of fiscal measures.[123]

The bill began to get bogged down again on the question of spending cuts. The $6 billion expenditure cut passed in the Senate bill was unacceptable to the Democrats; Carl Albert predicted that two-thirds of the House Democratic vote would be lost.[124] A meeting with Mills, Mahon, John McCormack (D–MA), and Boggs was set for the afternoon of April 30. At the meeting the Democrats decided to trade current spending cuts for future reductions and reached a formula of trimming $4 billion in expenditures, $6 billion in appropriations, and $12 billion in new obligational authority.[125] At the Ways and Means Committee meeting two days later, however, Mills "belittled the Appropriations Committee resolution [based on the 4-12-6 compromise], saying it was both inadequate in magnitude, and it did not really accomplish what it purported to do." Mills proposed a 6-14-6 package instead of the April 30 compromise. Zwick concluded: "Clearly this is a major retreat from his position of two nights ago. Either he is bargaining very hard, or trying to scuttle the Tax Bill."[126]

The administration was furious. Sanders wanted the president to "go after" Mills and the Republicans by discussing the effects of the cuts in the press conference. Mahon should give a background interview to the press on Mills's agreement and subsequent betrayal. Liberal groups such as the Urban Coalition should be mobilized to protest the cuts.[127] Califano called the situation a turning point in the Johnson presidency:

> For the past month we have been moving with increased power and ability to get things done, as well as an increased sense of confidence because the American people believe you are doing whatever you do without any ax to grind and only because it is right. This has all resulted from your pulling out of the race.
>
> But this remarkable accretion of power in a lame duck status could deteriorate rapidly if Wilbur Mills rolls over us on the tax legislation . . . If my instinct is right, then the importance of winning the tax fight transcends our fiscal problems.[128]

The next day Johnson publicly attacked Mills and other obstructionists in a press conference. Mills was not pleased: "It is too bad when a man gives an emotional answer and jeopardizes all the work that is going on." [129] Yet neither LBJ nor Mills washed their hands of the process. The president ultimately accepted Mills's numbers, on the advice of Henry Fowler:

> The stakes for the economy and the country are entirely too high to risk a loss of the legislation or a long, drawn-out delay. Either or both might be the consequence of a failure on the part of the Administration and the leadership to back up the Conferees' package. [130]

Even Sanders, loyal to the liberal view, agreed. "It is very tempting to let Mills lie in the bed which he has made . . . But failure of the conference report would, I am sure, cause severe problems in financial circles." [131]

The Coalition Strategy

In the face of general animosity to a tax hike, the administration turned to private sector support for its legislative agenda. August was filled with meetings between administration staff (primarily in the Treasury and Commerce Departments) and business groups. The White House had two goals: to develop a large, multisector group that would appear to call for the surtax with one voice and to persuade affected trade associations to testify.

The multi-industry tax group was reminiscent of the Business Committee for Tax Reduction developed to lobby for the 1964 act. Many individuals were members of both. The group was conceived at an August 10 luncheon; its initial meeting was attended by fifteen business and financial leaders and the president, Fowler, and Trowbridge. [132] The president presented a dire reading of the country's fiscal status and then called for a business/government effort to tame the unruly economy. Expenditures, originally estimated at $135 billion, were now expected to reach $143 billion in FY68. Revenues were $7 billion lower than expected; expenditures were $8.5 billion more than expected; and the surtax proposed in January (which would have produced $5.4 billion in revenues) had not been passed. The combination of these factors meant that the FY68 deficit would probably be $29 to $30 billion (including the $8.1 billion deficit already incurred). LBJ's solution was to pare down the deficit through the following formula: cut 25 percent, tax 25 percent, and borrow 50 percent. The president knew that passage of this program would not be easy. Therefore, he proposed that a group be formed to mobilize business and financial interests. All present agreed to participate except for Governor Allan Shiver (Chamber of Commerce), Werner Gullander (NAM), and Fred Kappel (AT&T). [133]

On August 24 the group, now 113 members, sent a wire to Wilbur Mills calling for a surtax and expenditure reduction. The 34 members of financial institutions and 79 from other business concerns asked for cooperation from "others who concur in principle to help gain understanding, support and acceptance for this program." Already facing some dissension from those who wanted the tax to be applied after the investment credit or to have a different effective date, the statement made clear that one could belong to the group and yet still disagree with particulars. "This does not preclude the right of anyone joining in this Statement to disagree with specific features of the Administration's tax proposal or to advance other ideas."[134] By September 13, 455 business leaders had signed the group's "Statement of Principles" calling for fiscal restraint. Almost a fourth of the signatories were from financial and housing firms.[135]

Besides its efforts to build consensus across the business community, the administration worked to convince specific trade associations to formally announce their support. Meetings were held with trade association members in the Treasury and Commerce departments. By August 18 approximately 125 organizations had met with administration officials to learn about the tax proposals. The administration concentrated its efforts on finance and housing groups, farm interests, and organizations of individuals on fixed incomes (veterans and retired persons).

Fowler listed the following successes: First, the American Bankers Association agreed to testify before the Ways and Means Committee after Fowler, Ackley, and Schultze met with their top personnel. Second, "there will be good representation before the Ways and Means on behalf of those concerned with housing and its problems": Mortgage Bankers Association, U.S. Savings and Loan League, National League of Insured Savings Associations, National Association of Home Builders, and National Association of Real Estate Boards. Third, twenty-nine farm organizations were approached; support was assured from the American Farm Bureau Federation and the National Grange. Twenty veterans' organizations met with the administration; a number promised support. "Useful testimony and support of the tax bill on the 'danger and damage from inflation' aspect ought to be forthcoming from the Life Insurance Association of America and the National Association of Retired Civil Service Employees."[136]

Apart from the generic August 10 group, the only other manufacturing groups addressed by the administration were a group of twelve transportation organizations led by Stuart Sanders of the Pennsylvania Railroad and NAM. Some members of the transportation group insisted that "the surcharge was saleable only upon demonstrable evidence of reduction of government spending."[137]

The administration asked sympathetic trade associations to help convince Congress to increase taxes. The Federal Home Loan Bank Board met with

White House staff in early August to plan strategies to develop support for the tax act. At the meeting the Board was assigned five groups to contact and mobilize. John Horne later reported that four of the five groups—the U.S. Savings and Loan League, the National League of Insured Savings Associations, the American Bankers Association, and the Mortgage Bankers Association—testified before Ways and Means in support of the bill. The fifth group, the National Association of Mutual Savings Banks, was also very supportive and sent mailings on the subject to its membership.[138] The National Association of Home Builders was also in favor of the surtax but demanded concessions for its endorsement. Larry Levinson wrote:

> I would have thought that the National Association of Home Builders would come out strongly for the President's tax proposal. As a group they stand most to lose by soaring interest rates. Now I find that they are holding out for concessions. They will not endorse the President's proposal unless we [accede] to their demands on this central mortgage banking facility . . . I hate to pay this price but I believe we should do it because of the influence that the Home Builders have particularly in the Ways and Means Committee.[139]

Sidney Weinberg (of Goldman, Sachs) testified that the tax surcharge was necessary if credit and capital markets were to be protected.[140] Wall Street executives met with key congressmen to impress upon them the need for a tax increase. In October, Gardner Ackley attended such a function with nine senators and forty Wall Street executives. The dinner was hosted by Bob Brimberg, head of a Wall Street firm and contributor to a number of campaigns. Ackley reports:

> The meeting was clearly staged to *provide an opportunity for the Wall Street people to lecture the Senators on the urgent need for a tax increase . . .*
>
> There was some pointed joking that *Wall Street Democrats would have no money to support election campaigns* if the financial markets plunged as a result of tight money and an unbalanced economy.[141]

Conclusion

Lyndon Johnson's vision of America—an imperial power abroad and a Great Society at home—required revenue. During the course of Johnson's tenure, the tax increase came to symbolize the viability of his presidency. Yet consensus in support of the Johnson agenda was prevented by economic and social disagreements and political power struggles.

The double threat of unemployment and inflation created incompatible economic goals; policymakers feared that a tax increase to curb inflation and balance-of-payment deficits would throw the country into recession. Indeed,

Table 4.1. Divisions in State and Society over Tax Options

Goals	Business	State	Policy
Inflation/balance-of-payment deficits	Finance	Most of administration esp. Treasury	Early surtax
Preventing unemployment	Manufacturing	Some support from CEA	Reluctance over surtax
Oppose Great Society	Small business	Mills/Congressional conservatives	No surtax/spending cuts
Oppose war in Vietnam		Congressional liberals	No surtax/military cuts

the experimental investment tax credit suspension in 1966 seemed to do just that. Conflicting noneconomic goals also galvanized reaction to the surtax: the war in Vietnam and the Great Society each had its own set of supporters and detractors.

The proposed tax increase divided the business community. Financial and housing interests were the earliest supporters of the surtax and the president's strongest allies in the struggle for legislation. Manufacturing interests were more reluctant to accept a tax increase, fearing economic downturn, but ultimately joined forces with the president. The original proposal was altered to bring in additional business interests: investment credits could be deducted before calculating the surcharge, the corporate surtax was made equal to the individual tax, and spending cuts were tied to the bill. Small business groups continued to oppose the tax increase, motivated by fear of a recession, fundamental disagreement with the welfare state concept, and general antigovernment sentiment.

Opposition from other factions within the government further hindered easy passage of the tax measure. As chairman of the House Ways and Means Committee, Wilbur Mills exercised his capacity to delay the act in committee for months and months. Mills worried that the tax would initiate recession and would be used to underwrite additional social programs. Liberals feared that the surtax would be used to pay for the Vietnam War. A personal animosity between the committee chair and the president also impeded smooth passage of the act. A jurisdictional dispute between the Ways and Means and Appropriation committees contributed to tardy action on the measure. Mills wanted to make spending cuts the price for tax reform; Mahon resented this usurpation of the Appropriation Committee's jurisdiction and resisted additional expenditure reductions. The camps constructed around opposing tax options are the subject of table 4.1.

The administration searched for tactics to circumvent Mills and other congressional enemies. One legislative possibility, ultimately rejected, was to have the Rules Committee report out the bill instead of Ways and Means. The president instead turned to corporate channels and formed an alliance with sympathetic private sector groups (initially finance and housing). A large multisector business group similar to the Business Committee for Tax Reduction was created for purposes of lobbying and legitimation. This group, together with traditional trade associations, was considered instrumental in the ultimate passage of the act. The coalition strategy paved the way to policy success.

5

The Economic Recovery Tax Act of 1981

Introduction

In 1981 Ronald Reagan ushered in another fiscal revolution in tax policy with a supply-side platform aimed at ending Democratic rule and the Keynesian consensus. Reagan's supply-side approach harked back to more traditional variants of neoclassical economics: rejecting a demand-led view of growth and government economic management while emphasizing accumulation. Yet supply-side economists joined Keynesians in accepting budgets that were out of balance. The rationale differed. Keynesians defended the unbalanced budget as a mechanism to stimulate demand during economic downturn. According to supply-side theory, the entrepreneurial activity unleashed by lower tax rates would quickly increase actual revenue intake.

The Economic Recovery Tax Act was the central policy manifestation of the new fiscal philosophy. The tax act, signed into law by President Reagan on August 13, legislated the largest tax decrease in the history of the United States. To stimulate accumulation (savings, investment, and work effort) the tax act disproportionately benefited upper-percentile individual and corporate income. Individual rates were cut across the board by 23 percent, the greatest savings concentrated in the upper brackets. The act radically expanded tax incentives for investment by creating a new kind of depreciation, the Accelerated Cost Recovery System, and enlarging the investment tax credit. Savings incentives received similar treatment with the expansion of the self-employed retirement funds and individual retirement accounts. Estate taxes were drastically reduced. A number of exclusions to the windfall profits tax were created (see table 5.1).

Slower rates of growth in the 1970s brought about this sea-change in economic thinking. A dramatic increase in international competition was partially responsible for the economic downturn. The economic distress focused attention on accumulation and away from consumption. First, economic malfunction had exposed the flaws in Keynesian macroeconomic stabilization: demand management seemed obviously inadequate to the task at hand. Second, the atmosphere of fiscal stress heightened class and group conflict. Growth had permitted the expansion of the public sector and the satisfaction of particularistic demands from many quarters. The new "zero-sum society"

Table 5.1. Primary Provisions of the Economic Recovery Tax Act

---

Individual marginal across-the-board tax rates cut by a total of 23 percent by 1984. These were based on cuts proposed by Jack Kemp (R–NY) and William Roth (R–DE).

Top marginal individual rate lowered from 70 percent to 50 percent.

Tax brackets indexed according to consumer price index increases beginning in 1985.

"Marriage penalty" reduced with the allowance of a new deduction for two-earner married couples filing a joint return.

U.S. citizens working abroad could exclude $75,000 from U.S. income tax in 1982, $95,000 by 1986. Replaced previous system of deductions and exclusions.

Accelerated Cost Recovery System (ACRS) replaced prior Asset Depreciation Range (ADR) system for depreciating tangible property. Created four asset classes with three-, five-, ten-, and fifteen-year lives. Three-year class consisted of autos, light trucks, and R&D equipment. The five-year class included most other equipment. The ten-year class included shorter-lived public utility property as well as railroad cars and mobile homes. The fifteen-year class included longer-lived public utility property and all real property (buildings).

Expensing allowed to businesses on $5,000 of personal property in 1982; up to $10,000 by 1986.

Investment tax credit applicable to $125,000 worth of investment in 1981; up to $150,000 in 1985. Had been limited to $100,000.

Safe harbor rule created by which the nominal lessor treated as the owner of property for tax purposes and could use the ACRS deductions and the investment tax credit.

Carryover period for unused net operating losses and investment tax credits extended from seven to fifteen years.

Rehabilitation of historic structures eligible for 25 percent investment tax credit.

25 percent tax credit for R&D expenditures above the prior year's level.

Corporate rate reduced on first $25,000 to 15 percent by 1983; second $25,000 reduced to 18 percent by 1983.

Incentive stock options reinstated; employee could count as capital gains when stock was sold.

Subchapter S corporation maximum number of shareholders expanded from fifteen to twenty-five.

LIFO inventory accounting simplified for small businesses.

Individual retirement account levels increased to $1,500 for individuals and $2,000 for couples.

Self-employed retirement plan deductions from income increased from an annual $7,500 to $15,000.

Qualified savings certificates ("all savers") created on which up to $1,000 in interest could be excluded.

Estate tax exemption increased from $175,625 to $225,000 in 1982; up to $600,000 by 1987.

Estate tax removed from transfer between spouses.

Gift tax increased from an annual $3,000 to $10,000.

Royalty owners allowed credit against the first $2,500 of windfall profit tax payment. By 1984 could exclude up to three barrels a day from the tax.

Stripper oil of independent producers excluded from windfall profit tax starting in 1983.

Windfall profit tax on newly discovered oil reduced from 30 percent to 27.5 percent in 1982 to 15 percent by 1986.

Source: Joint Committee on Taxation, *General Explanation of the Economic Recovery Tax Act of 1981* (Washington, DC: U.S. Government Printing Office, 1981), pp. 5–13.

altered this logic: groups scrambled for diminishing benefits and increasingly questioned one another's claims.[1]

Many advanced countries affected by the economic decline shifted attention to accumulation. Sweden experimented with a conservative regime after thirty years of social democracy. Mitterand's socialist France embraced austerity politics usually associated with rightist regimes. Yet Krieger points out that new policies in the United States and Great Britain constituted much sharper deviations from the existing order: "Why only in the Anglo-American world did the eclipse of Keynesianism result in such unabashedly pro-capitalist, anti-welfarist, and powerfully statist governments?"[2]

In the American case the answer can be traced to the president's ideological leanings, the array of interests in the business community, and the coalitions connecting the public and private spheres. American business responded to the economic downturn with a vigorous campaign to move the consensus on fiscal policy to the right.[3] Key business groups also sought to overcome sectoral differences over corporate taxation in order to present a united front in policy demands. Thus, 1981 witnessed an amazing period of consensus in the politics of tax policy: groups drew up a preference ordering of tax incentives and initially limited their demands. This class action served to delineate the policy debate. Both the Republican rulers and the Democratic challengers accepted business's corporate tax agenda.

To secure political support for his radical supply-side strategy of growth, Reagan offered a trade: action on the corporate tax priorities in exchange for business support for his personal cuts. But because winning the tax act was vitally important to the Democrats, they also tried to woo corporate supporters. Both parties adopted the coalition strategy to fight their political enemies; corporate tax provisions were the stakes in the partisan struggle. Ultimately, most business groups joined the president and organized the computerized lobbying operation which has been credited for much of the president's success. The considerable business unity and partisan conflict combined with aggressive use of the coalition strategy allowed business groups to secure many concessions. The process demonstrated classic pork barrel dynamics.

Macroeconomic Context

Tax legislation during the Reagan years must be viewed against the backdrop of significant economic malaise. The economy began a visible downward tailspin in the early 1970s. Although the decline was initiated by the 1973 oil crisis, the problems transcended the precipitating event.[4] One sign of a deeper trauma was the emergence of stagflation. Keynesian theory suggests a reciprocal relationship between unemployment and inflation; one can be used to cure the other. Yet with stagflation the economy began to experience slow growth and inflation simultaneously. By 1980 the growth rate of real income was almost zero, unemployment was up to 7.5 percent, and inflation was almost 10 percent.[5] Bosworth identifies the inability to explain stagflation as a major failure of the Keynesian model.[6]

Perhaps even more worrisome was the decline of the productivity growth rate in the United States. From 1948 to 1966 productivity grew at an annual rate of 3.3 percent; from 1966 to 1973, 2.1 percent; and from 1973 to 1978, 1.2 percent.[7] Although the productivity growth rate has declined in other countries as well, many nations have managed to narrow the gap between their levels of productivity and our own. For example, from 1960 to 1983 productivity (or real gross domestic product per employed person) grew only 1.2 percent in the United States. Comparable figures for other countries are 5.3 percent for Korea, 3.7 percent for France, 3.4 percent for Germany, 5.9 percent for Japan, and 2.3 percent for the United Kingdom.[8]

Trade deficits also worried policymakers. The merchandise trade balance first went into deficit in 1972; by 1984 it was $140 billion in deficit. The profit rate also suffered from the economic crisis: about 12 percent in 1965, it hovered between 4 and 6 percent during the 1970s and dropped to under 2 percent in 1981.[9]

State Factions: Economic and Political Agendas

Economic policy was perhaps the most important theme of the presidential campaign. Candidate Reagan campaigned on the promise to "get the government off the backs of the people" and generate entrepreneurial activity through tax cuts, deregulation, and deep curtailments in government spending. Early in the prenomination period, Reagan differentiated himself from his fellow candidates by endorsing supply-side economics.

Reagan's choice of the supply-side vision offered a bright counterpoint to Carter's failures. With the appointment of Paul Volcker to the Federal Reserve, Carter set dealing with inflation as his top economic priority.[10] Yet serious efforts to curb inflation may create recession; therefore, such a policy course is hard to maintain. Carter's administration went through many policy reversals, seriously undermining efforts to control inflation. In March of 1980 the Federal Reserve implemented new credit controls to bring the money supply down. During the next month the money supply dropped by 14 percent of the annual rate, the largest monthly decline since the Depression. But within three months it was again out of control, climbing at an annual rate of 15 percent. In April the prime lending rate was up to 20 percent; by July it was back down to 11 percent. Epstein concludes, "At no time since the Great Depression has the Federal Reserve followed such a contradictory monetary policy in an election year, exercised its power over the financial sector to such a degree, and yet seemed in so little control of the economy."[11]

Carter's inability to solve the inflation problem with policies that threw the country into recession played into the Republican campaign. Where Carter chose inflation fighting over domestic growth, Reagan and the Republicans offered to solve both problems with a mixture of monetary and supply-side prescriptions. The president-to-be campaigned on a platform that offered a stimulatory fiscal policy with 30 percent tax cuts to generate growth and a consistent, restrictive control of the money supply to control inflation. The new president offered a no-sacrifice solution to the contradictions of the economy.[12]

The Republican National Committee was captivated by the supply-side vision even before Reagan became its major spokesman. The Republicans were attracted to what Stein calls "the politics of joy" because it offered a vehicle for party rejuvenation and a way to break the New Deal coalition. Reagan, the first major candidate to endorse the new economics, converted in order to shake off the Goldwater mantle of austerity with which he was identified. As late as 1976 Reagan had cautioned that spending should be cut by $90 billion a year before a tax cut could be legislated.[13]

Once elected, Reagan had to test the utility of his new tenet. Yet the optimistic, supply-side vision did not enjoy uniform support within the administration: supply-siders, monetarists, and traditional neoclassical economists had very different concerns. Supply-siders were mainly interested in their now famous growth experiment: cutting taxes to increase personal incentives to work, save, and invest. Monetarists were committed to curbing inflation by slowing growth of the money supply. Traditional economists wanted to reduce government spending and balance the budget. These three goals and the means for accomplishing them were not totally compatible.[14]

The three groups had different ideas about how to revive the economy and what to do about taxes. Monetarists blamed the 1970s crisis on an excessive growth rate of the money supply.[15] The only way to cure the confusing stagflation of the 1970s was first to achieve price stability through restricted growth in the money supply and then to implement a responsible, predictable monetary policy. The money supply should be closely regulated through bank reserve ratios according to annually set targets. Monetarists discredited fiscal stimulation (since individuals adjust for it) and believed that unemployment and growth are assured under correct monetary conditions.[16]

Supply-side advocates placed low taxes at the center of their economic program. Like their neoclassical forebears, supply-siders believed that taxes constrain incentives to work, save, and invest, stifling entrepreneurial spirit and preventing capital formation. Taxes reach a point at which marginal increases so limit incentives that revenue actually drops, as is visually illustrated by the Laffer curve. The best way to achieve growth, therefore, would be to lower marginal taxes. Where supply-siders differed from neoclassical advocates was in their unconditional support for tax cuts, even at the expense of the balanced budget.

The neoclassical economists believed that any fiscal adjustments should be carried out in the context of a balanced budget. A budget deficit withdraws resources from the pool of savings available to private borrowers and, by raising interest rates, raises the price of money. High interest rates in turn impede growth. In this vein, Alan Greenspan informed the Ways and Means Committee that the tax cuts should be accompanied by budget cuts.[17]

Thus, neoclassical economists and monetarists were skeptical about supply-side fiscal policy. While rejecting government fine-tuning, neoclassical economists essentially accepted the logic of the Phillips curve: that inflation cannot be lowered without some accompanying unemployment. Therefore, they saw as untenable the supply-side belief that growth-producing tax cuts could also be noninflationary.[18] Monetarists feared that, given a fixed growth in the money supply, the increased borrowing by the government necessitated by the tax-induced deficit would crowd out private borrowing. At that point the Fed would be pressured to increase the money supply, thus compromising its efforts to fight inflation. Volcker testified before the Ways and Means Committee that the administration should see "concrete action on spending cuts before a final decision is made on the tax cuts." He explained that the financial market "would act adversely" should tax cuts be made before spending cuts. "I think it would be very skeptical that the spending cuts would ever come."[19]

Just as the monetarists feared that the tax cuts would negatively affect their efforts to fight inflation, the supply-siders feared that a restrictive monetary policy would thwart the supply-side experiment. Treasury supply-siders prepared the following memo the day after the inauguration:

> There is no way the President can carry out the main points of his administration . . . unless the Federal Reserve provides the right kind of monetary policy. The right policy is stable moderate and predictable money growth. There is no excuse for failure. If the Fed fails, the Reagan Administration fails.[20]

The ideological differences in the administration were manifested as a split between different departments. The Council of Economic Advisers with Alan Greenspan was the executive branch refuge of the traditional neoclassical economists. The Federal Reserve, the so-called fourth branch of government, with Paul Volcker at the helm adhered to a monetarist philosophy. The most ardent supply-siders were all located at the Treasury: Norman Ture, Craig Roberts, and Donald Regan.[21] David Stockman at the Office of Management and Budget (OMB) was originally viewed as a supply-sider; however, as the months unfolded, his arguments came more and more to resemble those of his traditional neoclassical counterparts.[22]

Taxation was also politically salient among congressional Democrats in 1981. The 1980 election was widely interpreted as a rejection of interest group liberalism and the multitude of spending programs it had spawned. The Republicans were thought to have a mandate to cut back government; the Democrats seemed confused about their role. Budget cutbacks seemed foreordained; the best the Democrats could hope for was damage control. The Democrats were badly beaten in the budget battle, and early evidence suggested that Reagan would approach the tax act with a similar take-no-hostages attitude.[23]

The Democrats, headed by Dan Rostenkowski of the House Ways and Means Committee, had to decide whether to try to beat the president on the tax act or to maintain integrity and lose gracefully. The second alternative, advocated by Morris Udall, entailed fashioning a progressive alternative to the regressive Reagan cuts. The Democratic leadership endorsed the former strategy: they attacked the individual cuts as inequitable and inflationary and moved to outbid the Republicans on the corporate provisions.

The Democrats chose this approach because they thought they had a chance of winning. Although Americans supported the president's spending cuts, they were at best ambivalent about the strange supply-side tax cuts. Dole reported that eleven Republican members of the Senate Finance Committee had serious reservations about the personal cuts.[24]

A second factor which may have given the Democrats hope for victory was the attitude of southern Democrats and the traditional Republican conservatives toward budget deficits. Sixty-three southern Democrats in the House, the so-called boll weevils, had broken rank with the Democratic leadership to vote with the administration on the budget act. Thirty-eight of these were part of the Conservative Democratic Forum. This was not surprising, since cutbacks in government spending had been an important conservative goal. Lower rates of taxation have also been widely supported by conservatives, who wish to restrain the growth of government. But the same southern Democrats tended to view budget deficits as an anathema and disliked the Kemp-Roth cuts. Speaker Tip O'Neill (D–MA) warned, "Reagan better get his own horses in line. There are 70 to 80 Republicans who campaigned against Kemp-Roth."[25]

Third, the tax arena offered Democrats "struggling to redefine their own identity" an opportunity to "put their stamp on economic policy."[26] The Democrats wanted to redeem themselves. A congressional staff person explained, "It's hard to describe the anxiety that was there. There were cheerleading sessions to get the lobbyists ready before the budget battle. Democrats who opposed the president, and his corporate supporters, were the big losers. They wanted a different outcome to the tax act." Allegedly, Jimmy Carter even called Rostenkowski and said, "Do what you have to do, but win."[27]

Fourth, the Democratic willingness to oppose the administration was facilitated by the special role of the Ways and Means Committee in devising tax policy and by the Democratic strength on that committee. By law, revenue acts begin the legislative process in the House. The Ways and Means Committee is responsible for designing the bills: determining which proposals should be included in the bill and hammering out the details. In 1981, Ways and Means, chaired by Dan Rostenkowski, had twenty-three Democratic members and twelve Republican ones. Since the House as a whole was only 55.8 percent Democratic, the 65.7 percent concentration on the committee made it "more left-of-center than the house as a whole," according to William Archer (R–TX). With that strength, the leadership felt that the committee could control the House tax agenda. Many Republicans agreed with Barber Conable's charge that the distribution was politically motivated: "The Democrats have stacked the committee to make it the cutting edge in a political counterattack if Reagan looks vulnerable." [28]

Finally, in a larger sense the committee's decision reflects the "right turn" of the Democratic party in the late 1970s and early 1980s. Ferguson and Rogers suggest that elite decision makers within the Democratic party moved the party to the right in order to protect moneyed interests threatened by the economic decline. [29] Edsall argues that the party explicitly decided that its future lay with the interests of the middle class and subsequently abandoned the claims of many of its traditional constituents. These developments made them less willing to consider an alternative economic policy. [30]

Insiders on Ways and Means report that all understood in advance that this approach to the tax battle would produce a flawed piece of legislation; however, they expected that the outcome would be less regressive than the president's proposal. In retrospect participants were disappointed: despite considerable overtures to the business community, Ways and Means ultimately lost. In the process many tax expenditures, left out of the administration's original proposal, were added to the act; many felt that the tax act was only made worse by the struggle. [31]

Pattern of Business Demands

Business demands in 1981 must be examined at two levels. Business was generally in favor of an accumulation-oriented economic policy. Yet, at the more detailed level of specific corporate tax provisions, sectors differed in their conceptions of growth-oriented taxation.

Financial sectors argued that saving incentives would solve the capital formation problem. The American Bankers Association wanted to expand the individual retirement account; the U.S. Savings and Loan League proposed the All Savers provision. This incentive would allow interest to be exempted from taxes on a special savings certificate worth not more than $1,000. Originally the money from the certificates was to be funneled into home mortgages; therefore, it was conceived of as a way to bail out savings and loan institutions. [32] Critics found the provision costly ($3.1 billion for three years), feared it would only divert funds from elsewhere (e.g., from tax-exempt municipal bonds), and calculated that upper-bracket taxpayers would be the primary beneficiaries.[33] Financial concerns were very skeptical of Reagan's supply-side personal cuts on revenue grounds. A group of financial trade associations wrote to Reagan in February, urging the president to be cautious in advocating the personal cuts and arguing that the deficits produced could lead to higher interest rates and inflation.[34]

High-technology firms wanted a 10 percent research and development tax credit and a restricted employee stock option. A trade task force within the American Electronics Association (AEA) identified the research and development credit as essential for innovation in knowledge-intensive industries. John Danforth (R–MO) in conjunction with the Electronics Industry Association in 1979 introduced legislation creating the tax credit. Treasury opposed the measure, fearing that the credit would fail to increase research and development activity and instead would create new opportunities for tax abuse.[35]

A capital formation task force within AEA identified the restricted stock option as the single most important policy solution to the industry's problems. Stock options were also a way of dealing with the tight market for good engineers: new companies with limited assets could offer stock options instead of higher salaries.[36] The association persuaded Bob Packwood (R–OR) and Gaylord Nelson (D–WI) in the Senate and James Jones (D–OK) and Bill Frenzel (R–MN) in the House to sponsor stock option legislation.[37]

Small business groups had their own roster of demands, endorsed at a White House Conference on Small Business in January of 1980. The individual and corporate income tax rates should be graduated up to $500,000, estate taxes should be relaxed, and a last in first out (LIFO) accounting system should be installed. Small business also wanted expensing (writing off all capital outlays in the first year) instead of accelerated depreciation since it greatly simplified accounting. The Tax Subcommittee of the U.S. Chamber of Commerce's Council on Small Business was instrumental in shaping the policy agenda.[38]

Capital-intensive manufacturing groups put a priority on depreciation reform to solve the capital shortage. The steel industry claimed that the United States had the longest depreciation schedule for steel in the world.[39] The timber and paper industry anticipated spending an additional $5 billion in capital investment by 1985 and feared that internal profits would be inadequate to the task.[40]

Credit and deduction refundability was a second priority for many manufacturing sectors. The steel industry's situation is illustrative. Beginning in 1977 the industry repeatedly failed to realize profit, paid no taxes, and began to accumulate carryover operating losses and investment tax credits. By 1981 the industry held $5 billion in carryover losses; 77 percent of the investment tax credits earned in 1981 were not realized.[41] The industry wanted to make the investment tax credit and depreciation allowance refundable, so that unprofitable firms could use the credits.[42] Current law, a lobbyist argued, discriminates against "poor" companies: "The rich get richer and the poor get poorer."[43]

Refundability was criticized from the left as a subsidy to business; conservatives thought it smacked of government handouts and redistribution of corporate wealth. There was also a jurisdictional problem. The House Appropriations Committee argued that, since the refundable tax credit would constitute money going out of the Treasury, it should be handled through appropriations. Supporters of the provision felt that this would be politically unfeasible—refundable tax credits would compete with other government programs—and pushed for it to be handled through Ways and Means.

A third priority for capital-intensive manufacturing was the repeal of the corporate minimum tax on tax preference items. The tax was designed to impose taxes on firms that escape paying taxes by means of dubious tax shelters. Yet, proponents argued, the minimum tax disproportionately burdened low-profit industries. Independent oil producers also wanted to repeal the windfall profits: phase out the tax on new oil, exempt the tax on stripper oil produced by independents, exempt two barrels daily for royalty owners, and freeze the depletion allowance at 22 percent.[44]

Mobilization within the Business Community

Sectoral differences were quite pronounced; yet business groups managed to agree on a priority of tax initiatives. Class politics rather than interest group politics characterized this period. This interesting development can be explained by an anxiety on the part of business about its general position. Edsall suggests that the pressure on business to act like a class originally came from the domination of the federal government by liberal Democrats in the wake of Watergate. Business was at a low ebb during the reformist fervor of the early 1970s; Watergate raised the general mistrust of private and public elites.[45]

In order to cope with this hostile climate, corporate lobbyists began meeting to discuss the dangers of the liberal agenda. The Business Roundtable emerged as the lobbying arm of big business. The American Council for Capital Formation (ACCF), founded in 1973 by Charls Walker, had a particular focus on economic policy. The Chamber of Commerce became more explicitly political after a hiatus in the early 1970s; its membership grew from 50,000 in 1970 to 215,000 in 1983. The Chamber, especially, has pursued a vigorous policy role: mobilizing its grassroots membership, organizing ad hoc coalitions among other trade associations, and issuing information about congressional campaigns.[46]

In the substantive area of corporate taxation, the necessity of organization and consensus was brought home to business leaders by the experience of the 1978 tax act. A rather astonishing turnaround in tax policy occurred in that year. An administration bill that resembled the tax reform acts of 1969 and 1976 in spirit and intent was transformed into a pro-business tax cut which reduced the taxation of capital gains.

Yet 1978 was marked by intense conflict and infighting in the business community. Although most businessmen and individual stockholders were happy to have reductions in capital gains taxation, such a tax change was not top on everyone's agenda. Timber interests (the founders of the American Council for Capital Formation), the securities industry, venture capitalists, and high-technology firms provided the core support for the 1978 cut in the capital gains tax rate. Capital-intensive manufacturing sectors preferred speeding up depreciation; small business sectors requested cuts in individual and corporate rates. One participant recalls: "Priorities were different about which approach to use. No one really got what they wanted because they were fighting each other. It was much easier for Congress to play one group off against the other. What provided the impetus for getting ACRS going was the experience in 1978."[47]

To avoid a repetition of the 1978 struggle, legislators Jim Jones (D–OK) and Barber Conable (R–NY) went on a campaign to unify the business community around future tax reduction. The legislators told corporate actors that they would work for a tax cut if two conditions were met: First, the vehicle must be extremely simple. Second, business groups must be unified in their goals and discipline themselves accordingly. As one staff person recalls: "Jones didn't like business telling him one thing in a group and another individually. So he told them to get their act together."[48]

The basic manufacturing sectors set out to build support in the business community for faster depreciation. Small business involvement was seen as critical for political appeal. A famous coalition called the Carlton Group provided a forum where the diverse interests could jointly pursue the goals of reduced corporate taxation. The Carlton Group was composed of representatives from a wide range of the business community: Richard Rahn (Chamber of Commerce), Paul Howard (National Association of Manufacturing), Cliff Massa III and Ernest Christian (Patten, Boggs, and Blow), Dirk Van Dongen (National Association of Wholesaler-Distributors), Jack Albertine (American Business Conference), James McKevitt (National Federation of Independent Business), and Mark Bloomfield (American Council for Capital Formation). The Chamber of Commerce, the National Association of Wholesaler-Distributors, and the National Federation of Independent Business all could claim to speak for small business. The American Business Conference presented itself as the voice for high-tech, fast-growing, small- and medium-sized firms. Thus, the Carlton Group seemed to extend across a broad section of American business.[49]

Cliff Massa III (the National Association of Manufacturers) recalls that until this time there was no regular, ongoing forum in which individuals with diverse interests could discuss tax strategies; therefore, very little coordination occurred. "All went about their own business." In 1975 and 1976, however, members of the business community were extremely alarmed by what they perceived to be the "high water mark of tax reform." Says one participant, "Out of absolute necessity, people had to get together." [50]

The Carlton Group began working on a compromise tax position in early 1979; Jones met with the group's tax analysts in February to establish the parameters of the legislation. The shape of the bill represented an effort to incorporate something for everyone. Tax unity hinged on a single provision: accelerated cost recovery, or "10-5-3." ACRS was a way of deducting depreciation allowances for fixed assets. Under the prior system each capital asset had an estimated useful life; the depreciation deduction was to be taken gradually over the course of the asset's useful life. There had been considerable dispute over the years regarding the exact length of the useful life, how much value was left in an asset if it were sold after its depreciation allowance had been used up, and how much of the depreciation allowance could be used up in the early years when a piece of equipment was functioning at its best. Inflation gave proponents of faster depreciation another argument: as inflation increased the replacement costs of equipment, depreciation allowances were even less helpful in replacing outmoded assets.

The accelerated cost recovery system replaced these asset lives with three general categories. Real estate could be written off in ten years; most equipment, in five; and trucks, in three. The concept of accelerated cost recovery was pursued in several arenas throughout the 1970s. NAM's taxation committee takes credit for devising the concept of 10–5 (ten years and five years being the two categories of asset lives which replaced the multitude of asset life estimates under the old system) in 1970. The Chamber of Commerce, the American Council for Capital Formation, and others also worked on the concept.

The sectors with the most to gain from accelerated depreciation were the heavy manufacturing industries. The "5" in "10-5-3" was of major importance to manufacturers of such products as steel, airplanes, and paper products—the constituents of the National Association of Manufacturers. Accelerated capital cost recovery with a five-year classification for equipment obviously was a major improvement over the prior ten- or fifteen-year asset lives.

Left out of the heavy industry consensus was independent oil. The oil industry supported "10-5-3" but doubted that accelerated depreciation would have much benefit for them. First, intangible drilling costs account for 70 percent of the costs for useful wells; depreciation does nothing to reduce these costs. Second, most of the independents' equipment is used rather than new;

rules for depreciating used equipment were much more restrictive. Finally, the industry was concerned about the comparative advantage of investments in oil fields vis-à-vis other opportunities. The 1981 act actually made oil investments less attractive.[51]

The finance and housing sectors were divided on the accelerated cost recovery provision. Housing sectors were drawn to the coalition because of the benefits of building depreciation: the "10" in "10-5-3" was designed to appeal to sectors which held most of their assets in structures. Under the previous law commercial and industrial buildings could be depreciated in twenty to twenty-five years; therefore, "10-5-3" made real estate investment extremely attractive. By comparison, it had little to offer the financial sector, since finance has very little equipment to be depreciated.

High-technology sectors also felt that the "10-5-3" provision had little to offer. Electronics equipment was already depreciated in seven years under the asset depreciation range (ADR) system, an accelerated depreciation system created in 1971. Dropping the asset life to five years was a marginal savings. The industry was unsuccessful in its push to make the depreciation life for computers and electronic equipment three years.[52]

Because none of the special small business provisions were addressed by the "10-5-3" proposal, small business groups were divided in their enthusiasm. The National Federation of Independent Business (NFIB) and the National Association of Wholesaler-Distributors (NAW) were active in the Carlton Group and were major proponents of the tax provision. The status of both groups on the national business scene had risen in the late 1970s. Both were included among the seven most influential business organizations. (The others were the Chamber of Commerce, National Association of Manufacturers, Business Roundtable, American Business Conference, and American Council for Capital Formation.) One Washington observer suggested, "Insiders generally cite NAW's new position as further evidence of the increasing role being played by smaller business in the critical Washington business group strategy."[53] A desire to remain significant players undoubtedly contributed to their participation.

Supportive small business groups were drawn to the coalition for material reasons as well. First, although small businesses have very little equipment, they have trucks, which could be depreciated in three years under the new rule. Second, extreme simplicity was valued; many small businesses had been unable to use the complex asset depreciation range system.[54] Third, some small business groups (the wholesaler-distributors and the retailers) were drawn to "10-5-3" for structure depreciation. Wholesalers and retailers are labor-intensive but own most of their capital assets in buildings. Finally, when "10-5-3" was tied to the president's supply-side cuts, small business was willing to accept the former for the sake of the latter. In 1976 almost 90 percent of the small businesses were organized as sole proprietorships, partnerships, and Subchapter S corporations. Such organizations are all taxed under the individual rates.[55] An NFIB representative reported: "It was a compromise situation. NFIB played along because they wanted personal rate reductions and indexing. They traded '10-5-3' for the personal cuts."[56]

The National Small Business Association (NSB) was the leader of the opposition. The ideological orientation of the two memberships rather than economic interests was responsible for their divergence. In the early 1970s, NFIB and NSB became somewhat polarized, NFIB moving toward the conservative end of the spectrum and NSB toward the liberal. NSB viewed the personal tax cuts as inflationary and "10-5-3" of little benefit to its labor-intensive type of firm. President Herb Liebenson explained:

> You have nearly 14 million businesses grossing under $2 million each, and they employ about 58 percent of the workforce . . . They produce 43 percent of the gross national product—but they got only 25 percent to 33 percent of the total business tax cut. A lot of our people supported this law without really understanding it.[57]

NSB was especially concerned about the fast write-off schedules under ACRS. The Small Business National Unity Council testified that neither the personal cuts nor the ACRS proposal "will benefit small business anywhere near in proportion to the importance of small business to the economy." The three-year asset life category under ACRS averaged three and a half years under the ADR system. This should be compared to the other categories: ten years under ACRS averaged thirty-two years under ADR; five-year write-offs averaged ten years under the old system.[58]

Despite the apparent unity behind "10-5-3" certain interests were noticeably missing. Although a great many sectors chose to participate in the initial industry alliance, not all held depreciation reform central to their interests. When the carefully constructed unity began to unravel, alternative demands became bidding chips in the political competition.

Proposal Development

Despite monetarists' and neoclassical economists' qualms, the president held firm to his endorsement of the 30 percent Kemp-Roth tax cuts.[59] To address the host of corporate tax proposals circulating the Washington community in 1980 would create a tremendous revenue loss. Therefore, even before the inauguration, Reagan's transition team began studying the range of tax proposals currently in the legislative hopper. The task force on taxation chaired by Charls Walker divided the list into those proposals which should be given top priority and those which were worthy of attention but could be delayed.

The composition of the tax act was a political problem. The president wanted the Kemp-Roth cuts desperately; however, business support was necessary for their passage. Without the restraint of corporate lobbyists, the legislative process with its sensitivity to special interests would produce a very different kind of tax act. The president had to find a way to get business lobbyists to support the Kemp-Roth cuts and to hold off on other demands. The problem was to choose the tax proposal generating the most political support. Administration staff analyzed the distribution of resources in the business community—money and power—and the means by which these resources were put to political ends: political action campaign information, grass roots organizing capabilities, and coalitions unifying diverse special interests. They identified accelerated cost recovery as the most widely supported tax provision in the business community. A high official in the administration explained: "It was a ready-made lobby with a ready-made plan. Eighty percent of the business lobbyists would go along."[60]

One corporate lobbyist admitted that a kind of exchange was made. He explained that certain trade associations such as the National Association of Manufacturers and the Business Roundtable "didn't like" the personal cuts. They "saw no connection between these tax cuts and the economy. But they were prepared to accept the personal cuts for ACRS."[61]

The concept and content of the two-stage tax act grew out of these political realities. The administration's strategy was to create two bills. The first bill would contain only two provisions: the Kemp-Roth personal cuts and the Accelerated Cost Recovery System. The second bill would contain all of the other provisions that special interests wanted enacted. The best way to get the Kemp-Roth cuts enacted as quickly as possible would be to couple these cuts with a provision that would keep the corporate lobbyists happy and interference in the legislative process at a minimum. On February 6 the administration held a meeting for twelve hundred business leaders to "explain and seek support for the administration's strategy in seeking targeted budget and tax reductions." The game plan was explained by Don Regan and Kemp: all provisions besides the Kemp-Roth cuts and "10-5-3" would be included in the second bill.

The Democrats responded with what they considered to be a competitive tax package. On April 9, 1981, Rostenkowski announced the broad outlines of the Democratic alternative during a speech before the Chicago Association of Commerce and Industry. Rostenkowski called for a one-year tax cut of $40 billion: $28 billion would go to individuals; $12 billion, to business. The individual cuts, unlike those in the president's plan, would be concentrated in the $20,000 to $50,000 income bracket.

Rostenkowski promised that his plan would also speed up depreciation; however, he rejected ACRS, feeling it discriminated against small, labor-intensive industries. He offered a number of other corporate tax provisions, designated by the Republicans for the second-stage bill. The three-year limit for carrying back unused investment tax credits would be extended. Small businesses were to receive as yet unspecified productivity incentives. Research and development incentives were promised as well as a larger exclusion for U.S. citizens working abroad.[62]

Ways and Means were to begin marking up their bill in early June. The two parties disagreed on four points. First, Rostenkowski wanted a one-year cut; Reagan, a three-year cut. Second, Rostenkowski wanted the benefits to be concentrated in the $20,000 to $50,000 annual income range; Reagan wanted to cut marginal rates. Third, Rostenkowski wanted to use part of the personal tax cuts to create savings incentives; Reagan wanted to leave the choice of savings up to the individual. Finally, Rostenkowski chose expensing as a form of speeded-up depreciation; the president, ACRS.[63]

Immediately after Rostenkowski's April speech, a calm passed over Washington: for a brief period compromise seemed possible. Rumors of "Reagan's new flexibility" appeared in the press. *Business Week* quoted Martin Anderson as saying "the best thing we can do is stay with the essentials of the 10-10-10 program" and then editorialized:

> The word "essential" still leaves the White House room to maneuver. In some quarters of the Administration, there is a growing realization that to get any kind of multi year tax cut, the White House must be prepared to accept some scaling back of the size of the rate reductions, a tilt to give more of the benefits to the middle and upper middle classes, and perhaps a tax cut of less than three years duration.
>
> Rather than running the risk of hanging tough and losing control of the tax-writing process to Congress, as President Carter did in 1978, even the most ardent Administration supply-siders are taking a more flexible line.[64]

Barber Conable (R–NY) recalls attending a tax strategy meeting at the White House after Rostenkowski had made a speech on "Face the Nation." The White House was interested in Rostenkowski's two-year personal cut proposal but did not want to make the first overture. Someone suggested that a call from Rostenkowski to Regan would be helpful; Conable was elected to call Rostenkowski and present him with the idea. Conable recommended that Rostenkowski propose a two-year personal increase, dropping the top rate from 70 to 50 percent, and "10-5-3." In return, the president would let Congress handle the second-stage bill. Rostenkowski responded enthusiastically but did not immediately contact the Treasury. Conable tried to find out why the Democrats were hesitating; Rostenkowski replied that he had to "talk to his boys." A week passed, and Conable and Regan concluded that the Democrats were stalling. It was decided that Regan should approach the southern Democrats. Chief of Staff James Baker III and Donald Regan approached Kent Hance (D–TX) and Phil Gramm (D–TX) and identified several adjustments in the bill necessary for southern Democratic support. Estate taxes would have to be lowered, the marriage penalty adjusted, and the exclusion on dividends expanded.[65]

At this point Conable was still hopeful that a compromise could be achieved. He explained to Regan that, since the southern Democrats were willing to make a deal, the Democratic leadership would undoubtedly go along. Rostenkowski promised to "talk with the boys" in a week's time. Meanwhile Conable had a meeting of the minority Ways and Means members "to hold my own boys in line." He wanted to keep them committed to leaving out the provisions in the second-stage bill.[66] Rostenkowski and Senator Bob Dole (R–KS) met the day before Rostenkowski was to meet with White House staff. Afterward Rostenkowski optimistically remarked: "Senator Dole and I are pretty much on target. I'd say there's more agreed upon than disagreed." Dole contributed to the spirit of hope as well: "We feel we are close enough that we ought to discuss it with the administration. If it were left to us we think we could reach agreement."[67] Yet, when Rostenkowski and Dole met with Regan on May 28, the attempts to compromise ended in failure. The length and form of the personal cuts were the manifest sticking points.[68]

There is a Democratic version and a Republican version of why the efforts to compromise failed. Democratic insiders say that the problem was that the Democrats were forced to negotiate with Don Regan but that Regan was unauthorized to make deals. Rostenkowski was expected to state his bottom line to Regan, who then had to report back to Jim Baker and the president. Rostenkowski wanted to negotiate directly with the president: he wanted to avoid giving away Democratic secrets without reciprocal behavior from the Republicans. Republicans claim that the problem lay with a split Democratic leadership.

> Although Rostenkowski was willing to accept two years of the personal cuts and a trigger, Jim Wright said no. Danny, Tip O'Neill, [and] Jim Wright met with Regan, Baker, and the president, and nothing could be worked out. The Democrats hadn't come together, didn't have their act together. Regan tried to make a deal, but it didn't work.

There may also have been a problem with the Rostenkowski-Dole announcement. The president had been perplexed over Dole's public readiness to endorse a compromise position. The administration's view was still that the Democrats must make the first overture.[69]

The Bidding War

After the hopes of compromise were dashed, the bidding war began in earnest. Rostenkowski and the Ways and Means Committee showed signs of gathering strength in May. Many of the southern Democrats, concerned about the fiscal responsibility of the personal cuts, indicated that they were less willing to break partisan rank than they had been during the budget battle. Although the Ways and Means bill would not actually be reported out of committee until July 23, industry representatives were guaranteed provisions much earlier. The Democratic alternative included refundable tax credits for basic manufacturing, research and development credits for high technology, individual retirement accounts for the financial sector, graduated income tax rates and job credits for small business, and special tax credits on old and historic buildings to attract real estate.[70]

On June 4, Reagan fought back, radically revising his tax act so that it would bring constituents back into the fold. The Republicans included provisions under Democratic consideration and proposed liberalizing estate and gift taxes, extending the one-year exemption from the windfall profits tax for small royalty owners, and making permanent the exclusion on dividends and interest. These provisions were clearly concessions to the southern Democrats, whose constituents in large part were composed of farmers and oilmen. Kent Hance (D–TX) remarked: "As long as they need our votes, we're a political faction that's going to have to be dealt with . . . The only reason the White House called on our group is because we've got the swing vote."[71] Barber Conable recalls: "The president switched to the coalition strategy after the Democrats didn't play ball. Rosty sought Republican constituencies: realtors, home builders, and small business. Since the Democrats put all these in, the president was made to play ball also. Rosty is easy to underestimate."[72]

In order to pay for these additional tax expenditures, the administration proposed cutbacks in ACRS. "10-5-3" was changed to "15-10-5-3"; all buildings were now to be written off in fifteen years rather than ten years. The percentage of depreciation that could be taken in the early years was also revised; the 200 percent declining balance schedule was changed to a 150 percent declining balance schedule.[73]

Cutting back the ACRS provision offended one very important constituency: the coalition of corporate lobbyists who had worked so hard to bring it about. There is some indication that the administration was surprised by the business community's response. One insider recalls Don Regan saying that he knew something about the business community and that what they wanted was a decline in the long-term capital gains rate. The Friday after Black Thursday, as that June 4 came to be known, saw an angry response from these Washington professionals. In Friday morning's *Wall Street Journal,* Richard Rahn accused the administration of a "breach of faith." Cliff Massa called Rob Lennart, staff of the Ways and Means Committee, and reported that the president's sudden change of heart "presented the Democrats with an opportunity to pull in some aspects of the business community." On Friday afternoon corporate lobbyists including Charls Walker (ACCF), Richard Lesher and Richard Rahn (Chamber of Commerce), Dirk Van Dongen (NAW), Cliff

Massa and Ernest Christian (Patten, Boggs, and Blow), and Mike Mckevitt (NFIB) met with top-level administration officials Jim Baker, Elisabeth Dole, Don Regan, Norman Ture, and Buck Chapotan to demand a policy reversal. Baker and Dole were there as political experts in the administration; Regan, Ture, and Chapotan were there to deal with the substantive aspects of the change. After an emotionally charged meeting, the Treasury agreed to a compromise: ACRS would be implemented in stages, with the percentage to be taken in the early years gradually increased over time.[74]

The press reported that corporate executives descended on Washington after the June 4 revision to demand that the president reinstate the cuts. Corporate lobbyists, however, recall that the White House spent the weekend contacting the chief executive officers of major corporations to garner support for the altered version. These executives in turn contacted their trade associations and demanded that the political lobbyists support the president. Remarked one lobbyist, "If the CEOs had been brought in earlier by the president, we wouldn't have gotten anything back at all."[75] The experience of June 4 impressed the "10-5-3" business coalition that haste was extremely important in legislating the tax bill. *Business Week* reported:

> Whatever form the business tax cut ultimately takes, the greatest risk for the corporate community lies in a protracted bidding war that could cause the tax bill to balloon in size. The Administration has already displayed a willingness to sacrifice business cuts to make room for the pet proposals of individual members while preserving the bulk of its personal rate cuts.[76]

Following the Rose Garden speech was a series of rapid concessions to special interests on both sides. During the first three weeks in June the Ways and Means Democrats adopted a series of proposals to break up the president's coalition of Republicans and conservative Democrats. The administration's June 4 revision was introduced in the House in mid-June by Barber Conable (R–NY) and Kent Hance (D–TX) and was called Conable-Hance I. On July 24, the day after the Ways and Means Committee reported the Democratic bill out of committee, the administration updated its bid for legislative and corporate support with Conable-Hance II. The Republicans also responded to the Democratic bids in the Senate Finance Committee's markup.

Financial groups were wooed with the All Savers provision, a provision heavily pushed by a coalition of housing and mortgage interests led by the U.S. League of Savings Associates. The coalition carried out their campaign with "scores of full-page newspaper ads, studies from economic research firms and aggressive lobbying."[77] The coalition originally approached Treasury's Buck Chapotan, who responded that inclusion of the provision in the president's package was impossible. The home builders then approached Rostenkowski, who agreed to include it in the markup in exchange for support.

Although All Savers eventually found its way into the Republican bill as well, the National Association of Home Builders was one of the few trade associations to stay with the Democrats throughout the legislative process. The Senate Finance Committee endorsed the All Savers provision as part of its savings strategy. The committee was heavily lobbied to accept the provision: in June two-thirds of the Senate Banking Committee wrote a letter to Finance asking them to support All Savers. The business coalition considered this a turning point. The House provision had more restrictions than the Republican version: it would only be granted to savings and loans and was tied more closely to home mortgages.

The high-technology lobby consisted of five industry groups: the American Electronics Association, Electronics Industry Association, Semiconductor Industry Association, Computer and Business Equipment Manufacturers Association, and Scientific Apparatus Makers Association. Paul Oosterhuis, tax counsel at Hogan and Hartson, was retained by the coalition to help in the research and development fight.[78] The high-tech group was originally disappointed with Reagan's overtures. Ken Haggerty of AEA explained: "When Reagan came to town he wasn't very plugged into high tech. High tech wasn't as visible as other sectors. Reagan sat down with business and they told him that they wanted '10-5-3.' But '10-5-3' did nothing for high tech."[79] The American Electronics Association reported:

> After the 1980 election, AEA faced a new set of problems. Though bills and sponsors were ready to go, AEA found itself on the outside looking in. Instead of a president who wanted no tax bill at all, we had acquired a new one who did want a bill, but limited to only personal rate cuts for individuals (Kemp Roth) and accelerated depreciation for business ("10-5-3"). He was supported by a large, powerful and vocal coalition of business groups in Washington which had buried differences to work together on this bill. This coalition combined with the administration to recommend that stock options and research and development credits should await for a promised second tax bill.[80]

But the industry tried to make use of the political divisions between the Democrats and Republicans in the bidding war. As one industry spokesman explained, "Reagan was unsympathetic, so high tech sold their ideas to the Democrats."[81] This was helped by the fact that several long-time Democratic sympathizers sat on the Ways and Means Committee. Despite the administration's apparent lack of interest, the group lobbied Treasury and found Undersecretary Norman Ture sympathetic.

When the Kemp-Roth/"10-5-3" exclusive package began to unravel, the coalition of high-tech firms perceived an opening. The American Electronics Association sent out an action alert to member companies: "The chances for meaningful tax help for high technology companies have soared in the past two weeks . . . This is the key time to contact the House Ways and Means members who must make the initial decisions." [82]

The industry increased its lobbying effort in the Senate, and the administration finally gave approval to Finance Committee Republicans to accept a limited research and development credit, consisting of a 25 percent credit on incremental increases in wages and salaries related to research and development. Then the House Ways and Means Committee, led by Jim Shannon (D–MA), put a comprehensive research and development credit in the Democratic bill. The comprehensive credit would apply to all research and development expenditures. The Shannon version would cover all materials, laboratory supplies, and computer time. Industry analysts calculated that the alternative would lose about 50 percent more revenue than the administration version. [83] But later the president allowed the full credit to be included in the Hance-Conable substitute. [84]

Stock options were being considered but were not yet included in the version before the Ways and Means Committee when the American Electronics Association had its annual capital caucus. One hundred sixty executives came to Washington for this event and held eighty-three meetings with key individuals in the two branches. Shortly thereafter, stock options were finally accepted by the administration for inclusion in the Senate Finance bill. The industry credits Bob Packwood for playing a major role in this effort. The House Ways and Means Committee followed suit, led by Jim Jones. The final 1981 act included most of what the electronic industry wanted. Jack Robertson observed, "Elated electronic industry officials last week watched as rival Democratic and Republican tax bills vied to offer the most research and development tax incentives, [the most] accelerated depreciation, and [the] lowest corporate income tax rates." [85]

Small business groups also entered into the bargaining sessions. The National Federation of Independent Business (part of the original "10-5-3" coalition) remained consistently behind the president's bill. But members of the National Small Business Association were early supporters of the Democrats and helped Ways and Means write the small business provisions in their alternative: graduating corporate tax rates up to $200,000, cutting the top corporate rate from 46 to 34 percent, and increasing the amount a firm could accumulate before it must pay accumulated earnings taxes. Expensing, developed as an alternative to ACRS and the investment tax credit, helped small business by greatly simplifying accounting and by equalizing some of the disparity in effective tax rates paid by capital- and labor-intensive firms. [86] The National Association of Wholesaler-Distributors formally supported the president throughout the bidding war but privately worked with Ways and Means on the estate and gift tax clauses.

Politicians on both sides offered refundability schemes to basic industry's "sick six": steel, autos, railroads, paper, airlines, and mining. The Democrats were the first to be interested in the concept and started working on the refundable tax credit in April 1981. Don Bailey (D–PA) spearheaded the effort; industry representatives such as Bethlehem Steel's Don McCambridge helped design the bill.

Meanwhile, efforts were being made to get a sympathetic ear on the Republican side. Neither the administration's initial tax package nor Conable-Hance I included a refundability provision. The Republicans developed safe harbor leasing, a variation on the refundable tax credit theme, at the midnight hour to ensure the loyalty of the basic industry lobbyists. Safe harbor leasing allowed unprofitable companies to sell their assets and then lease them back again at very low rates and with no need to repay residual values at the end of the leasing term. The accelerated cost recovery system and the investment tax credit would be available to the nominal owners, the profit-making firms; the unprofitable firms got the use of capital assets at much lower rates. The administration preferred this to refundability, because the market rather than Treasury would reimburse companies. Of course, the actual impact of the provision was to reduce revenue. Some in industry regarded safe harbor leasing with suspicion: many continued to prefer a less complicated refundability provision. Many trade associations did not formally endorse either bill.

Independent oil producers originally supported the president's two-stage process despite an interest in repealing the windfall profits tax act. After the administration's June 4 revision, it became obvious that many other provisions originally designated for the second bill were being included in the first. The oilmen decided that, if changes were to be made in the windfall profits tax, they would have to be included in the current legislation. Oil industry congressmen Senator Lloyd Bentsen (D–TX) and David Boren (D–OK) tried to get oil provisions included in the Senate legislation. Bentsen introduced an amendment to exempt the first one thousand barrels daily for independents and royalty owners. Boren introduced a measure exempting new oil from the tax. These amendments failed, but the Finance Committee compromised with a vote to reduce the windfall profits tax from 30 percent to 15 percent.

On June 25 the Independent Petroleum Association of America (IPAA) held a strategy meeting including representatives of eighteen oil and gas corporations. Participants feared that their previous "attitude of cooperation was purposely misinterpreted as acceptance of the status quo. The industry's critics in Washington were projecting the misunderstanding that 'the industry really isn't all that concerned about the windfall profit tax.' " They decided that a "geographically representative group of independents" should meet with Senate Finance to increase the visibility of the industry. Rod DeArmant, chief counsel, met with forty-five independents on July 6 to explain why the administration couldn't address the windfall profits tax at that time.[87]

The oilmen were not satisfied with the Finance Committee meeting, so Bob

Dole arranged a session with the administration leadership. On July 8 the group met with Regan and Chapotan in Dole's office. The group reminded the administration that independent oil had been among the president's strongest supporters. The president's campaign platform had included the repeal of the windfall profits tax.

On July 9 the president himself met with a representative group of oilmen. George Bush, Bob Dole, Elisabeth Dole, Max Friedersdorf, Martin Anderson, and Buck Chapotan were also present. One participant reported that the president made a strong case for loyalty: "You're used to having me ask for money, but this time I want blood." [88] Reagan agreed to restate his opposition to the windfall profits tax in a public letter to the Independent Petroleum Association of America. But the president reiterated that current repeal of the windfall profits tax was not politically feasible. The *New York Times* reported that the purpose of the meeting was to cool off the independents. [89] John Miller (IPAA chairman) reported that he was not pleased with the president's lack of commitment to the oil cause. [90]

The independents continued to try to get their provisions included in the Senate Finance Committee bill but without success. They informally polled a target list of sympathetic senators to gauge the extent of support for the Bentsen and Boren amendments and to determine if a second-stage bill was considered likely. Forty-two senators reported support for Bentsen; forty-nine, for Boren. Ninety percent doubted that there would ever be a second tax act. On the basis of this response, the oil representatives decided that considerable support existed for their bill.

Kent Hance and Tom Loeffler (R–TX) began a movement to exempt the first one thousand barrels of oil daily from the windfall profits tax. Oil interests persuaded 208 members to cosponsor this bill. Hance and Charles Stenholm (D–TX) met with White House and Treasury staff during this period urging them to action. Over the July 17 weekend, Hance and 15 other Democrats were flown to Camp David to discuss taxation with the president over hamburgers. The following week, the oil tax dispute became the "principal issue" in the tax debate.

On July 21 the Bentsen amendment (the thousand-barrel exemption) was defeated on the Senate floor sixty-one to thirty-eight. Only nine of the fifty-three Senate Republicans supported the amendment; the president's will was upheld. A ten-barrel exemption for royalty owners was also killed.

On the last day of the markup session, the Ways and Means Committee adopted a set of oil provisions designed to woo southern Democrats away from the president. Hance argued for the thousand-barrel exclusion. Bill Archer of Texas offered an amendment similar to the Boren amendment (eliminating the tax on new oil). At first most of the Democrats on the committee were opposed to these two measures, although the Republicans supported them. Finally, at 2:30 A.M., the Democrats endorsed the oil provisions in pursuit of boll weevil support.[91] A daily exemption of five hundred barrels was allowed from the windfall profits tax, costing the Treasury $7 billion over five years. Ways and Means also upped the ante on estate taxes, increasing the exemption from $175,625 to $600,000.[92]

After the administration learned that the House Democrats had caved in on oil, it decided to follow suit. Later in the afternoon of July 22, the White House told Hance that oil representatives had a meeting with the president at 10:00 A.M. the next morning to present their desired windfall profit tax changes. IPAA's Lloyd Unsell and Bud Scoggins met that evening with Hance, Loeffler, Stenholm, Anderson, and staff member Jim Rock. Hance explained, "What we need is a package that won't cost an arm and a leg in revenues but that independents across the country can get enthused about." Industry lobbyists and congressional staff stayed up all night hammering out the industry's position. The next day the Conable-Hance alternative was presented to the House, complete with an expanded set of oil concessions designed to claim the hearts of southern Democrats forever.

Fifty independents came to Washington July 27 to monitor the successive House votes. Contacts were made with boll weevil Democrats who had earlier committed themselves to the Ways and Means bill but were now encouraged to go with the Conable-Hance alternative. Finally, the House voted for the Conable-Hance bill 238 to 195.[93]

One task remained, the reconciliation of the House and Senate bills by the Joint Conference Committee. The Senate bill held less advantageous measures for the oil industry. Since Rostenkowski controlled the debate on the House bill, he could simply acquiesce to the Senate alternatives. Bud Scoggins (Independent Petroleum Association of America) monitored the process, consulting with Dole and those sympathetic to the industry. The sticking point was the percentage depletion allowance freeze. At 2:00 A.M. after arguing for four hours Rostenkowski told the group, "We just won't have a bill" and left the room. The remaining conferees continued meeting. Dole discussed the impasse with the White House and lobbyists for the industry. Finally at about 4:00 A.M. industry participants signaled to Dole that they were willing to forgo the allowance. As an industry representative explained: "We knew from the outset that we wouldn't get anything on percentage depletion. But we knew that the longer we held out, the more we would get that time and the next time around."[94]

In a desperate move to cover all the bases, the administration contacted the Securities Industry Association (SIA) during the last week of the legislative battle. The industry had been lukewarm about the tax act. A Data Resources study commissioned by the SIA ranked the original Reagan proposal the lowest of seven tax proposals in terms of economic activity generated for revenue lost. The industry had not, however, formally opposed the tax act. Some executives explained that their general sympathy with the administration prevented such action. Don Regan himself had been a stockbroker.

Despite initial reservations, the industry became an active ally in the last phases of the battle. An exchange was made: the securities industry people promised to go out and "burn the telephone wires" generating support for the administration in return for the lowering of the holding period on capital gains from one year to six months. The *Wall Street Journal* reported:

> Within hours of the White House meeting the SIA cranked up a full-throttle lobbying drive to push the Reagan bill through the House. With securities firms operating branch offices in every state, the industry commands a powerful lobbying machine. The SIA set up "phone squads" to uncork a flood of calls to Capitol Hill, particularly to undecided members of Congress from their own districts. National brokerage firms such as E. F. Hutton and Merrill Lynch and Co. wired all their branch managers to urge them to call their Congressmen and push for the Reagan bill. Meanwhile, an SIA computer spun out names of brokerage industry officials friendly with particular members of Congress . . .
>
> Between the Friday meeting at the White House and the House passage of the bill the following Wednesday, the securities industry generated as many as 20,000 calls to members of Congress . . . Others involved in the campaign estimate that the five-day total ran as high as 35,000 calls.[95]

Despite the securities industry's efforts, the six-month holding period was dropped from the bill during the conference committee. The industry was approached only after the Senate bill had been completed; therefore, the holding period reduction only appeared in the House version. During the House-Senate conference to reconcile the two bills, Rostenkowski offered to defer to the Senate's position on the measure.

The Coalition Strategy

On June 29 the House of Representatives voted to pass the president's tax bill 238 to 195. Forty-eight Democrats defected to the Republican camp, most of whom were the southern Democrats to whom both sides had offered concessions. The Senate voted on its own bill the same day, passing it 89 to 11. Thirty-seven of the 47 Senate Democrats supported the bill; there was no Democratic version.[96]

Why did the president ultimately succeed? Not to be overlooked were the ties between the Republican party and most sectors of the business community at the time of the 1980 election. Many lobbyists had worked hard to get the president elected and felt that Reagan had consistently supported the corporate perspective. One oil lobbyist explained, "You dance with him that brung ya." [97] Although the Democratic package was very advantageous to some sectors, its sponsors were regarded with suspicion. Many believed that, once Rostenkowski had won, he would revoke the measures in conference. Richard Rahn explained: "I think there's a lot of cynicism in the business community. The Democrats were appealing more to business for support, but they were also destroying any intellectual credibility they ever had." [98]

The natural disposition of business to go with the Republican party was reinforced by a highly sophisticated lobbying effort on the part of the administration. The president held a series of meetings on the tax cuts to generate support for his plan. In February several thousand executives were invited to learn about the president's economic strategy. On June 11, shortly after the Rose Garden speech, the president held a reconciliation reception for the three hundred business groups that had supported his budget battle.[99] Less public efforts to retain the loyalty of the business community were also pursued from the early days of the administration. A tax steering committee was set up in the business community to generate support for the president's bill. This group had computerized records of swing congressmen and members of the business community with ties to those congressmen.

This core of corporate supporters helped to engineer the final passage of the act. On July 27 the president appeared on television to request support for the cuts. At the end of the speech he called upon the American people to contact their congressmen and demand the Republican version. During the next forty-eight hours, key congressional offices were flooded with telephone calls favoring the president's program. The administration claimed that this represented mass support for Reagan's agenda. In fact individuals involved on the corporate side have admitted that there was a concerted effort by the business community with the tacit participation of the administration to flood the offices of less-than-sympathetic congressmen. Employees of participating firms were directed to "tie up the lines" of the targeted congressional offices, thus preventing the expression of opposing views.[100]

Individual deals also helped to fix final passage. Bill Goodling (R–PA) was promised that $37 million would be allocated to clean up Three Mile Island. Charles Hatcher (D–GA) was assured of the continuation of the peanut program. Ways and Means Democrats claim that this action, signaling the exodus of the Georgia delegation, marked the beginning of the final defection of southern Democrats. *Dun's Business Month* observed:

> In the end, however, the White House outmaneuvered the Democrats. Abandoning its original idea of a "clean" bill consisting only of a straight three-year tax cut and stepped-up depreciation for business, the White House developed its own Christmas tree version that

matched Rostenkowski's on most items and outdid it on breaks to oil and farm interests—the key to the Southern vote.[101]

Conclusion

In the history of corporate taxation the Economic Recovery Tax Act constitutes a bench mark. Earlier tax efforts sought to balance the dual elements of the commercial Keynesian growth strategy: capital-intensive investment and mass consumption. The 1981 act sharply diverged from Keynesian demand management (at least in theory) and targeted accumulation as the sole source of growth. The legislation greatly expanded incentives for investment and savings, and concentrated personal rate cuts in upper-income levels, where individuals were least likely to spend. Thus, the act greatly curtailed progressivity.

The new tax approach was prompted by the economic malaise of the 1970s. Yet economic decline alone cannot explain the rise of hyper-accumulation, since other countries experiencing similar troubles developed different solutions. Rather, this new growth strategy was made possible by a drive for unity in the business community and severe partisan conflict, which heightened corporate power. Table 5.2 lays out the divisions.

During the prelegislative period, business groups undertook a concerted campaign to overcome sectoral differences and forge a class agenda in support of the "10-5-3" proposal. This accounts for the relative unity of business at the beginning of the policy process. Later, during the political competition for business support, this relative business class unity began to disintegrate. As corporate concessions became the medium of exchange in the bidding war, business groups abandoned solidarity in order to reap the harvests of political conflict. Yet the initial high level of unity allowed business to proscribe the agenda for corporate taxation; virtually no other options besides an invest-

Table 5.2. Divisions in State and Society over Tax Options

Goals	Business	State	Policy
Increase accumulation, lower rates	Manufacturing, some small business	Supply-side in administration and House GOP	Growth measures, big personal tax cuts
Reduce inflation, increase accumulation	Finance	Monetarists in Fed, CEA, neoclassical economists	Growth measures, smaller individual cuts
Increase accumulation, retain some progressivity in individual rates	Some small business	Democrats, Rostenkowski	Growth measures, less regressive individual cuts

ment-oriented cut were considered in 1981. The individual tax cuts were the center of controversy; the corporate provisions went practically undisputed.

Business unity was matched by considerable state-centered conflict. Republicans and Democrats both fervently wanted to deliver the tax bill. Candidate Reagan, like candidate Kennedy before him, had used economic issues to differentiate himself from the incumbent. Although the two men worked from very different views of economic functioning, both promised to cut taxes to stimulate economic growth. Congressional Democrats also badly wanted to win the battle, perceiving the tax cut as a vehicle for political redemption among an unhappy electorate. Democrats hoped that the voters and southern Democrats would oppose the president's deficit-producing personal cuts on the grounds of fiscal irresponsibility.

In this atmosphere of intense partisan competition, business groups became external resources to alter the balance of power; corporate tax provisions, the medium of exchange. The political salience of the tax act made both sides go to extraordinary lengths to win: business groups were the ultimate victors. The privileged position of business shaped policy in the many special concessions granted for political support. Reagan's coalition strategy was instrumental in securing passage of the 1981 act.

6

The Tax Equity and Fiscal Responsibility Act of 1982

Introduction

Almost immediately after passage of the Economic Recovery Tax Act, pressure began mounting to reverse the monumental tax cut. One year later on September 3, 1982, President Reagan signed the Tax Equity and Fiscal Responsibility Act (TEFRA), the largest peacetime revenue increase in the postwar period.[1] In spirit and practice, TEFRA was a partial repudiation of the Economic Recovery Tax Act (ERTA), legislated only eleven months earlier. Although the individual tax cuts, the centerpiece of ERTA, were left untouched, the corporate provisions were scaled back considerably. With repeal of the ACRS provisions scheduled to take effect in 1985 and 1986, about one-third of the depreciation benefits of ERTA were rescinded. The basis for depreciation was also lowered by half the investment credit taken on it. In addition, the investment credit was curtailed by restricting the amount of income it could offset. Safe harbor leasing was repealed, and corporate tax payments were accelerated. A withholding requirement was placed on dividends and interest income, a provision that was later to be repealed (see table 6.1).

What accounted for the dramatic reversal in taxation between 1981 and 1982? To some extent TEFRA may be thought of as an effort to address the abuses of ERTA. The 1981 bidding war allowed a multitude of provisions to find their way into the bill that would have greatly changed the original revenue calculations. Yet the climate in which TEFRA was enacted, as well as the impact of the bill, suggests that a more fundamental change had occurred in the perception and process of taxing. The concerns of 1982 were for fiscal solvency, a balanced budget, and low interest rates. Reform was seen as the way to accomplish these goals. TEFRA, as its name suggests, combined the dual concepts of equity and fiscal responsibility.

Precipitating the revisionist thinking was ERTA's failure to bring about economic improvement. Despite the considerable investment inducements, capital expenditures continued to decline. Anti-inflationary monetary policy negated the fiscal stimulant and strangled any chance of recovery. Only one dramatic change appeared in economic forecasts: unfortunately this was the

Table 6.1. Selected Major Provisions of the Tax Equity and Fiscal Responsibility Act

Adjusted the basis of assets for depreciation purposes so that the value was lowered by one-half of the investment tax credit (includes energy and historic structure investment tax credits). If the investment credit was 10 percent, the asset's basis would be lowered by 5 percent.

Reduced the amount of tax liability that could be offset by the investment tax credit from 90 percent to 85 percent.

Repealed the ACRS provisions in ERTA that were scheduled to be implemented in 1985 and 1986. Consequently, about one-third of the ERTA accelerated depreciation benefits were repealed.

Repealed safe harbor leasing.

Scaled back several corporate tax preferences by 15 percent: percentage depletion for coal and iron ore, excess bad debt reserves, oil companies' intangible drilling costs, rapid amortization of pollution control devices, and mining exploration and development expenditures.

Accelerated corporate tax payments so that companies had to pay 90 percent of the current year's liability in estimated tax payments. Had been 80 percent.

10 percent withholding on dividends and interest imposed effective July 1, 1983.

Placed restrictions on industrial development bonds.

Tax benefits from mergers and acquisitions restricted.

Independent contractors or certain sales persons who were direct sellers would be treated for tax purposes as self-employed persons rather than employees.

Added several new tax preferences to the individual minimum tax.

Itemized medical expense deductions were to exceed 5 percent of income, had been 3 percent. Also limited casualty loss deductions.

unprecedented budget deficits created in large part by the stillborn tax act. Policymakers were presented with a Hobson's choice: raise taxes to correct for the revenue loss or tolerate the largest peacetime deficits in U.S. history.

Macroeconomic conditions pointed to a dilemma rather than to a clear course of action. The business community gave mixed signals as well. In 1981 nearly unanimous business support vaulted capital investment incentives to the center of the president's corporate tax proposal. Alternative interests were at least initially kept at bay. Yet fundamental divisions within the business community made the 1981 accord inherently unstable. In 1982 these divisions surfaced, resulting in a multiplicity of demands and little intracorporate cooperation.

Ultimately, the administration was persuaded that the budget deficits posed a more formidable political problem than slowed economic growth. Democrats agreed, fearing that the deficits would be used in the future to assault the social welfare state even further. But although a tax increase seemed necessary, no one wanted to do the dirty deed. Political factions in both parties and branches felt overwhelmed by the severity of the economic problems and by the lack of consensus over the appropriate course of action. To reduce the political stress created by the difficult choice between conflicting priorities, coalitions were formed. Yet the permutations of 1982 present an intriguing twist to the coalition strategy. The most interesting alliance in that year was the one formed by the executive branch, Senate Republicans, and House Democrats.

Macroeconomic Context

Several things happened between 1981 and 1982 to alter people's perceptions of the president's economic program drastically: budget deficits of over 4 percent of the GNP, a deep recession despite the expansionary fiscal policy, and double-digit unemployment. The FY82 deficit was originally projected to be $45.0 billion for FY83. By February the administration had increased its projection to $98.6, making it the largest budget deficit ever. Underestimating the budget was not unprecedented: budget projections for FY80 and FY81 were $29 and $15.8 billion, yet the actual numbers turned out to be $59.6 and $57.9 billion. Errors in deficit estimates, however, had never before been so dramatic.[2] The revised budget deficit estimates precipitated an enormous drop in the stock market in August 1981, only weeks after ERTA was signed into law.

Budget deficits are generally considered a macroeconomic stimulus; yet the country was thrown into a deep recession in 1981. Real GNP grew by only 0.7 percent in 1981 and actually declined by 1.2 percent in 1982. Despite the hoped-for effects of the tax cuts on business spending, real business fixed investment dropped 8.4 percent from the last quarter of 1981 to the last quarter of 1982. Between 1977 and 1981 business spending had increased at an annual rate of 5.2 percent. Orders for new plants and equipment were hit especially hard, dropping 12 percent in the year's time.[3] Unemployment climbed to over 10 percent in 1982, its highest level since 1940. It had been 7 percent when the president took office in 1981. The main good news was that inflation had indeed dropped, in large part due to the recession. Consumer prices rose 12 percent in 1980 but went up less than 4 percent in 1982. When it became apparent in the middle of 1982 that the economic indicators were unlikely to improve, real interest rates dropped. Yet they did not fall as fast as inflation, with the result that real interest rates actually went up between 1980 and 1984.[4]

In formulating a fiscal strategy for 1983, the administration had to decide whether to address the deficit problem or the recession. A logical way to reduce the deficit would be to cut government spending and increase taxes. Yet contractionary fiscal policy is generally thought to be the wrong approach to use in a recession. Deficit reduction during the recession would "reduce the total demand for goods and services and thus aggravate the contraction and slow the subsequent expansion." But any fiscal stimulation seemed to be constrained by the high interest rates, which most non-supply-side economists thought were a result of the deficit. Joseph Pechman explained the irreconcilable differences between the expansionary fiscal policy and a contractionary monetary policy:

> Fiscal and monetary policies appear to be on a collision course in the years immediately ahead. The budget implies large and increasing deficits while the monetary authorities, who have the full support of the administration, are determined to slow inflation further by maintaining a policy of restraint . . . In circumstances such as those now prevailing in the economy, output and employment may grow for brief periods. But any sustained expansion is likely to be choked off by rising interest rates, as increasing credit demands run up against the tight monetary targets.[5]

Pattern of Business Demands

Prior to the 1981 act there had been a major effort by a network of corporate lobbyists to unify the business community around accelerated cost recovery. Although the unity and discipline broke down during the bidding war, the initial effort had served its purpose: "10-5-3" was passed. No such unity or consensus existed regarding the 1982 tax proposals; the business community was bitterly divided over whether a tax increase was necessary and the form such an increase should take. With neither a class-wide agenda nor agreed-upon priorities, many business groups set out to defend previously won concessions in the zero-sum competition to avoid increased tax burdens.

The financial and housing lobby was most receptive to a tax increase. Even in 1981 the financial sector worried about the inflationary impact of the personal cuts; the deficit projections and stock market plunge accentuated these fears.[6] Few bankers believed that the Federal Reserve would be able to maintain its restrictive monetary course; the pressure to pay off the deficit through inflation and lower interest rates was enormous. Henry Kaufman of Salomon Brothers, one of the administration's most vocal critics, remarked, "Washington's current policies make acute financial conflict inevitable."[7]

In keeping with the general spirit of mistrust surrounding the president's financial program, the dollar dropped 11 percent from August 10 to September 18, a "rather frightening decline" according to the vice-president of the World Bank. Currency trader Martin Schubert, president of Rosenthal International, observed, "Sentiment has turned completely against the dollar in the belief that, despite what Volcker says, the administration is putting severe pressure on him to reinflate the economy and reduce interest rates."[8]

The housing industry was also very badly affected by the high interest rates and threat of reinflation. Gil Thurm, National Association of Realtors, testified in March that housing had declined for forty months and that the past twelve-month drop had been especially steep. Thurm called it the worst housing depression since the 1930s.[9]

Financial and housing groups participating in the Business Roundtable considered the obvious solution to be an increase in individual taxes; the third year of the personal cut should be dropped or delayed. These groups also favored some corporate changes, most notably the repeal of safe harbor leasing. Many credit corporations had substantial leasing units before safe harbor leasing was invented. Under the traditional leasing rules, equipment had to be sold for the residual value if the lessee decided at the end of the leasing period to purchase the asset from the lessor. Safe harbor leasing changed this. Because the safe harbor rules did not demand that a residual value be assigned to equipment at the end of the leasing period, the lessees could negotiate deals whereby they could lease an item for much less. Corporate lobbyists in the basic manufacturing sectors charged that traditional lessors realized 40 percent profit rates on their investment before safe harbor leasing, and only about 18 percent thereafter.[10]

Housing trade associations were publicly neutral on the subject of leasing, although the National Association of Home Builders came close to endorsing its repeal. As a lobbyist from another trade association put it: "There was no reason to go out and publicly gorge one area over another . . . Certainly in private we may have railed against it, but no public stand was taken on the leasing issue."[11]

The financial and housing groups split over the issue of the minimum tax. Two preference items made commercial banks a major target for the minimum tax: the bad debt deduction and the tax-free interest on municipal bonds. The industry estimated that the minimum tax would increase banks' corporate taxes by 53 percent.[12] The realtors and home builders, labor-intensive sectors, paid high effective tax rates. The minimum tax would have little impact on them; therefore, they officially supported a "reasonable" minimum tax.[13] A housing representative explained: "Everything we do is geared toward interest rates. That's why we support the idea of an alternative minimum tax. We supported it in 1969 and we support it now."[14] The financial and housing sectors fought a proposal to place a withholding tax on interest and dividends. Housing trade associations opposed repealing the All Savers certificate and placing a limit on deductions for personal property tax and consumer interests.

The capital-intensive manufacturing sectors were on the defensive in 1982. ACRS, the largest corporate provision in 1981, was most beneficial to these sectors. The safe harbor leasing provision made accelerated cost recovery and the investment tax credit accessible to the cyclically profitable firms. Therefore, protecting the accomplishments of 1981 and preventing the minimum tax were the cause célèbre of these lobbies.

Trade associations in these sectors did not participate in the deficit reduction movement and took no stand on the proposal to rescind the individual tax cuts. One lobbyist explained: "Companies don't lobby very hard for deficit reductions. They lobby for their own concerns." [15] The National Association of Manufacturing publicly called for retention of the individual tax cuts. [16] Privately, however, NAM preferred delaying the third year of the individual cuts over any changes in corporate taxes. Lobbyists from these sectors explained that the individual cuts were of minor importance to them. Their concern with preventing erosion of the corporate tax cuts left little time or interest in attacking or defending the individual cuts. [17] NAM denounced changes in corporate taxation as an abandonment of the goals of growth and capital formation:

> NAM believes it is essential to retain the business tax cuts enacted in the Economic Recovery Tax Act of 1981 (ERTA) . . . raising business taxes at this time would entail a serious risk of throwing the economy into deeper recession. Tax increases would further reduce business cash flow, forcing companies to increase their reliance on short term debt at a time when they are already highly leveraged and suffering the effects of high interest rates. If the problem of business liquidity is so compounded, existing productive capacity will continue to be underutilized and there will be less new capital investment. [18]

Efforts to scale back the corporate tax cuts legislated in ERTA were concentrated in three provisions: repealing a portion of the ACRS benefits, repealing safe harbor leasing, and strengthening the corporate minimum tax. The large, capital-intensive manufacturing firms, which were best able to make use of the ACRS and investment tax credit provisions, violently opposed the minimum tax on several grounds. First, unprofitable firms argued that it would only increase the discrepancy between profitable and unprofitable firms, since the former's use of the growth incentives already gives them an edge over the latter. Second, the minimum tax would cancel out the effect of growth-stimulating incentives such as the investment tax credit. Finally, abuses in the law should be corrected individually. A broad brush approach such as the minimum tax distorts individual circumstances. [19] Unprofitable sectors such as steel concentrated on fighting the repeal of safe harbor leasing.

Small business trade associations were divided over the necessity of a tax increase. As in 1981 the two major small business trade associations found themselves on opposite sides. The National Federation of Independent Business (NFIB) resisted a tax increase, a position they held to be consistent with their membership's aversion to a tax increase at any time regardless of the circumstances. The Chamber of Commerce and the National Association of Wholesaler-Distributors (NAW) joined them in the opposition.

In 1982 the National Small Business Association (NSB) joined the realtors, the home builders, and the American Business Conference as the earliest supporters in the business community of a tax increase. Small business trade associations had a very good reason to be alarmed. Small businesses typically must pay several percentage points above the prime rate for loans. According to NSB it was the expectation of future budget deficits that had kept interest rates "in the 20 percent range . . . for almost 2 1/2 years." NSB linked these high interest rates to the catastrophic rate of business failures:

> Those conditions resulted in over 17,000 business failures last year (according to Dun and Bradstreet). This represented a 45.1 percent increase over calendar year 1980, and a 96 percent increase over the average of the previous five years. It is within a whisker of the 1961 total, which was the highest since the Depression.[20]

Three of the four groups that ultimately opposed the president's bill were major representatives of the small business community.[21] Given the impact of high interest rates on small businesses, why did some representatives of small business support a tax increase while others opposed one? Opposing associations say the answer lies in the preference of their members. The NAW membership had never supported a tax increase. NFIB agreed that, although their members hated the deficits and suffered from the high interest rates, the best way to lower interest rates was to cut spending, not increase taxes. Opposing groups suggest that the policies of NFIB, NAM, and the Chamber of Commerce represent a conservative Republican orientation. Allegiance to the Republican party was strained in 1982, however, when the president endorsed a tax increase.

Once the issue of a tax increase had been settled, the small business groups were more unified. The financial sector wanted to delay the third year of the personal tax cut; small business groups violently opposed this solution, since many small businesses are partnerships or sole proprietorships, paying individual taxes.[22]

The entire small business community was also favorably disposed to the repeal of safe harbor leasing. NSB and NFIB actively promoted the leasing repeal. One lobbyist explained that leasing was in no way beneficial to small firms; they simply did not have the accounting manpower to negotiate such complicated deals. Safe harbor leasing only served to exacerbate the distortions in the tax code that favored large, capital-intensive sectors. Steven Holuk (Laventhol and Horwath accounting firm) captured the feeling of small business when he remarked, "They left it wide open for the Occidental Petroleums and IBMs, but they effectively knocked the little guy out of it [the safe harbor leasing market]."[23]

In direct opposition to basic industry, small business was sympathetic to the minimum tax proposal: the tax "pitted the high-tax guys against the low-tax guys." Small business trade associations at first tried to ignore or quietly support the minimum tax rather than to actively work for it. One lobbyist remarked, "You don't raise somebody else's taxes." [24] A representative of the National Small Business Association testified:

> Since the majority of smaller incorporated business already pay taxes with effective rates well above 15 percent, NSB does not feel that this provision will have any direct significant impact on small business. To the extent that a 15 percent minimum might result in substantial additional Treasury revenues which would help reduce deficits and relieve some of the upward pressure on interest rates, NSB believes this provision should be given careful consideration. [25]

But in the struggle to avoid minimum tax legislation, General Electric, United States Steel, some multinational oil companies, and other firms in basic manufacturing recommended that Congress legislate a surtax instead of a minimum tax. A surtax, an across-the-board increase of everyone's taxes, was said to be a more equitable means of raising revenue. [26] The labor-intensive, small business trade associations were appalled by this suggestion. A percentage increase would naturally tax sectors with high effective rates more than those with low effective rates. A respondent explained, "10 percent of zero is still zero." At this point a number of groups began actively promoting the minimum tax. NAW changed its formal position: it still opposed all tax increases; however, should an increase occur, it should be a minimum tax. [27] To avoid a surtax, an antisurtax coalition was formed which later evolved into the Coalition to Reduce High Effective Tax Rates. The group had two main goals: first, to defeat all surtax proposals; second, to reduce high effective tax rates. This coalition was composed of small business, food-processing, and high-technology firms and trade associations: National Federation of Independent Business, National Association of Wholesaler-Distributors, American Retail Federation, American Business Conference, IBM, 3M, General Foods, and General Mills.

State Factions: Economic and Political Agendas

From the first days of the Reagan regime, it was obvious that there was an inconsistency in the goals of the various factions participating in high levels of the administration. The *Wall Street Journal* remarked that the "tax cutters, tight-money advocates and budget balancers" could not all succeed at once. [28]

This conflict was never adequately addressed during the 1981 tax legislative process. Yet the conflict between tight money, expansionary tax cuts, and a balanced budget surfaced in the administration's budget deficit forecasts for FY82. Earlier in the year the administration had predicted that the budget deficit for FY82 would be $42.5 billion; by FY84 the deficit was to have disappeared altogether. This forecast was based on optimistic assumptions of growth rates of over 4 percent, higher than any rates since the mid-1960s.

According to the supply-side magic, the infusion of tax cut capital and expectations of reduced inflation would stimulate the economy to new heights.

The forecast also assumed that the requisite spending cuts would be made. Yet, throughout OMB's budget proposal, asterisks appeared where spending reductions were yet to be specified. This plus the elimination of cuts in the legislative process left the total budget reduction $75 million short. Chase Econometrics' Lawrence Chimerine warned that the deficit "could reach $100 billion in each of the next several years," thus keeping interest rates high by "preventing an improvement in inflationary expectations." [29]

Public realization that the budget deficits were to be far higher than predicted combined with the consequent drop in the stock and bond markets forced the administration to confront the trade-offs in its mutually exclusive goals. On the one hand, the administration was very committed to the tax cuts, the core of the supply-side experiment. Many saw the tax cuts as a means of forcing spending cuts and reducing the size of the government, the president's personal mandate. On the other hand, the huge budget deficits were an anathema to both financial markets and traditional Republican philosophy. When the president argued in December that the deficits were less serious than people realized, he was greeted with a huge outcry from his own constituents.

The administration was split along predictable fault lines. The traditional economists within the administration led by OMB waged war on the deficits, attacking the forecasts. On August 12 a memo from Larry Kudlow to David Stockman argued that OMB should "post significant revisions from the mid-session forecast." The memo warned that the recession should be linked to fiscal rather than monetary policy: "High interest rates should not be blamed on the FED. Instead, in order to dovetail into the September Offensive, high interest rates should be blamed on government deficits and borrowing." [30]

Monetarists also called for a fiscal solution to the budget deficits. Although Volcker pressured for spending reductions as a first solution, by November he called publicly for tax increases in the event that requisite spending cuts failed to materialize. In a speech at the University of Nebraska the Federal Reserve chief explained that a deficit in FY82 was appropriate: the current recession demanded an expansionary fiscal policy. Yet a tax increase would be necessary to offset deficits in the years thereafter. [31]

The supply-side contingent in the administration, not surprisingly, wanted to retain the tax cuts. Regan and the Treasury emerged as the major proponents for this scenario. Regan complained of "worrywarts in the bond market" and blamed business for failing to respond to the tax incentives with increases in capital spending. Regan and other supply-siders argued that delaying the individual cuts had compromised the experiment. [32]

Throughout the fall and winter the president was caught between opposing approaches, each with its own set of constituents. The administration vacillated, and the president himself seemed reluctant to make any major changes in his economic policy. In late September he asked for additional spending cuts of $13 billion in FY82 combined with $3 billion in tax increases from some reform measures. With these fiscal changes he revised his deficit forecast for FY82 to be $43.1 billion.[33] These minor changes only served to irritate legislators, who felt that they had suffered enough in the major budget and tax battles of the year. Encountering political opposition, the president abandoned the plan and instead promised to introduce tax and budget initiatives in January.[34]

Throughout January there was speculation that the revenue needs would be met through an increase in federal excise taxes. The rumors grew so intense that finally the president told his staff that "it would be unwise to engage in additional speculation" while he made up his mind. Baker, Stockman, and Senate Republicans were in favor of the increases. Against them were the House supply-siders, who argued that the move would hurt "the little guy." The Chamber of Commerce has been credited for helping the president arrive at the final decision to reject the excise tax increase.[35]

The Democrats found it even more difficult to formulate a tax plan. Upon completion of the 1981 tax increase, Democratic legislators who supported the president went home expecting to be congratulated on the achievement. After all, they had been told that the country was firmly behind the president's economic program; hesitant congressmen had been the target of a telephone campaign whose vigorousness they had seldom experienced in their legislative careers. But instead of appreciation, constituents offered criticisms of the continuing high interest rates and the pro-business sentiment of the act. One congressman explained that legislators went home during the August recess "in a state of euphoria" and returned "in a state of panic." The country seemed frightened and angry about the high interest rates rather than delighted with the fiscal victories.[36]

The feeling that the 1981 act had been a mistake was intensified during the autumn by the exposure of safe harbor leasing abuses in the press and the failure of the ACRS provision to spur capital spending. Congressmen had been told that additional funds would prompt U.S. industry to invest in capital goods; this should have led to an upturn in the economy. Yet companies such as Northwest Industries, Bendix, Seagram, Control Data, and Gulf Oil used increased investment funds to buy back their own stock. A merger frenzy was an unexpected side effect of the increase in depreciation benefits. That United States Steel had demanded special assistance as a firm in an unprofitable industry and then had offered $6.4 billion for Marathon Oil seemed hypocritical at best.[37]

The perception that business had received more than was fair was strengthened by a Treasury analysis of ACRS. With the scheduled increases to 175 percent declining balance in 1985 and 200 percent declining balance in 1986, ACRS plus the investment tax credit would actually be more profitable than expensing in the first year.[38]

Trounced in 1981, the Democrats were determined not to engage in partisan struggle over economic policy in 1982. Rostenkowski explained: "What was done last summer is done . . . Any proposals for change or rollbacks must come from Republicans." Tip O'Neill agreed that the Democrats would provide no alternative budget and tax plan. They would only support a tax increase proposal which had been endorsed by the president himself. O'Neill explained: "All they wanted were political victories over us. Well, they got their political victories. When the President admits his program was a mistake, then we'll extend the hand of friendship."[39]

Another reason why the Democrats were reluctant to pursue a tax bill had to do with a reluctance to alienate independent oil. The independents were largely Democratic before Carter and the windfall profits tax, but largely Republican thereafter. That the Democrats badly wanted to regain this moneyed constituency was illustrated by their drive to capture boll weevil support in 1981. In 1982 the newly won oil provisions were an obvious source of revenue; however, most Ways and Means members deferred.[40]

This left it to Senate Republicans, especially Budget chair Pete Domenici (R–NM) and Finance chair Robert Dole, to take the lead in the tax increase struggle. Dole's motivation for pushing a balanced budget was undoubtedly strengthened by his ties to financial sectors and his Kansas farm constituency. Large deficits hurt farmers by keeping interest rates up and indirectly by keeping the dollar's value high in the international currency market. Others have suggested that Dole's role as tax reformer had in part to do with his presidential aspirations.[41]

Proposal Development

In his long-awaited State of the Union message President Reagan announced his budget and revenue plans for the year ahead. Instead of a major increase in excise taxes, the president chose a solution which enabled him to keep his 1981 agenda intact and still raise revenues—reform. The proposal focused on loophole closing: it proposed to expand and strengthen the corporate minimum tax, restrict the use of tax-exempt industrial bonds, forbid the completed contract method of accounting, and repeal energy tax credits. Compliance measures were also recommended: withholding on interest and dividends, and enhanced Internal Revenue Service enforcement. Yet, despite this impressive array of reform and compliance measures, the tax proposal would increase revenues only by $12.8 billion. The total revenue increase would total only $55.9 billion, leaving a deficit of $91.5 billion for FY83.[42]

In the face of the administration's reluctance to endorse a brave new tax increase, Bob Dole and the Senate Republicans took charge. On February 19 Dole identified the repeal of safe harbor leasing as a likely candidate for revenue generation. The business community was put on notice that any safe harbor leasing deals after that day might be subject to repeal.[43] On February 25 Dole announced that the Senate Finance Committee would consider "a whole array of other tax breaks to raise revenue." On March 16 the Finance Committee hearings began.[44] Dole and Senate Finance began examining the minimum tax proposals; GOP leadership determined that as much as $35 billion could be generated.[45]

The new minimum tax provision would replace the old. Corporations would pay the higher of two taxes: either their regular income tax or 15 percent of their regular tax plus the value of their tax breaks from certain tax preference items. The concept was aimed at preventing corporations from wiping out all tax liability with the use of tax incentives such as excess intangible drilling costs and the deferral of export income through domestic international sales corporations.[46]

Insiders say that Dole originally wanted to raise taxes on the oil industry but that the president would not consider this approach. Instead, the senator concentrated on a few big ticket items: the corporate minimum tax, safe harbor leasing, and withholding on interest and dividends. Dole feared that a general reform bill could be torn apart by private interests.[47]

The president's tax program did little to assuage financial market fears. The revenue gains seemed paltry compared to the deficit projections. In the FY83 budget presented to Congress on February 8, the president predicted $246.3 billion in budget deficits from 1983 to 1985.[48] When Reagan failed to propose a major tax increase in his State of the Union message, demands for deficit reduction intensified. Toward the end of February, a coalition of banking and housing trade associations made public a joint letter to the president calling for a tax increase. They wrote, "More than anything else, it is the specter of an overwhelming volume of deficit financing which haunts housing and financial markets and poses the threat of economic and financial conditions not seen since the 1930s."[49]

The Business Roundtable had pushed for deficit reduction since the fall of 1981. A representative of the group explained that it "came to the forefront of the deficit before anyone else." Although the Business Roundtable preferred to reduce the deficit through spending reductions, it would go to taxes as a last resort. Taxation task force chair Ted Brophy met with the president to urge action on the deficits including a reconsideration of Kemp-Roth. The Roundtable would be glad to assist the administration in determining which tax cuts should be delayed. President Reagan's initial response had been that the country would grow out of the deficit.[50] In early March the Business Roundtable publicly announced the plan they had previously suggested to the president in private: the third year of the individual tax cuts should be delayed.[51]

Financial people were also angry about the nature of the limited tax increases the president had proposed, since they favored a delay in the personal cuts. The White House responded by chastising the financial sector: Regan told securities specialists that this suggestion had "spooked" the Congress. If they continued to make such demands, they might suffer "the consequences" of higher capital gains or reduction of the "10-5-3" benefits.[52]

Parts of the tax package as well as the idea of a tax increase generated strong opposition from the business community. Small business representatives, led by the Chamber of Commerce, continued to oppose any tax increase vehemently. The minimum tax was heavily opposed by financial firms and the unprofitable basic manufacturing sectors, which paid little tax. Sectors began to meet regularly at the National Association of Manufacturers to develop strategies for opposition. Twenty companies in steel, railroads, shipping, and utilities hired the public relations firm Gray and Company to lobby against the provision. Gray and Company published a survey indicating that their members would be forced to pay 47 percent higher tax bills under the minimum tax than they had paid before ERTA. The Chrysler Corporation actually argued *for* a gasoline tax; it seemed they preferred this measure to a minimum tax.[53]

Seeking an alternative to the minimum tax, basic manufacturers recommended a surtax as a more "equitable" means for raising taxes. According to General Electric's John McCoy, the minimum tax would be borne by 5 percent of the corporate taxpayers whereas a surtax would be spread broadly. Commercial banking joined manufacturing in calling for a surtax since the bad debt reserve was one of the identified tax preferences. Lindley Clark explained:

> Administration officials poke fun at the businessmen because they can't agree on what taxes should rise. That's buck-passing of the worst sort; government, not business, enacts tax changes. If there is a worry about whose ox is to be gored, a slight increase in all taxes might be the answer.[54]

Small business groups were furious: labor-intensive firms typically pay high effective tax rates and would be hit hardest by a surtax. The National Association of Wholesaler-Distributors, hitherto opposing any tax hike, amended their position. If taxes were to be increased, a minimum tax should be the vehicle. As Dirk Van Dongen explained, "Somebody else started the cannibalization process." The National Federation of Independent Business remained "neutral" toward a minimum tax but was tempted to follow the wholesalers' example. Another problem with the surtax, according to the

American Retail Federation, involved its effect on small business spending. According to the federation's Lloyd Hackler, "Consumption is going to be the thing that leads us out of the recession." [55]

The battle over the minimum tax is a good example of the business community's divergence from their usual mutual noninterference during a tax increase. Senate Finance Committee counsel Bob Lighthizer thought such "cannibalization" was a healthy development:

> Business guys in this town tend to say to each other, "you go after yours, and I'll go after mine, and I won't tell anybody what a joke yours is if you won't tell anybody what a joke mine is.
> "They ought to realize that when things are tight, if you get yours, the odds are less likely that I'm going to get mine." [56]

Although safe harbor leasing seemed destined for extinction, it nevertheless generated a battle in the process. In mid-November, during the final fifteen days before the leasing deadline, the press gleefully recorded stories of million-dollar deals that would enable large corporations to wipe out their effective tax rates. General Electric Credit Corporation paid $250 million and got tax breaks of over $1 billion for equipment which would subsequently be leased back to the asset users. IBM was the largest purchaser: it bought $200 million in benefits from Ford and $100 million from CSX Corporation. [57] General Electric Credit Corporation actually advertised for leasing deals, running full-page ads showing how many "shopping days" were left until the November 13 cutoff date. [58]

The race to complete big leasing deals only exacerbated the image of safe harbor leasing as a big business giveaway. One congressional staff member explained, "Leasing has become a symbol of the excesses of last year." As revenue needs became apparent, safe harbor leasing appeared to be an easy target for change. In February, Dole declared that the leasing provision would be either repealed or tightened. [59]

Lobbyists blamed the negative attitudes toward leasing on two factors: the attention given to the provision in the popular press and the attack on it by the traditional leasing industry. Said one lobbyist: "General Electric really screwed everybody. General Electric utilized it to the fullest but saw in it the decline of the leasing industry." Also, at a time when the government was looking for revenue, it seemed easier to phase out a recent tax expenditure than a long-standing one. As one lobbyist explained, "Get the new kid on the block." [60]

The industry nonetheless tried to rescue its pet provision. Several coalitions were formed to protect leasing. Charls Walker formed a group to oppose the repeal but allegedly charged $50,000 for the right to join. The Walker group hired a public relations firm, Wagoner and Berudie, to counter the negative publicity given the provision in the popular press. John Meaghar of LTD formed the Safe Harbor Leasing Coalition consisting of representatives from the steel, auto, airline, paper, railroad, and farm equipment sectors. This group subsequently became the Basic Industries Coalition, an important policy and lobbying forum for mature manufacturing firms.

The leasing coalition reasoned that one way to avoid total repeal would be to develop a compromise position. As participants saw it, there were several possible scenarios. One was to cut safe harbor leasing altogether. A second was to cut back the benefits to the lessors but keep the concept alive. To this end the coalition developed an alternative version of safe harbor leasing that would cap the benefits to lessors at 50 percent of their tax responsibility. Since one of the basic problems was that the leasing provision could be used to "zero out" tax liability, the coalition's proposal would allow only one-half of a firm's taxes to be offset. The industry groups offered their compromise to Congress, arguing that the major abuse of safe harbor leasing was that big profit-making industries were able to avoid paying taxes. The compromise provision would solve this problem, yet still allow cyclical industries to generate badly needed funds.

The compromise position found its way into the Senate bill through the efforts of Senator Durenberger (R–MN), a major congressional contact for steel and other basic industries. Durenberger opposed Bob Dole on the interest and dividends withholding provision in order to get leverage on safe harbor leasing. Dole needed Durenberger's support on withholding; therefore, he agreed to keep leasing alive and endorsed the coalition's compromise. Durenberger also proposed repealing the deduction for taxes on real property as a substitute for measures adversely affecting capital-intensive sectors.[61]

The Gang of Seventeen: A Coalition of Political Factions

The split in the business community over the tax/deficit issue was mirrored in Congress. Conflicting priorities seemed to rule out a bipartisan consensus or even agreement within the Republican party itself. Moderate Senate Republicans wanted deficit reduction. Democrats tended to share that goal but were too traumatized by the events of the previous year to take the initiative toward achieving it. Among the House GOP were the ardent supply-siders, who opposed a tax increase at all costs.

In the face of this political dissidence, a group began meeting to try to forge a consensus on the budget/revenue issue. The group, nicknamed the Gang of Seventeen, met for a period of several months with the explicit goal of resolving the budget dilemma. The public's negative reaction to the president's 1983 budget proposal motivated the formation of this group. As one White House staff person put it: "The budget was dead on arrival. The Democrats walked away from it. The Republicans refused to endorse it." The legislators worried about the election-year implications of further budget cuts.[62]

The administration realized that the adversarial approach it had taken on the budget in 1981 would not work and instead decided on a compromise strategy. The president authorized selected high-level staff members to meet with bipartisan congressmen and senators to formulate a compromise budget. One participant explained that the Gang of Seventeen worked like a think tank: Its primary goal was to solve the deficit problem. All possible courses of action with the exception of altering the personal tax cuts were open for debate.

The group negotiated in secret for several months until it finally dissolved because of irreconcilable differences over the third year of the Kemp-Roth cut and over social security reform. Senate Democrats decided that the price of their cooperation on the social security cost of living allowances (COLAs) was the delaying of the third year of the individual tax cut. The Senate GOP leadership were inclined to think this wasn't such a bad idea and hoped to forge a deal between the Democrats and the president. If the Democrats would accept the social security cuts in exchange for a delay in the third year of the individual cuts, the president might be persuaded to modify Kemp-Roth for slashes in social security.

Any hopes of achieving a social security/Kemp-Roth compromise were dashed, however, when House Republicans launched a campaign against it. Thirteen conservative GOP congressmen led by Roth wrote to Reagan promising to "use every legislative and preliminary option at our disposal" to prevent change in the personal tax cuts. Any alteration of the Kemp-Roth provision, they threatened, "would be tantamount to a complete abrogation of one of the major promises of your campaign and that of the Republican party platform."[63]

Although the Gang of Seventeen was ultimately unable to achieve its mission and reach consensus on the larger social security/budget issue, the broad outlines of TEFRA were successfully negotiated. The two parties agreed to a formula of $1 of tax increases to $3 of spending cuts. The president was finally persuaded to support this package by Baker, Darman, and Stockman. Revoking a tax cut promise would cause political problems for a short period of time, but the budget deficit would haunt him politically every day for the rest of his tenure. Even Regan asked rhetorically, "Do you think that this administration can stand a deficit of over $100 billion?"[64]

The Legislative Process

In May the administration began to support publicly some of the corporate tax measures which had emerged in the Senate Finance hearings. The individual tax cuts continued to be off-limits. For the first time, however, Regan indicated that the administration would support a modification of the safe harbor leasing benefits. Specifically, it would endorse the compromise advocated by the safe harbor leasing coalition: to cap the percentage by which profitable firms could reduce their tax responsibilities. Regan also allowed that changes in depreciation were acceptable to the president. ACRS had been greatly criticized: the fast depreciation deductions combined with the investment tax credit actually offered more tax benefits in the first year than outright expensing. To soften the opposition to the minimum tax, Regan said that the investment tax credit might be allowed to offset it. The president then endorsed the Senate Budget Committee's proposal to link $1 of tax increases to $3 of spending cuts: taxes would be increased by $95 billion and spending decreased by $319 billion over a three-year period.[65]

The Senate voted on July 23 for the set of provisions that had been hammered out during the preceding months. The vote, fifty to forty-seven, was largely along party lines. (The final vote on the conference bill in the Senate was fifty-two to forty-seven, with eleven Republicans opposed and nine Democrats in favor.) The Senate Democrats proposed a substitute bill which would defer the final 10 percent Kemp-Roth tax cut; however, it was defeated.[66] The consensus conceived in the Gang of Seventeen was partially upset by some rivalry between Bob Dole and Russell Long. Long and the Democrats on the Finance Committee were angry with Dole because the final bill had been developed in a Republican caucus instead of in the official committee markup session. Long maintained that the Democrats could have made their mark on the bill at the committee level, if given a chance. Dole responded that the provisions in the bill had been developed months in advance.[67]

By law, tax acts are to be initiated in the House Ways and Means Committee. During this period, the Ways and Means Committee should have begun marking up its own tax bill. The only two exceptions to this requirement have occurred during the legislation of the 1968 surtax and TEFRA. The Ways and Means Committee initially delayed action on the bill until mid-July. On the night of the twenty-second, the Democrats on the committee caucused to review the plan put together by Rostenkowski and Conable. The Democratic version was to be very much like the Senate's bill with a few exceptions. The minimum tax provisions were tighter, and some increases on oil were included. However, as the all-night meeting became progressively hostile, it became obvious that no consensus existed for any kind of tax bill, much less one that was even more stringent than the Senate's version. Only three people on the committee—Rostenkowski, Jim Shannon (D–MA), and William Brodhead (D–MI)—were willing to consider the bill. One participant recalled:

> Rostenkowski proposed a bill to peal back a lot of the special interests in 1981. Everybody took a hit, but it deep-sixed the oil stuff.

From a political perspective, Rostenkowski was anxious to pay the guys back. He had learned a big lesson in 1981. Rosty wanted to show them.

At six o'clock the night before [the markup] Rostenkowski called a caucus of the Democrats and had a staff pass out the proposal. It was real scorched-earth stuff. The caucus degenerated into a real angry, tense discussion about what they were doing. Beryl Anthony [D–AR] said we had to leave oil alone. Anthony had really crossed the line: we had to leave these guys alone because we've raised a lot of money from them and we promised we would. Rostenkowski then adjourned the meeting abruptly.[68]

After this ill-fated meeting, the Ways and Means Committee agreed to go directly to conference without a tax bill. This would mean that the House would have little role in formulating the tax act. Jim Shannon argued fervently against the committee's relinquishing its jurisdiction, but Rostenkowski said he simply didn't have the votes. Republicans criticized this failure to take responsibility, stating that the Democratic leadership was trying to make the Republicans take the blame for 1981. Democrats justified their course of action as an effort to minimize responsibility for what they saw as a correction of the president's failure.

Lack of public Democratic participation in TEFRA's development did not signify lack of support for the tax increase. Unlike in the Senate, much of the support for TEFRA in the House came from the Democratic side. When the president threw his weight with the tax increase, he angered the House Republican supply-siders, who had been his strongest supporters of the 1981 act. In the view of the House GOP, Reagan and the Senate Republicans had sold out. The hard-core supply-side contingent, led by Jack Kemp (R–NY) and Newt Gingrich (R–GA), revolted against the administration's position, vowing to fight TEFRA at every step. Kemp and others started meeting with opposing business groups, especially the Chamber of Commerce, to fight the administration's own lobbying organization. Lyn Nofziger was originally part of this group; however, the White House persuaded him to come back to the White House and lead the counterattack to bring the recalcitrant Republicans back into the fold.

Faced with disobedience in its own camp, the administration needed considerable Democratic support. Yet Democrats were very reluctant to push openly for a tax increase. As one key Democratic congressional aide put it, "There was a lot of paranoia." Many House Democrats were fearful that they would be portrayed as the party of tax increasers in the 1982 election. Therefore, the Democratic leadership agreed to provide the votes if the administration could "get the GOP up front." To reassure the Democrats and assure enough Republican support for the tax bill, administration staff set about to recruit House Republicans to lobby for the tax bill. Reagan's men initially targeted some of the senior members of Congress: Chalmers Wylie (R–OH), Stewart McKinny (R–CT), and Bill Broomfield (R–MI). Next they sought pivotal opinion leaders who represented the more moderate Republicans: Conable, Bill Frenzel (R–MN), Guy Vander Jagt (R–MI), and Willis Gradison, Jr. (R–OH). The administration also made overtures to some of the supplysiders and managed to recruit a few of the most adamantly opposed. A key selling point to the Republican legislators was that the tax increases would help get the spending cuts. Many were persuaded to go along because of the 3-to-1 formula: $3 in spending cuts to $1 in tax increases.[69]

The spirit of cooperation set up by the Gang of Seventeen characterized the rest of the legislative period. One insider recalls: "Republicans went over vote lists with Foley and Rostenkowski. With some Democrats Republicans had better access, and vice versa." Dole and Rostenkowski frequently consulted on the bill. Every effort was made to keep political competition to a minimum and to avoid any embarrassment of the other party. Television speeches from that period were less polemic than usual. Reagan promised personal letters of thanks to protect Democrats against criticism of their support of TEFRA by Republican opponents.[70]

TEFRA passed in the House on August 19, 1982, by 226 to 207. One hundred twenty-three Democrats supported the measure. Of those 123 Democrats, 96 had voted against the president on ERTA and all other critical 1981 economic measures. Twelve Democrats who had supported the president in 1981 voted against TEFRA. Eighty-nine Republicans voted against it. Freshman representatives, largely the hard-core supply-side contingent, were the greatest defectors, with 23 for the bill and 32 against. Most members elected before 1978 voted for TEFRA.[71]

Business Participation in the Alliance

Close cooperation between the White House, Senate Republicans, and the Democratic leadership helped to secure the passage of TEFRA. The administration also worked to secure political support for the act in the business community. Originally only the financial community supported a tax increase, but throughout the spring other trade associations were persuaded to join forces. The National Association of Manufacturers, the Business Roundtable, and the American Business Conference indicated in April that they would be willing to support some type of tax increase. They remained divided, however, as to what type it should be.[72]

Having made a commitment to the tax increase, the president set about to persuade the business community to back the program. In May the White House met with the leadership of all the top trade associations to lay the groundwork for the tax increases. Subsequently, White House staff went to trade associations and big corporations, one by one, to request support. Horizontal groups (associations containing more than one industrial sector) were contacted first: the National Association of Manufacturers, the Chamber of Commerce, the American Business Conference, and the National Federation of Independent Business. Jack Albertine of the American Business Conference immediately agreed to back the tax increase and emerged as one of the leaders of the effort. Next, the administration approached trade associations representing single sectors.

Groups in the housing sector were the easiest to convince to support the legislation, since they were the most concerned about the implications of the budget deficit for interest rates and inflation. The National Association of Home Builders was one of the earliest groups to make a commitment. The home builders supported the bill for two reasons. First, they were extremely concerned about the deficits. Second, they had opposed the president's bill in 1981 and were anxious to get back into the good graces of the White House. As one administration official put it, the home builders were "presoftened" in 1982.[73]

The National Association of Realtors started supporting a tax increase effort during the budget reconciliation process. Bob Dole and others from the Gang of Seventeen had solicited the industry's support to get the budget passed. While the realtors preferred spending cuts to a tax increase, they nonetheless decided to go all out for deficit reduction.[74]

Manufacturing groups were less anxious to join the coalition. General Electric, one of the first firms to join the administration's effort, was a notable exception: GE's huge leasing business undoubtedly motivated its participation. The National Association of Manufacturers agreed to support the administration at a very late date. As has been mentioned, basic manufacturing violently opposed both the safe harbor leasing repeal and the minimum corporate tax provisions. Yet many of these sectors and trade associations had a lot of other interests. In 1981 the administration had asked industry groups to submit a list of their ten least favored regulations. The mature manufacturing sectors wanted the Clean Air Act revised, the Environmental Protection Agency curtailed, pollution controls decreased, and natural gas deregulated. One way to secure compliance from these sectors was to promise action, or threaten nonaction, in other policy areas. Thus, some groups were willing to trade support on TEFRA for future action in other policy areas.

The president faced his greatest challenge from small business. The National Small Business Association, as noted, was with the president from the beginning. It was extremely concerned about the impact of the deficit and interest rates on its membership. Yet the small business groups who had supported the president in 1981—the Chamber of Commerce, National Association of Wholesaler-Distributors, and National Federation of Independent Business—were adamantly opposed to the tax increase.

Reagan lobbied these small business groups vigorously to get them to support his view. The president called the chairman of the National Association of Wholesaler-Distributors from *Air Force One* to ask him for his support. On another occasion the entire NAW board of directors were brought in for a White House meeting. The association was deeply torn; it had never supported a tax increase. Finally, the board decided to continue to oppose the bill formally. To soften their opposition to a president for whom they felt strong allegiance, staff delayed a mailogram urging members to contact their congressmen until it was too late for mass mobilization.[75]

The administration used similar tactics with the National Federation of Independent Business. NFIB members, according to insiders, were also traditionally adamant against tax increases. Spending cuts were preferred to solve the deficit problem. Again, President Reagan made a personal appeal to their president and talked with their board. A trade association representative recalls that NFIB's "hands were tied, since we don't make policy internally. We formulate policy according to members' preferences. We can't bargain for things, so we didn't give the administration a way out."[76]

The most notorious example of the administration's coercion of a trade association during the tax legislation occurred during its dealings with the U.S. Chamber of Commerce. The Chamber's board had steadfastly opposed the tax increases throughout the winter and spring. Yet in May its president, Paul Thayer, suddenly switched positions. Thayer was invited to the White House for a presidential conference with the leadership of top trade associations. Immediately after the meeting Thayer was asked to meet alone with the president to discuss tax issues. Thayer was persuaded by the president to change positions and immediately afterward was taken out to the White House lawn to announce the Chamber's support before television cameras.

The Chamber was ripped apart by this development. Dick Lesher, who succeeded Thayer as Chamber president, and much of the board were committed to maintaining their opposition. Yet Thayer wanted to come out for the course he had announced on prime time. The Chamber's tax policy committee was to meet in May following Thayer's White House announcement to make recommendations to the board on what the Chamber's position should be. The meeting was unusual in the amount of attention accorded it by nonparticipants. Jack Kemp asked the group if he could deliver an address urging opposition to the tax increase. The White House wanted to send Ed Harper to present its point of view and asked Jack Kemp not to attend. Scheduled to be in Texas on the day of the meeting, Thayer proposed addressing the group via telecommunications. Many members expressed outrage at what they saw as excessive outside interference.

The divisive atmosphere continued in the Chamber's executive committee meeting. Thayer, a former naval pilot, told the group that he had responded to his commander-in-chief on the issue. Don Kendall, although he had been intensely involved in the Reagan candidacy, remarked, "I don't care if Ronald

Reagan or Jesus Christ himself wanted to increase taxes, it's wrong." The executive committee agreed to support Thayer; however, many members privately expressed considerable dislike for the outcome. Thus, while publicly committed to the tax increase, members privately lobbied intensely on the Hill against the act.[77]

In these ways the administration set about to gain the support of, or at least to neutralize, important business groups. Once organized, the coalition of business interests was used to apply pressure to opposing legislators and recalcitrant trade associations. A sophisticated "boiler room operation" was headquartered in the National Association of Home Builders. The operation was a private sector endeavor, but there was much contact with the White House Office of Business Liaison. The group met twice a week with a White House aide. A card file was kept on all congressmen and senators; the material was also computerized. The group kept a running tally of votes, organized by four categories: "for, leaning for, leaning against, against." Individual trade associations and business executives were given assignments to put pressure on legislators. Individuals were assigned to a case if they had plants in a given legislator's district or personal associations with a congressman or senator.

Participating trade associations also applied considerable pressure during the periods shortly before the votes were to take place. The realtors, for example, used their extensive grassroots network to target two hundred members of Congress. All local boards were organized, the national headquarters sent out calls for action, and full-page ads appeared in various newspapers.

Safe harbor leasing was eventually repealed; however, some firms were able to negotiate special dispensations. Public transit received an exclusion; safe harbor leasing is still applicable to nontaxpaying entities. Ford, United Airlines, American Motors, and Scott Paper negotiated extensions. The steel industry received an extension after the markup session was officially ended. The House Steel Caucus approached Rostenkowski and the Ways and Means Committee members to urge them to reconsider an extension for steel. At 11:45 the markup session was reopened for the purposes of considering this request. Barber Conable opposed the concession, calling these transition rules "a school for scandal." Vice-President Bush called Conable to urge his cooperation, and the committee decided to grant the extension. An industry representative remembers being called at six o'clock the next morning to provide the language for the extension, which was put into the bill in a handwritten note.[78]

Conclusion

In 1981 policymakers legislated a fiscal revolution in tax policy: monumental cuts were made in upper-income and corporate rates in order to stimulate supply-side recovery. The language of the Economic Recovery Tax Act was entirely neoclassical, many pronounced Keynesian economics dead. Yet the new strategy's dominance was short-lived. The slow growth which had prompted ERTA was left unchanged by the president's fiscal intervention. Instead, the Federal Reserve's monetary policy pushed the country even deeper into recession. The most stunning effect of the 1981 tax measure was the creation of monumental budget deficits. Many believed that the deficits would keep interest rates high, thus further choking any possibility for recovery.

Disillusioned with the failure of accumulation-led recovery, policymakers pursued a very different tax strategy in 1982. The Tax Equity and Fiscal Responsibility Act questioned the fairness and equity of the selective growth incentives and revoked about one-third of ERTA's corporate savings. Although budget deficits motivated the tax initiative, the experience generated new questions about the viability of the hyper-accumulation growth strategy.

The specter of a tax increase aroused conflict in the business community. Businessmen found themselves disagreeing about both the immediate vehicle for revenue enhancement and the larger strategies for growth. Financial and housing groups demanded a tax increase to reduce the budget deficits and interest rates. They generally supported rescinding the third year of the individual tax cut. Manufacturing groups wanted to protect the 1981 growth incentives at all costs and were less concerned about the deficit. Small business groups opposed a tax increase; however, should one be necessary, they favored reducing the corporate tax incentives and retaining the individual cuts (see table 6.2).

In the face of strong conflicting macroeconomic requirements and elite demands, both Democrats and Republicans felt paralyzed. The stock market decline and the drop in the strength of the dollar created a huge political uproar over the budget deficit projections. Reagan vacillated for months over which macroeconomic course to pursue, torn between his promise not to raise taxes and the multiple problems caused by the deficits. He ultimately opted for political damage control, deciding that the deficit presented a more damaging political problem than his promise not to raise taxes. Rostenkowski was

Table 6.2. Divisions in State and Society over Tax Options

Goals	Business	State	Policy
Stimulate domestic economy	Manufacturing	Supply-siders in House and executive	Keep ACRS, safe harbor, personal cuts
Decrease deficits	Finance, housing, high tech	The Fed, Senate GOP, CEA	Reduce ACRS, safe harbor, personal cuts
More equity	Small business, high tech	Some House Democrats	Reduce ACRS, no surtax, keep individual cuts

unable to mobilize enthusiasm for any kind of tax initiative among his Ways and Means compatriots.

To manage these conflicting requisites, a coalition was formed. Yet the resulting alliance presents an intriguing twist to the coalition approach: the opposing factions formed a coalition with one another. The administration negotiated a deal with House Democrats and Senate Republicans to jointly pursue the TEFRA tax approach and fight House Republicans. Business groups from the financial and housing sectors joined the bipartisan coalition.

The unusual cooperation between partisan factions limited concessions to special interests. Yet the bipartisan alliance used business allies to secure passage of the legislation. Business groups were especially helpful in fighting House Republican supply-siders, who made up the major opposition. A coalition of factions in state and society worked together for passage of the bill.

7

The Tax Reform Act of 1986

Introduction

The Tax Reform Act of 1986 documented a third fiscal revolution: a final blow to progressivity and a radical rejection of the capital-intensive investment orientation characteristic of both the "commercial Keynesian" and "hyper-accumulation" growth strategies. The individual rate cuts were profound. Before tax reform, there were eleven rates, ranging from 11 to 50 percent; the tax act condensed the brackets into two and lowered the top rate to 28 percent. The standard deduction and personal exemption were increased, removing some 6 million individuals at the lower end from the tax system altogether. The act also lowered the corporate rate from 46 percent to 34 percent.[1]

To compensate for lost revenue, the act eliminated or scaled back many of the selective tax incentives to achieve social and economic ends that had upset horizontal equity in the past. Among these were major corporate provisions: the investment tax credit, the individual retirement accounts, differential taxation of capital gains, and accelerated depreciation allowances. A major source of revenue was the curtailing of "passive" losses, or losses to investors who were not active participants in a business.[2] Many of these measures had been important parts of the revenue code for years. Previous efforts to eliminate them had been unsuccessful.

The bill greatly altered the balance between the individual and corporate income tax, shifting about $120 billion to corporations and returning the corporate share to pre-1980 levels.[3] In the process the reform measure redistributed the tax burden among corporate sectors. Major losers were commercial real estate interests and capital-intensive sectors. One observer noted:

> Companies whose capital stock is not concentrated in depreciable capital would thus have a net tax reduction. In contrast, those whose capital stock is concentrated in depreciable property or who benefit from the special tax provisions that the Treasury proposes to eliminate would tend to have a tax increase.[4]

Another interesting aspect of the reform process was its "state-centered" nature. Tax reform was initiated by policy entrepreneurs: Birnbaum and Murray document the rousing story of the heroes of tax reform.[5] Conlan et al.

emphasize the role of Treasury Department professionals in setting the agenda for tax reform and attribute their relative autonomy to the existence of a professional consensus about how the tax system should work.[6] State actors attempted to restrict concessions to special interests with a revenue neutrality rule (lending the process a zero-sum nature) and with a high degree of bipartisanship. President Reagan and Congressman Rostenkowski (D–IL) appeared on television with a bipartisan plea for tax reform, and with occasional lapses continued jointly to support the effort.

The radical aspects of tax reform challenge "politics as usual" explanations. How did this nonincremental piece of legislation get passed? The prevailing wisdom has portrayed tax reform as a triumph of equity over growth. Over time, loopholes in the tax code had allowed individuals and companies with similar incomes to pay vastly different taxes, causing widespread dissatisfaction. Birnbaum and Murray write: "In part, the deterioration of the tax code had gone so far that something had to be done. The American people were disgusted with the system, and that disgust represented a latent political force waiting to be tapped."[7]

Kuttner suggests that Republicans sought to harness this discontent and achieve a critical realignment, shifting mass allegiance to the Republican party and cementing the Reagan legacy.[8] Shefter and Ginsberg agree that "yuppies" were a critical swing vote: tax reform benefiting middle-class professionals was an attempt to establish a durable link between these groups and the Republican party.[9]

The individual changes do seem linked to an effort to generate mass populist appeal. Yet equity by itself is an insufficient explanation. Analysts have questioned whether the tax changes, essentially gutting vertical progressivity, were truly reforms.[10] Most of the reform measures had been on the agenda for twenty years. Nor can the equity explanation account for the seeming increase in government commitment and capacity to pursue policies which, according to many, would offend much of the business community. The equity analysis also is incapable of explaining the extensive redistribution of the corporate burden.

It is argued here that, in addition to a search for equity, tax reform was made possible by a shifting perception among key actors about the productive investment strategy necessary to stimulate economic growth. The emerging strategy has a very different emphasis from the capital-intensive investment orientation of the earlier period. Therefore, the distribution of the corporate tax burden under tax reform has assumed a much different cast.

Conventional wisdom also suggests that reform was made possible by a unique process in which bureaucratic experts were able to keep special interests at bay. The partisan consensus on the importance of tax reform reduced state-centered political conflict and thereby lowered concessions to outside interests. Yet the transformation in policy focus was not accomplished totally without business intervention: a core group of business devotees were critical to passage. An emerging industrial coalition helped to change the consensus around growth and keep tax reform alive at key points in the legislative process. This coalition also sought to secure the conditions for radical policy change by seeking to limit the particularistic demands among private sector interests. One industry lobbyist explained:

> Tax reform represented a big reset button: clearing the decks of political deals made by previous generations of lawmakers and allowing them to enter into new political deals with the new powers that be. The economy is changing and it is appropriate that there be adjustments in the fiscal system to reflect changes in the economy. This is the good part. We got rid of a lot of preferences that were no longer justifiable and improved the overall legitimacy of the tax code.[11]

Macroeconomic Context

The economy began to recover after the recession in 1981–82; by 1984 the GNP had increased 6.8 percent and inflation had dropped considerably. Yet, according to a Citizens for Tax Justice study, the 1981 investment incentives were not responsible for the economic revival. Plant and equipment investment fell 15.1 percent and companies' dividends were raised 17 percent between 1981 and 1983. The fifty companies with the lowest tax rates were most disappointing, decreasing their investment by 22 percent. By comparison, companies with the highest tax rates (for whom consequently the tax incentives would have the least impact) increased investment by 4 percent.[12]

Despite the improvement in some economic indicators, federal budget deficits remained out of control. The stringent monetary policy used to control inflation combined with the climbing budget deficits increased interest rates; these in turn drove up the price of the dollar in international currency markets. A higher dollar increased the price of and decreased the desire for goods manufactured in the United States; by 1984 the trade deficit was $125 billion, three times that of 1982. According to Jefferson, the strong dollar imposed a 50 percent surcharge on U.S. goods sold abroad; the trade deficit cost more than 2 million jobs.[13]

Microeconomic malaise varied by industrial sector. Capital-intensive manufacturing sectors continued to fare poorly in the world economy. Especially worrisome was the increase of imports to and the decline of exports from the United States. Imports were only 13.9 percent of the GNP originating in the U.S. manufacturing sector in 1969; by 1986 they were up to 44.7 percent.[14] Internationalization and the increased mobility of capital meant that many industries now did much of their manufacturing elsewhere. Therefore, investment incentives for domestic production became relatively less important.

State Factions: Economic and Political Agendas

Three policy solutions to the economic conundrum circulated the academic and congressional corridors. The first was sponsored by a group of politicians, bureaucrats, and scholars who thought that the key to economic health was deficit reduction. Thus, Lawrence argued that solving certain macroeconomic problems—namely, the high budget deficit and overvalued dollar—would return American manufacturing sectors to their previous hegemony.[15]

The second approach was a radical reevaluation of the capital-investment policy package. Although capital-intensive investment continued to be important, its limits were articulated. Adherents to this view worried that bad investment decisions, or investments made in an inadequate climate, were responsible for many of our economic ills. Bailey blamed bad investment decisions in the 1970s, resulting in premature obsolescence, for the drop in quantity of output produced per unit of capital after 1973.[16] The U.S. semiconductor industry's decline has been attributed to excessive product innovation. Excessive investment in new technology has limits as well: service employees have discovered that "sophisticated machines in many cases have been hampering their work." Inadequate knowledge and reliability problems constrain the potential of computer technology. For example, despite the computerization of cash registers in the retail industry, productivity growth has remained at an annual 1 percent. The productivity growth rate of workers in industries such as health care, law, and accounting has actually declined.[17]

Recognition of the limits of capital shifted attention to the human resources necessary to make firms productive. Since productivity depends on the human climate in which equipment is introduced, existing technology is not always used to its maximum. Therefore, management strategies, worker-management relations, and the general skill level of the work force will all influence productive outcomes.[18] The importance of management strategy on productivity levels was pondered over in the pages of the *Harvard Business Review*. Skinner wrote a seminal article in the mid-1970s arguing that the productivity crisis is a problem of "how to compete." Managers who focus on a "narrow product mix for a particular market niche" will achieve higher performance rates than their conventional competitors.[19] In their study of twelve factories, Hayes and Clark found those factories with the greatest complexity and confusion had the lowest rates of total factor productivity.[20]

This reevaluation of the investment strategy resurrected an old tax debate. Some economists had long been worried about the effect of the investment tax credit and accelerated depreciation on the composition of capital assets in the economy. They feared that the tax incentives favored some kinds of investment over others, so that the incentives would change the composition of investment rather than increase the total amount of capital.[21] Auerbach's findings are characteristic: the corporate tax system skews investment from structures to equipment. Income generated by structures is taxed at roughly 30 percent; that generated by equipment, at approximately 20 percent.[22]

A third policy option of the mid-1980s was to continue the status quo. Not everyone agreed that a sound economic future required shifting resources from basic industry to high technology. Zysman points out that the principal exporting companies remain the mature, capital-intensive industries.[23] Others argued that a capital-intensive investment strategy was precisely what was needed to promote competitiveness. According to this analysis, high-technology firms must be innovative in order to retain market share; high rates of innovation require considerable capital investment. Even before reform the cost of capital was higher in the United States than elsewhere. Hatsopoulos and Brooks calculate that U.S. firms have paid three times as much for capital as their Japanese competitors.[24]

Tax reform would worsen the disparity. Landau calculated that Treasury II would actually increase the cost of capital by 1 percent. Thus, the cash flow of U.S. corporations might decrease by $222 billion over five years; the tax burden on corporations would increase by 24 percent from 1986 to 1990.[25] Charls Walker argued that the Ways and Means version of reform would increase the capital cost of investing in equipment by 18 to 20 percent and would quadruple the effective corporate tax rates on equipment investment. The capital cost recovery on these investments would drop 59 percent. Robert Holland, president of the Committee for Economic Development, predicted that tax reform would inspire the relocation of many U.S. firms overseas to take advantage of better rates of return on capital investments.[26] Landau concluded:

> Supply-side incentives of all kinds need to be retained and indeed strengthened if the United States is to retain a balanced competitive economy with adequate job formation. Some of the comments on Treasury II seem to gloat over the fact that it basically favors high tech over smokestack industries, and thus the "winners" over the "losers." This again betrays complete ignorance of the workings of the economy, where high technology requiring large capital investments is spreading into virtually every industry, if it is to remain competitive and permit adequate economic growth. The health of the economy is even more dependent on manufacturing than before, not only for competitiveness and inflation resistance, but also because the higher productivity levels in manufacturing lead to a great impact on business cycles when manufacturing turns down.[27]

The Reagan administration began its tenure in 1981 in the third camp; but by 1986 the second solution package had captured the imagination of many administration officials. Thus, the 1986 tax act was explicitly motivated by a different view of growth from the older emphasis on capital investment.

First, given the current economic structuring, economists worried that investment resources were being directed toward the wrong parts of the economy. Tax reform sought to correct for this by creating tax neutrality or a "level playing field" with respect to investment capital. Tax neutrality would shift investment from tax-motivated targets to opportunities chosen on economic bases. Richard Darman wrote, "A depreciation system that is nearly neutral across classes of investment will lead to a more efficient allocation of capital."[28] Tax neutrality was achieved at a cost: removing the investment incentives would increase the cost of capital. But this was thought to be justified. More efficient use of capital would compensate for higher costs.[29] Ballentine explained:

> While tax reform will have a negative effect on the level of U.S. savings, it will have a positive effect on the productivity of our savings and the investment financed by that savings. This arises because tax reform results in more equal tax treatment of alternative business investments. Proponents of reform have rightly said that by treating all investments more equally, tax considerations become less important in making business decisions, and the underlying economic and profit realities become more important.[30]

Second, reform was expected to revive investment in human resources. To this end the President's Commission on Industrial Competitiveness recommended restructuring the tax code to equalize investment in physical and human capital.[31]

Third, by improving the utilization of resources, tax reform was expected to improve competitiveness. Lyon wrote:

> The traditional approach to economic growth has called for increasing output per capita by increasing the capital stock of the economy. However, economic growth can also be achieved by utilizing the capital stock more efficiently . . . The Tax Reform Act recognized that tax incentives can cause less productive investments to be chosen over more productive investments.[32]

Fourth, the major remaining selective tax incentive, the research and development credit, was expected to shift investment into new sectors. Darman wrote, "With the elimination of most other credits, the research and development tax credit will be more attractive, and increased R & D will improve productivity."[33]

Finally, the tax act at least symbolically signified a relative deemphasis of the role of the federal government in directing economic growth.

The impact of the act also reflected the new approach to investment. The elimination of the investment incentives reversed a twenty-year trend by shifting the tax burden back onto capital-intensive industries. Fullerton, Henderson, and Mackie found the total effective tax rate of capital investment in equipment under prior law to be 4 percent; after tax reform this rate increased to 42 percent. By comparison, structures bore total effective tax rates of 44 percent before and 49 percent after; inventories, of 49 percent before and 47 percent after.[34]

Despite the aggregate increase in the corporate tax burden, many sectors actually benefited from the tax act: the rate cuts helped high technology, small business, and the service sector at the expense of heavy industry. A study of the effect of tax reform on small business found that 60 percent of the sample thought that tax reform would *not* lead to higher taxes. Of small manufacturing and construction firms, 44 percent feared a tax increase, but only 25 percent in service companies worried about this.[35] Sara Lee, a food processing company which spends a lot on marketing, thought that tax reform would increase earnings by at least 10 percent. Hardwich Simmons, vice-chair of Shearson Lehman Brothers, said of the Senate Finance bill, "If the bill becomes law as it is, we're in fat city."[36] One journalist called the Ways and Means bill "a bill that is pro-consumption and anti–capital investment, one destined to accelerate the nation's already powerful shift from a manufacturing to a service economy."[37]

Why did this new approach to growth succeed in capturing the tax agenda? Disparate issues drew Republicans to tax reform: an attraction to the new growth strategy, concerns about competitiveness, a desire to please high-technology supporters, a desire for electoral realignment, and a desire for low rates.

First, at least some within the administration seemed to be persuaded by the arguments of professional economists about the effects of the growth incentives. Rudolph Penner (Congressional Budget Office) argued that the new tax regime can be linked to the power of ideas: "These economists have more influence than is generally perceived even by themselves. What they think gets into the legislative process by staff, including CBO, reading their work and translating it into more accessible English for the members."

Second, tax reform initially appealed to Reagan's supply-side followers as a way to continue their cutting edge agenda. "Tax reform became a code word among conservatives for tax reduction. This gave the thing enormous impetus."[38] Regan was the primary representative of this view within the administration.

The supply-side contingent was extremely influential in the president's initial decision to endorse reform. Birnbaum and Murray describe a poolside meeting in 1983 in which twenty supply-side politicians and intellectuals gathered to determine a slate for the 1984 election. Irving Kristol recommended that the group endorse the Bradley-Gephardt reform proposal as a mechanism for achieving a central supply-side goal of lowering tax rates. Some members with strong corporate connections opposed—namely, Richard Rahn and Paul Craig Roberts. They disliked the reduction of investment incentives for business. But the group finally decided that Kemp should propose a variation of Bradley-Gephardt. The Kemp version differed from Bradley-Gephardt in increasing business investment incentives with rapid depreciation allowances for equipment.[39]

Third, the president's interest in tax reform was linked to concerns about international competitiveness. Several years before passage of the tax reform act, Jack Albertine (American Business Conference) recalls that Boston industrialists presented President Reagan with findings about the effects of Massachusetts' Proposition 2 1/2. They argued that the tax reduction effort had stimulated economic growth: the hodgepodge of selective incentives combined with higher rates stood in the way of a happy economic future. This presentation was made around the time that the President's Commission on Industrial Competitiveness was formed. Part of the commission's task was to think about the relationship between competitiveness and the tax code.

Policy concerns were reinforced by good politics. A fourth Republican concern was that Democrats would make an issue of tax reform in the 1984 election. Although this did not happen, Republicans felt compelled to respond to the Democratic industrial policy initiatives. With the failure of the early Reagan interventions to resuscitate the economy, the Democrats began a campaign to seize control of the economic agenda. In their 1984 bid for election the Democrats put forth an idea that had gained currency with economic analysts associated with the party: economic restructuring through industrial policy. The Center for National Policy organized a panel led by Felix Rohatyn, Lane Kirkland (AFL-CIO), and Irving Shapiro (DuPont) to draft an industrial policy platform. Timothy Wirth (D–CO) and Richard Gephardt (D–MO) sponsored a bill to create an Economic Cooperation Council to analyze problems of specific industries. Stan Lundine (D–NY) and David Bonior (D–MI) proposed legislation creating a National Industrial Bank.[40] The latter was patterned on Felix Rohatyn's concept of a business-government partnership to revitalize those parts of the economy which held the greatest potential for growth. The bank was to be a 1980s version of the New Deal Reconstruction Finance Corporation (RFC). It would advance capital to industries in exchange for union concessions in wages and work rules and acceptance of guidance by management.[41] Bonior noted the political benefits of industrial policy: "You cannot meet Reagan to beat Reagan. You have to stand for something, and it doesn't have to be socialism . . . It can be a cooperative working relationship between industry and government."[42]

Advocates of industrial policy also recommended tax reform; however, this was a sideshow to the main program. To Thurow corporate tax "distortions are so large that if the current tax incentives are allowed to continue for any length of time they will burden the economy with an inefficient pattern of investments that will severely handicap America's efforts to compete with the rest of the world."[43]

Listening to their own constituents in high technology, the Republicans realized that they must also develop policy to enable the transformation of the American economy. Stokes explained:

> In recent years, many liberals have advocated an industrial policy to revitalize failing industries . . . In contrast, the conservatives' approach would improve productivity by restructuring the tax code, liberalizing antitrust laws and beefing up federal support for R & D, all spurring export-oriented economic growth.[44]

Republicans viewed industrial policy as an inappropriate vehicle for economic restructuring because it could create market distortions and could ultimately hinder productivity growth. Critics also doubted the efficiency of industrial policy and worried about its excessively interventionist nature. Economic restructuring occurs gradually; the annual magnitude of change in the economy is small. Productivity growth has declined in many sectors; therefore, offering help to one or more sectors will not greatly alter aggregate productivity performance.[45] Business was also suspicious of greater government intervention: a Harris poll in January 1984 found only 33 percent of the business executives sampled favoring central strategic planning to save declining industries.[46]

Instead, the Republicans sought a solution in a policy area which had always been used to further economic goals: the tax system. Tax reform offered a mechanism for negating the skews in investment incentives and redistributing resources toward rapidly growing sectors, while minimizing state intervention. In this vein, the Committee for Economic Development's Kenneth McLennan argued that tax reform avoided some of the targeting problems of industrial policy but accomplished many of the same goals:

> The Democratic Party's need to develop an alternative policy agenda to the Reagan Administration's approach has led to the advocacy of an industrial strategy based on policies which favor the development of specific economic sectors . . . In contrast, the Reagan Administration favors permitting the market system to identify and support the expansion of promising economic sectors and to permit the automatic and gradual decline of sectors of the economy which have lost their comparative advantage . . . The issue is which of these extremes should play the dominant role in determining the nation's economic strategy for the next decade.[47]

Fifth, electoral realignment was a political motivation; tax reform would "bring Joe Six Pack into the Republican party." In fact mass public demand for tax reform was actually somewhat questionable. Some polls did indicate considerable support for the reform effort: a January 1985 poll showed 75 percent agreeing that the "present tax system benefits the rich and is unfair to the ordinary working man or woman."[48] In an Advisory Commission on

Intergovernmental Relations comparison of the perceived fairness of various taxes, the federal income tax moved from first place in 1972 to last place in 1979.[49] But other polls reflected a disengaged public. One January 1985 poll showed 41 percent believing that the current tax system was basically fair.[50] In other polls that month, 48 percent had not heard of the Treasury Department's tax reform proposal, and 72 percent wanted individuals to continue to pay at different rates depending on their income.[51]

Hansen's view of policy changes during critical realignments may be consistent with findings of questionable public pressure for tax reform. She agrees that dramatic changes in the tax code have historically taken place at points of electoral realignment. But in her view, policy transformations are *not* an acknowledgment of public outcry but a post hoc response to the realignment made possible by the increased capacity of the ruling party to legislate policy initiatives.[52]

Within the Democratic party many originally preferred deficit reduction to tax reform. The House Democratic Study Group, the left wing of the party, believed that the revenues raised by closing tax loopholes should be directed toward deficit reduction.[53] Yet Democrats also embraced tax reform for a variety of reasons.

First, some Democrats brought to tax reform the traditional reformer's desire to close loopholes. (Other Democrats, it is true, were involved in the creation of the selective tax incentives and accepted reform only under duress.) Bill Bradley was the earliest political reformer; he began building support for tax renovation in 1982. As a pro-basketball player, Bradley had been appalled by the tax system. He once allegedly remarked to Ronald Reagan, "Mr. President, you came to this [tax reform] because you were an actor who paid at the 90-percent rate; that's why you want a lower rate. I came to this because I was a depreciable asset."[54]

Joe Minarik worked with Bradley to construct a reform plan with three rates: 14 percent, 26 percent, and 30 percent. The corporate rate was lowered from 46 to 30 percent. A few deductions were retained for home mortgage interests, for charitable contributions, for IRAs, and for state and local taxes. Bradley and Gephardt introduced the bill as the Fair Tax Act of 1982.[55]

The traditional tax reformer's commitment to reform also emerged in staff input. A technicians' prejudice existed among the staff that the tax code should not be used as a social and economic tool. Many reformers were intrigued by the possibility of reforming the cumbersome tax code and worked to influence their political bosses. Within the Treasury, Regan left many of the details of reform up to experts Ronald Pearlman and Charles McLure. Rostenkowski worked closely with the Joint Committee on Taxation.

Another important tax reformer with close ties to the Democrats and labor was Bob McIntyre, head of the Citizens for Tax Justice. In the early 1970s McIntyre began publishing *People & Taxes,* a low-budget, high-spirited rag which railed against the inequities of the tax system. In a 1985 report, "Corporate Taxpayers & Corporate Freeloaders," McIntyre published the names of 275 companies that paid less than 15 percent and 50 companies that paid no taxes at all (see appendix 7.1). Another group of influential reformers were the staff of *Tax Notes*. Their publication of vastly uneven effective tax rates across industrial sectors captured the attention of individuals within both business and government.

Second, Democrats also seemed to believe that a sound economic future was linked to tax reform. Discussions of the economic impact of tax reform were critical during the Ways and Means Committee's early meetings on tax reform. One participant recalled: "We are talking about tough decisions—but promoting economic growth and cleaning up the tax system . . . We concluded that we wanted to come up with a great tax bill . . . I walked out of there and thought: Jesus, public policy really becomes important!" Another reported, "A lot of the discussion was about what was good for the economy, good for growth, and this and that." [56] "There was a feeling that the code had a bias toward the metal benders," revealed another participant. Although the level of discussion about alternative economic paradigms was evidently not very sophisticated within Ways and Means, members believed that business would be better off if all got taxed the same. The buzzword of "level playing field" drew a sympathetic response. [57]

Third, when the Republicans made reform a major policy issue, the potentially realigning nature of tax reform generated Democratic involvement. The *New York Times* noted, "Because the issue has enjoyed wide bipartisan support, it will be difficult for either party to gain a lot of political mileage for tax revision in the November election." [58] The Democrats were also generally motivated to retain a partisan claim to tax reform as an equity issue. According to one lobbyist, Rostenkowski said "that in the spring the rivers will thaw, the waters will rise, that will start the erosion of the Republican Senate, and we will get back the White House." [59]

Finally, tax reform was aided by the change in fiscal climate due to economic decline and the budget deficit. Weaver points out that a climate of fiscal austerity changes the incentives of government actors. During periods of fiscal stress, policy decisions are likely to be unpopular; therefore, politicians look for ways to avoid blame. A "circle-the-wagons" strategy allows politicians to avoid blame by seeking agreement among themselves and presenting a united front to the public at large. Recent years have demonstrated a trend toward automatic government. Automatic formulas, such as the Gramm-Rudman-Hollings Act, alleviate decision-making overload, limit discretion, and help politicians avoid taking repugnant policy decisions. [60]

Blame avoidance figured in at many points of the process. One staff explained that "Rostenkowski never claimed that tax reform was going to happen. All the Chairman wanted to do was to get the bill out of the House. If it died after that, it would be OK." Likewise, Finance staff recalled their favorite metaphor for the death of tax reform in the Senate: a dead cat left at the doorstep.[61]

Pattern of Business Demands

The split has created a kind of class warfare, with capital-intensive companies contending that the President's plan is unfair to them and service-oriented industries arguing that it gives them more tax equality. The divisions are just as deep on larger questions, such as what the plan will do for the country's over-all economic growth and competitiveness in international markets.[62]

Tax reform represented a realignment of power in the business community.[63]

Divisions in business over tax reform were reminiscent of those in 1982. Basic industry remained committed to the status quo of selective tax incentives and uneven effective tax rates. Tax reform was supported by those parts of the business community most discriminated against by the earlier system: high technology, small business, and service. These sectors actively worked to put reform on the public agenda and provided considerable lobbying power during the legislative process.

The high-technology industry's interest in tax reform stemmed from their belief that the Accelerated Cost Recovery System (ACRS) discriminated in favor of heavy manufacturing. Products and equipment become obsolete more quickly in high technology; therefore, accelerated depreciation only marginally quickened the write-off period. Because high-technology companies also tend to be "information-intensive" and dependent on human resources, these firms sought a tax code more neutral to labor and capital. These firms also believed that tax reform could improve competitiveness in the world economy.[64]

Despite general support for reform, certain tax preferences continued to be important to high technology. First, since the industry tended to meet capital needs through stock rather than debt, the capital gains differential was of primary importance. Second, the industry valued research and development incentives to encourage innovation. In 1986 the treatment of research and development as a preference in the alternative minimum tax was a major issue. Finally, the international character of the industry (in markets and production) made taxation of foreign affiliates important.[65]

Small business and service firms also sought tax reform to equalize the effective tax rate between sectors. These businessmen hoped that a more neutral tax system would increase investment in their firms. At the same time, these sectors believed the lower rates would generate more disposable income for consumers.[66] The tax preferences of these sectors included graduated rates for small business and tax deductions for fringe benefits.

These private sector supporters of reform organized themselves into a broad-based group called the Tax Reform Action Coalition (TRAC). TRAC was an offspring of the Coalition to Reduce High Effective Tax Rates, formed to oppose the proposal for a corporate surtax in 1982.[67] That group had become somewhat dormant since the passage of TEFRA, although leading members continued to stump for more equitable effective tax rates. The administration's proposal jolted the group into action. Jack Albertine was so visible during this period that he appeared on a list of overcited sources that the *Wall Street Journal* circulated to its reporters. In the week after Reagan's May 28 tax reform speech, Albertine appeared on seven television programs to support the bill.[68]

Although initial reaction to the administration's first proposal (Treasury I) was quite skeptical, Jim Baker and the Treasury staff constructed a second proposal (Treasury II) to draw in these natural business allies. The administration told business contacts that it would like to "have people out there supporting the rate cuts." A few days after Treasury II was announced, the Tax Reform Action Coalition was formed. TRAC first met on June 11, 1985, and was run by a management committee consisting of three CEOs and three trade association representatives.

TRAC members worked steadily to increase membership during the summer of 1985. They constructed a list of potential recruits by examining the financial structure of industries and identifying sectors with shared interests. A list of firms in each sector was developed; the management committee wrote letters and made follow-up telephone calls to each firm on the list. For example, there were 8 food-processing firms in the initial TRAC group. The leadership determined that the food-processing industry would benefit from reform and set out to enlist every food processor in the sector. By the end of the summer TRAC had enlisted 175 members; by the time tax reform was enacted, 700 groups and CEOs had joined. (See appendix #2 for a list of the TRAC Steering Committee.)

The goal of the group was to keep the legislative eye focused on the prize of the corporate rate cuts, and not allow it to give in to more sectarian demands which could push tax rates up again. To belong to TRAC, members had to offer public support for lower tax rates; involvement in other tax battles was a private affair. Although the sole goal of the group was the low rates, there was also a realization that negotiation on other provisions could threaten to push the rates up again. "TRAC [as an organization] never tried to kill anybody else's preferences" and refrained from opposing specific provisions. But when faced with a damaging proposal, members had to "soul search" whether or not to support it, knowing that noncompliance could hurt the rates. This made the members set priorities for themselves and restrain their demands for specific provisions in a way not seen in other tax bills. Later, during the Senate markup sessions, TRAC members made a formal promise to support the bill in its entirety.[69]

The CEO Tax Group was a big-business parallel to TRAC: a coalition of chief executives from twenty Fortune 500 companies.[70] The group was organized by Lawrence O'Brien and Rod DeArment. To belong, a company had to pay a fee and endorse the basic tenets of tax reform: lower rates and closed loopholes. Where TRAC excelled at massive grass roots mobilization, the CEO Tax Group offered targeted intervention from the nation's leaders of industry. In practice the two groups cooperated closely.

The Grocery Manufacturers of America (GMA) also launched an early grass roots campaign to seek tax reform legislation. One tactic begun in 1984 was to hold breakfast meetings for members of the Ways and Means and Finance committees in the members' home territory.[71] The group's chairman, John Bryan (chair of Sara Lee), put together a computer file of 300 tax and business editors with whom he had regular contact. Bryan also convinced 359 other corporate CEOs to allow him to represent them before Congress. GMA worked closely with the Citizens for Tax Justice, a liberal research organization which has long lobbied for tax reform. A Citizens for Tax Justice study documenting the disparities existing in corporate taxation served as a consciousness-raising exercise for high corporate taxpayers. The Citizens originally provided Bryan with the list of 359 companies he later represented. GMA also distributed the Citizens' *Money for Nothing,* a report on the failure of the investment tax incentives, and contributed $3,000 to Citizens' budget.[72]

The primary opponents of tax reform were basic manufacturing and real estate. Capital-intensive mature manufacturing industries had been the greatest beneficiaries of the old regime and therefore had the most to lose from the new. These industries objected to the general thrust of the tax reform act. As one lobbyist put it, "The whole theory of tax reform was to neutralize investment, but in fact it shifted to non-risk, non-capital-intensive investment." The opponents of reform offered a vastly different conception of the interaction between growth and the tax code. Their arguments centered on two points: that capital investment was necessary to a healthy economy and that basic manufacturing was necessary to world trade. Charls Walker argued: "Computers are nice. But you can't eat computers, you can't sleep in a computer, you can't wear a computer. I really believe a nation can't live by eroding its industrial base and taking in each other's wash."

Central to this vision of growth were the investment tax credit and accelerated depreciation allowance. In addition, many sectors had more particularistic gripes about the reform measure. For example, the oil industry strongly objected to the passive loss provisions. Multinational industries strongly opposed the bill's treatment of foreign source income.

To put forth their views, mature manufacturing industries formed several groups. The American Council for Capital Formation, founded by Charls Walker, worked to build support for policies to foster capital-intensive investment. For the more specific purpose of fighting tax reform, Walker and others formed a group called the Coalition for Jobs, Growth, and International Competitiveness. Chief executives of fifteen big capital-intensive companies paid $40,000 each to belong. (Small firms could join for $1,000; and trade associations, for $5,000.)[73] Another group, the Basic Industries Coalition, was founded in 1982 when attacks on the investment incentives first materialized in TEFRA. These groups commissioned a variety of studies to support their position. Birnbaum and Murray whimsically recall some of the arguments:

> Data Resources was only one of a host of hired guns who made hay preparing studies on the supposedly disastrous effects of tax reform. When added together, they suggested the president's tax bill would create a cataclysm. According to various studies circulated on Capitol Hill, the bill would force "a dose of Jonestown-type cyanide" on the construction industry, raise apartment rents by 20 percent to 40 percent, destroy old urban neighborhoods, and jeopardize "the oral health of the American people." Horse breeding would fall 18 percent, American Samoa would be devastated, and canned tuna would become obsolete. The president's tax plan, according to these studies paid for by anti-tax-reform lobbyists, would precipitate all evils short of famine, pestilence, and plague—even plague wasn't entirely out of the question.[74]

In the tax reform battle, real estate interests were riveted around two issues: the second home interest deduction and passive loss rules. To protect the second home interest deduction the industry carefully calculated the number of second homes in each legislator's home state. The second home was thereby shown to be a middle-class American's investment with wide political support.

Passive loss rules were changed in the 1986 act to prohibit passive investors (nonparticipants in productive activity) from offsetting their other income with tax losses from this investment. This provision was intended to channel investment into more productive activities and away from unproductive tax shelters. The real estate industry contended that passive loss rules were necessary to build partnerships and predicted that the changed rules would increase rents in low-income housing. The industry now claims that the tremendous reduction in low-income housing since 1985, increased homelessness in America, and the downfall of the thrift industry are all direct results of this tax change.

The real estate industry also initiated a massive grass roots campaign against reform. The National Association of Home Builder's Congressional Contact Program identified individuals with close ties to members of Congress. The goal of the program was to generate twenty contacts for each legislator. Sympathetic legislators identified colleagues who might be persuaded to the industry's side and alerted the industry to key points. Members were sent a political update for their state and encouraged to join the lobbying effort. The political affairs staff of the association provided technical assistance and staff support to local associations and held seminars to help builders with local races. Members would often become involved through local political efforts, such as stopping antidevelopment drives, and then would be encouraged to become active on national policy issues. Seminars were also developed to teach local groups how to build PACs; the association hoped to get $2.7 million in PAC money for the 1985–86 elections. The association also tried to recruit candidates to run for Congress. To educate members on which candidates were sympathetic to development issues, the home builders offered a "Technical Race Analysis" analyzing each legislator's voting record. Candidates who had not yet developed voting records were interviewed to this end. The association also offered scores on average voting records for each state to determine which states excelled in pro-housing candidates. The home builders raised $1.4 billion to fight tax reform.[75] The Business Roundtable was unable to reach consensus on the 1986 tax reform act, since its members fell into both camps.[76]

Proposal Development

The first reform proposal produced by the Treasury Department was largely a product of experts. Secretary Regan had a limited understanding of tax issues and left most decisions up to his staff. The staff knew that the proposal might end up as a study but welcomed the chance to "fill the hopper with good ideas."[77]

The proposal was based on rates of 15, 25, and 35 percent, with a corporate rate of 33 percent. Treasury analysts originally proposed rates of 16, 28, and 37 percent; however, Regan didn't like the sound of this. Raising the corporate rate from 28 percent to 33 percent could make the plan work but would increase corporate taxes by $150 billion. Regan originally hoped to maintain the balance between individual and corporate burdens.[78]

The proposal eliminated the investment tax credit, the capital gains differential, and scaled-back depreciation allowances; only the research and development credit survived. Large increases in the standard deductions, personal exemptions, and indexing for inflation were included as sweeteners, along with the lower rates. The tax treatment of business was negotiated in an early debate between two Treasury officials, Charles McLure and Manuel Johnson. Johnson wanted to incorporate an expensing provision in the act which would allow the cost of the equipment to be written off in the first year. McLure pointed out, quite accurately, that expensing would continue to shift the tax burden away from capital-intensive industries and onto service and high technology.[79]

The proposal was made public on November 27. Already fearing the political consequences, Regan announced that the proposal had been written on a word processor and could be changed. President Reagan immediately distanced himself from the proposal, saying he would "listen to the comments and suggestions of all Americans, especially those from Congress," before offering his own plan.[80]

Shortly before the proposal was unveiled, Treasury staff met with high-technology representatives "to tell us how much we would like it." The response was quite the opposite. The American Electronics Association told the *Wall Street Journal* that the plan would sap "the very lifeblood of America's high risk, high-technology companies." High technology had the most trouble with the proposal to eliminate preferential treatment for capital gains, which would reduce the availability of venture capital. Robert Perlman (Intel) observed: "I think the Treasury is trying to find an ally who will go out there and help them beat back the smokestack guys. But I'm not sure high-tech is ready to go out and take on the world for an issue they are lukewarm on."[81]

Other sectors heaped criticism on the proposal as well. After an extremely acrimonious meeting with Treasury staff Tim McNamar, the oil industry "pulled out all the stops with Congress, saying how devastating the change would be."[82] The day after the proposal was released, President Reagan expressed surprise that corporate taxes had been increased so much by the "Treasury bill."

At this point a fortunate and fortuitous occurrence changed the course of tax reform: Jim Baker and Don Regan traded jobs. Baker was tired of being a staff person and wanted to become a principal in an important substantive area within the administration. Regan felt excluded from the White House; having run a large organization, he felt well prepared to assume the administrative duties of chief of staff. Baker's lateral move to the Treasury was critical to tax reform, because Baker understood the power distribution in Washington and would make the political compromises necessary for the proposal to work. As one observer remarked, Baker and his assistant Darman "were two guys who knew how to get things done on the Hill." Don Regan's new position at the White House provided him ample opportunity to sell his creation to the president.

Baker's early months at the Treasury were spent meeting with potential business allies to garner support for a new version of reform. For example, the National Association of Wholesaler-Distributors commissioned Arthur Andersen to determine how Treasury I affected their constituency. The study discovered that the elimination of the corporate tax gradations actually increased the tax burden on wholesalers and distributors. The National Federation of Independent Business's primary concern was to retain the graduated corporate rates and to prevent changes in estate taxes. Representatives of the organization met with Baker and promised the support of the small business community for desired action on the proposal. Said one industry representative, "Treasury under Baker was a lot more supportive than I ever expected them to be." Baker ultimately agreed to reinstate gradations in the corporate income tax for small-sized firms.[83]

High technology made the capital-gains differential its highest priority and set about to lobby Congress and the administration as soon as the contents of the proposed bill were made public. (The industry also objected to the inclusion of the research and development deduction in the alternative minimum tax.) Many administration officials were sympathetic to lower capital gains and apologized for the proposal, explaining that it was "black-boxed out of the bowels of Treasury." The president himself met with twenty-eight high-technology executives on February 5 and indicated sympathy for their position. Treasury quickly reinstated the differential and gained the allegiance of many high-technology groups. A proposal to recapture depreciation benefits was eliminated after heavy lobbying from General Motors and IBM; high-technology groups were also pleased with the extension of the research and development tax credit.[84]

The passive loss provisions in the Senate bill which later alienated real estate interests were taken out of Treasury II. Finally, Baker and Vice-President Bush met with Regan and the president to argue for the reinstatement of oil and gas incentives. President Reagan was persuaded; consequently, apart from minor reductions, oil benefits were left unchanged. Only 60 percent of drilling costs could be deducted in the first year instead of the full amount. The changes benefiting the oil industry cost $50 billion.[85]

How can one account for the initial dramatic purity of the Treasury proposal and the equally dramatic subsequent reversal of many of its key provisions? One participant claimed that no one expected Treasury I to be accepted but that its purity was an important part of the process:

> It was the classic trial balloon. A great deal of work was put into it, because they really wanted a reaction of specifics . . . They played it very well: came out with a purist package, sent it up as a trial balloon, let them define the proposal and let them know where constituencies were. They could then buy constituencies on the legislation by putting their concerns into the bill.[86]

Tax Reform in the House

After Treasury II was announced, tax reform was taken up by the House Ways and Means Committee under the leadership of chairman Dan Rostenkowski (D–IL). At first glance Rostenkowski was hardly anyone's idea of the traditional tax reformer. Coming from a political heritage of back room dealmaking, Rostenkowski was a lobbyist's congressman. Yet the Illinois congressman took up the cause of tax reform with vigor. Reagan and Rosten-kowski campaigned for reform in May and June of 1985; after a presidential address on television, Rostenkowski pledged his support and urged the public to write to "Rosty, Washington, D.C."

Why did the congressman participate so enthusiastically? As stated earlier, the Democrats viewed tax reform as a potentially realigning issue and wanted to retain control over the process. In addition, there was evidence that Rosten-kowski and the supporting members on Ways and Means believed in the eco-nomic benefits of reform. The retreats organized around tax reform and the breakfast meetings with reform-minded CEOs served as a vehicle for ideo-logical transformation.

Finally, Rostenkowski had personal reasons for wanting reform: it repre-sented a vehicle for career building. The congressman explained: "I was look-ing for reform. You know, I've kind of lived in the shadow of Wilbur Mills."[87] Also, experience had taught Rostenkowski to value bipartisan co-operation on fiscal policy. "Rostenkowski's political record was that when he did stuff with the president, he won; but when he fought, he lost. He likes to be at the center of things, likes to win. So Rostenkowski had a choice to either say 'no' which would take him out of the action, or to be the guy that did tax reform." Rostenkowski's considerable negotiating skills also entered into the calculus: the chairman believed that he could "get the president into the pit, and figured that Reagan was so dumb that he could get Reagan to do what he wanted."[88]

The strategy for passage generated some debate among the administration and the House leadership. Baker wanted Rostenkowski to take a blitzkrieg approach (like that used to garner support for the Omnibus Budget Reconcili-ation Act of 1981) and to construct a precooked deal similar to the strategy used by the Gang of Seventeen with TEFRA. Baker and Darman started hold-ing secret meetings with the tax reformers in Congress (Bradley, Gephardt, Kemp, Kasten, Rostenkowski, Duncan, Packwood, and Long) to figure out what the compromise would look like.[89]

Rostenkowski resisted this strategy. First, the Democrats wanted to draft a bill more favorable to the middle class. Second, as a Ways and Means staff person explained, "Rostenkowski feels very strongly that you can't lead un-less you know where the people are." Instead of rushing the bill through, the Ways and Means chairman sat down with his members one by one and asked: "What do you want? What can't you accept?" The chairman tried to locate the political center of the committee and started with this package for the markup.[90]

The chairman began meeting with committee members and business groups to put together a coalition of core supporters. An early decision was made to endorse graduated corporate rates to attract small business groups. Other in-terests were likely to be included in the package: Barbara Kennelly (D–CT) had insurance; Jim Jones (D–OK), oil and gas; Robert Matsui (D–CA), tax-exempt bonds; and Ronnie Flippo (D–AL), commercial banks.[91]

Rostenkowski was defeated on two procedural rules for considering the bill. First, he wanted all changes to be revenue neutral, so that a congressman would have to pay for a proposed change. Second, he wanted the committee to work from the staff option rather than from existing law, so that members would be forced to put their tax expenditures back into the bill. Both of these devices were later successfully used by Packwood; however, Rostenkowski could not persuade his reluctant committee to comply. This made the early markup very difficult, and Rostenkowski began to lose control of the bill.

A major setback was the inclusion of an amendment by Ronnie Flippo (D–AL) to expand the bad-debt-reserve deduction for banks, a loophole the administrative staff wanted to scale back. Lobbyists cheered when the committee voted in favor of Flippo, and the chairman adjourned the markup indefinitely in disgust. Those sympathetic to the chairman's efforts contacted the press and suggested that they explore how much bank money finds its way into the campaign funds of Ways and Means Committee members.[92]

Rostenkowski resumed the markup a week later, determined to move the committee out of deadlock. One strategy was to form working groups to work on major substantive areas such as small business, agriculture, low-income housing, and tax-exempt bonds. Each group had four Democrats and two Republicans. Another was to organize a compromise to retain the deduction of state and local taxes; the chairman determined this to be a central political concern.

The drive to save the deduction of state and local taxes was spearheaded by the Coalition against Double Taxation, a group organized by David Rockefeller (formerly of Chase Manhattan Bank), James Robinson III (of American Express), and Laurence Tisch (of Loews Corporation). The group spent $1.5 million in one and a half years on a campaign run by a New York real estate developer, Lewis Rudin.[93] Governor Cuomo lobbied the committee extensively in support of the measure, asserting that, if Abe Lincoln were alive, he would oppose the repeal of state and local tax deductions.[94] Also, Democrat Thomas Downey worked to link state and local tax deductions to the protection of oil incentives to get both major deductions protected by the act.[95] The campaign paid off. Congressman Norman Lent (R–NY) received a letter warning: "Congressman, if you vote for the tax bill, may all your teeth fall out but one. And may you have a toothache for the rest of your life."[96]

Meanwhile, antireform business efforts began to take shape. The U.S. Chamber of Commerce's sixty-five-member board of directors voted unanimously at a closed meeting to oppose the Ways and Means bill. Richard Rahn explained that from the outset the Chamber only agreed to support tax reform if it enhanced capital formation, job creation, technological advancement, and competitiveness. Chairman Frank Morsani promised to do everything possible to kill the bill.[97]

The Chamber of Commerce and the National Association of Manufacturers lobbied vigorously against the Ways and Means version, convincing House

Republicans that the bill was unacceptable. On November 1, Vin Weber (R–MN) and Newt Gingrich (R–GA) with thirty-six other House Republicans wrote the president, urging him to reject the Democratic package. They accused Rostenkowski of selling out to special interests and losing the potential for true tax reform. Rostenkowski's decision to increase the personal exemption to $1,500 (instead of to the $2,000 favored by the president) demonstrated that the bill had lost its pro-family flavor. The Republicans cited the committee's treatment of depreciation, corporate tax rates, and capital gains as antigrowth.[98] The president publicly complained that his vision of reform was being "watered down" by the Ways and Means Committee. Rostenkowski complained in response, "It's amazing how much bipartisanship there is until you start voting."[99]

On December 3, the day that Rostenkowski delivered the Ways and Means bill, the House Republicans offered their own bill. The Republican measure preserved a 5 percent investment tax credit, indexed the depreciable basis of assets, scaled back the minimum tax, only increased corporate taxes by $105 billion over the next five years, and lost money. Senator Robert Dole (R–KS), Senator Strom Thurmond (R–SC), House Minority Leader Robert Michel (R–IL), House Minority Whip Trent Lott (R–MS), Representative Jack Kemp (R–NY), Representative John Duncan (R–TN), and Representative Vander Jagt (R–MI) met with the president to plead support for the Republican alternative.

Many within the administration expressed skepticism about the Ways and Means bill and were anxious about opposition from business allies on other issues. Don Regan and Trent Lott both urged the president to disassociate himself from Rostenkowski's product. Regan wanted to give the Republican alternative a chance, arguing that "true tax reform is imperative." Baker and Darman wanted the president to support the Ways and Means measure, since they had participated in its creation and wanted to keep the bill alive until it got to the Senate. This dissension between Reagan's top advisers paralyzed the president, who then refrained from endorsing the Ways and Means measure.[100]

The president's silence inspired a House Republican revolt, implemented in a move to defeat the rule vote allowing the bill to come to the House floor. The Democrats blamed the president for not having offered more support. Tip O'Neill (Speaker of the House) publicly wondered if Ronald Reagan had become a "lame duck" and warned that the rule would be considered again only if the president could deliver fifty Republican votes.[101]

When the rule was voted down, TRAC mobilized its supporters in a major grass roots campaign. A special action bulletin was sent to all of the members of TRAC, and each group or company was encouraged to send a similar document to its own members. This created a "barrage of pressure from home." TRAC organizers also contacted the press, complaining that the real problem with tax reform was not the president but rather Don Regan. One participant called Mrs. Reagan and urged her to intervene, arguing that Reagan's influence was threatening her husband's most important second-term initiative as well as his place in history.[102]

At this point Reagan was sufficiently shaken up to begin actively lobbying for the measure. On December 16 he met with 160 House Republicans and urged them to support the bill until it could be taken up by the Senate. The massive lobbying campaign paid off, and tax reform was passed in the House.

Action in the Senate

The phrase "the Senate will fix it up" is the moral equivalent of "I'll respect you in the morning." (Representative Bill Frenzel, R–MN)[103]

On the basis of ideology and interest, Senator Packwood (R–OR) was no tax reformer. As recently as February 1986 he had voiced a strong belief in the tax code for the allocation of social goods such as low-income housing. Known as "Mr. Packman," the Finance chair had received over $6 million in campaign contributions between 1981 and 1986.[104] Yet Packwood was compelled to give the measure more than passing attention. First, tax reform was a major initiative that had to be taken seriously. Second, Packwood also had to be careful not to alienate the president. On the left on certain key social issues, especially abortion, Packwood was "already out of synch with the administration."[105]

Democratic support in the Senate Finance Committee was also less than forthcoming. Ranking minority member Russell Long (D–LA) had many oil interests to protect. As chairman of the committee for many years, Long had developed many parts of the code now under attack. During a special retreat with the Finance Committee, Packwood found sixteen of the committee's nineteen members opposed to reform.

Packwood began his efforts with a patchwork strategy: the idea was to put together a bill by making enough deals. Obvious interests immediately emerged. Packwood, with senators George Mitchell (D–ME) and David Pryor (D–AR), was bound to consider timber interests. Oil and gas provisions generated concern among Dole, William Armstrong (R–CO), Steve Symms (R–ID), Long, David Boren (D–OK), and Lloyd Bentsen (D–TX). Senators John Heinz (R–PA), Armstrong, Symms, and William Roth (R–DE) worried about capital formation incentives. Dole, John Danforth (R–MO), Charles Grassley (R–IA), and Max Baucas (D–MT) asked that special attention be given farmers.

Senator Packwood also attempted to organize an industry coalition to back the measure. The original Finance proposal appealed to a segment of business very different from the core supporters of the House measure. The Chamber of Commerce was sympathetic because Packwood's initial measure had a better capital cost recovery system. The Basic Industries Coalition made a deal with Packwood: their support in exchange for a proposal which would allow companies to cash out accumulated investment tax credits at a rate of seventy cents on the dollar. Packwood was willing to negotiate, and the coalition joined reformers in the Senate. Packwood made a separate appeal to the National Federation of Independent Business, offering direct expensing of equipment up to an annual $50,000 in exchange for small business support. This direct expensing would have been one of the best small business capital-recovery systems in the world. The expensing provision was later discarded when senators representing heavy capital and investment pushed for changes in ACRS over direct expensing.[106]

Notably underrepresented were many of the business groups which had supported tax reform in prior stages. Packwood admitted that his plan set out to reverse the "favorable treatment" accorded wholesalers and retailers in the president's and Ways and Means' bills.[107] Rather, tax reformers should "pay for lower rates." For example, Senator Packwood's proposal extended the depreciation life for buildings to thirty years but speeded up the depreciation of machinery and equipment. This helped traditional manufacturing but hurt small business sectors such as retailing and wholesaling whose major assets were in buildings. Another provision repealed the installment sales rules which allowed the industry to delay taxation on the sale of items bought under the installment plan until the customers had paid in full.[108]

To raise revenue, Packwood suggested an entirely new tax constructed around denying deductions for federal excise taxes and tariffs. The Basic Industries Coalition testified in favor. But TRAC members hit the ceiling, some believing that Packwood was "deliberately out to get them."[109] The American Trucking Association mobilized representatives of the transportation, wholesale, retail, cigarette, and alcohol industries to fight the proposal in a group called the Coalition against Regressive Taxation. *Tax Notes* observed:

> Some of the tax revision's strongest supporters, most of whom were willing to back the House tax bill, are discouraged by the shape tax revision is starting to take in the Senate Finance Committee . . . [Packwood's] controversial proposal to disallow the deductibility of business excise taxes and tariffs is proving to be the issue that is driving away former proponents of tax reform. Disenchanted business groups are concerned that any benefits they may have reaped from lower corporate rates will be lost because of increased excise taxes, while consumer groups, who supported the House bill's tax reduction for the poor, contend that the excise tax proposal is highly regressive.[110]

One insider explained that Packwood hoped to use this alternative business coalition so that he wouldn't have to rely on TRAC. "Packwood did not like TRAC because he felt that TRAC was trying to run the show." chief aide Bill Diefenderfer held a meeting with this new group of business interests at the Phoenix Park Hotel shortly before the chairman's bill was released. He urged, "I want everyone to stick with us through the whole thing, and we will stick with you." [111]

Packwood encountered resistance from the banking community, which opposed his proposal to repeal the bad-debt-reserve deduction. Treasury had originally proposed repealing the deduction, concerned that banks would set up excessively large and unnecessary bad debt reserves for tax purposes. Rostenkowski set up a two-tiered system: banks with assets over $500 million would lose the deduction; smaller institutions would retain it. The American Bankers Association began a campaign to resist the proposal and ran advertisements in twenty-three newspapers, eighteen of which were in the home states of Finance Committee members. [112]

During markup Packwood began with timber and resource issues; he considered these easy, because of the many senators on the committee with large timber and oil constituencies. Bradley attempted to phase out percentage depletion allowances over a three-year period in keeping with the position of Ways and Means. Half of the percentage depletion benefits, according to Bradley, went to ninety thousand individuals. Also adopted from the House was a proposal to amortize intangible drilling costs over a twenty-six-month period. Finally, Bradley tried to repeal capital gains treatment for timber cut on federal land. None of these proposals drew sympathy from the committee; resource provisions were preserved intact. [113]

Next, a depreciation package was approved which would actually allow for *more* generous depreciation of equipment with the introduction of a new class of "productivity property." This category applied to manufacturing equipment but not to service sector machines, since equipment in the service sector was not productively used. Bradley criticized the proposal as "purely arbitrary. The whole service industry is treated worse than chicken coops, pig pens and jewelry." At this point John Heinz (R–PA) motioned to move rental tuxedos from the five-year to the three-year class of property, initiating a debate over the useful life of a tux. Darman admitted, when pushed, that his tux was seventeen years old; the amendment was ultimately rejected six to five. [114]

Packwood's patchwork strategy, however, failed to deliver the hoped-for committee allegiance to the markup legislation. Gradually the chairman lost votes on revenue-generating measures. For example, Armstrong was going to propose an amendment curbing the deduction for business entertainment. American Express lobbied heavily against this amendment and informed Bill Diefenderfer that the committee did not have the votes to go through with it. Packwood had to break the bad news to Armstrong, who responded angrily, "Is this for lobbyists or is this for us?" [115]

An early mistake was Packwood's initial failure to require that amendments be revenue-neutral. John Colvin, Senate Finance Committee chief counsel, explained: "It makes it easier to resolve these questions on the merits. It's better if we do one subject at a time." This decision later allowed the process to get out of control.[116]

Because the senator had attempted to construct business support from groups naturally hostile to reform, there was very little private sector lobbying in favor of the bill in the early days of the markup session. As one Senate Finance aide remarked, "Senator Packwood tried to get rewarded business groups to help keep the bill on track, but they just weren't there for him." Meanwhile the core group which had supported the bill in the House was thoroughly disillusioned with the Senate version.

Depressed about the state of the markup exercise, the Senate Finance staff urged Packwood to have a kind of group therapy session with the committee, beginning with the statement "I think we have a problem." The members responded that they didn't feel that they were getting any reform; to them, the entire exercise seemed futile.

On April 18, 1986, Senator Packwood adjourned the markup session indefinitely. There were essentially three options: to scrap the markup entirely, to construct a minimal reform package (revoke the investment tax credit and put the rates in the low 40 percentile), or to endorse radical reform. The now famous story is that Packwood and his chief aide Bill Diefenderfer went out for lunch and, over two pitchers of beer, calculated what it would take to get real tax reform. In a moment of daring, they decided to go the radical route: with low enough rates they could conquer the political constraints which had plagued them. When the low-rate option was first introduced, no one thought it would be adopted. Rather, as one Senate staff person put it, "since you are going to lose, you might as well lose by being holier than thou and say that you are trying to do the right thing."[117]

Packwood had for some time been intrigued by the idea of very low rates. During the Ways and Means markup, Packwood asked the Joint Tax Committee to develop a tax package using a top rate of 25 percent. During the Senate hearings, he had routinely asked industry representatives how much the rates would have to drop for them to relinquish their demands. At first Dave Brockway, chief of the Joint Tax Committee, thought that the order to explore much lower rates was a political ploy. The idea was "to stake out a position that was totally unrealistic, and then reject the reform proposals that were realistic. You can afford to be against it, if you are in favor of true reform." Later he concluded that Packwood had long been considering the radical plan.[118] The radical low-rate idea also had backing in the business community; for example, the Chamber of Commerce had been pushing for a 19 percent flat tax, which Steven Symms (R–ID) pitched to Packwood a few days before Packwood adjourned the markup session.

Packwood asked Brockway to go to work on a new radical tax proposal. Brockway had been hitherto relatively excluded from the process, as the Senate measure had been largely developed by John Conlin. Brockway spent the weekend putting together a package that drew on work done for Packwood in 1985 as well as the Bradley-Gephardt, the Kemp-Kasten, and the Ways and Means proposals. The very low rates immediately presented an equity problem: how to distribute the tax reduction over all income groups. For Brockway this was a moral as well as a practical issue; he was personally committed to eliminating tax shelters and removing horizontal inequities. He identified two items for mandatory inclusion: changes in the passive loss rules, and elimination of the capital gains differential. Packwood and the Finance staff decided to leave corporate changes unspecified for the time being. These measures would be the most bitterly fought, so it would be better to bring them up at the end, when the momentum for tax reform had increased.[119]

Packwood reconvened the Finance Committee and presented the new, revised version as "Brockway's plan," in part to distance himself from the radical measure and in part to give the proposal the credibility accorded to Joint Committee documents. The Finance Committee members were cautiously enchanted with the low-rates idea; Senator Malcolm Wallop (R–WY) remarked, "This is closer to real reform, maybe I can do this."

Senator Packwood now insisted that markup be based on this new proposal and demanded that alterations be revenue neutral. The Joint Tax Committee prepared a short summary of the new plan so that members could understand the broad outlines. The first proposal had been excessively elaborate.

> It was totally incomprehensible to a layman. The Senators didn't understand any of it. So that the only thing that you can do is, you have a constituent who has a bitch so you can argue about that. There was no overall policy role. Nobody was working to pull anything together because they didn't create it.

Senator Packwood also wanted to work from the new document "to make members prioritize their deductions and see what happens to the rate every time they add a deduction."[120]

Packwood put together a core group of bipartisan Finance senators to support him. To belong to the core group, a senator had to promise not to offer amendments on the Senate floor. The group was used to lobby other senators; every day new assignments were given. The core group's activities were also coordinated with TRAC's efforts: the senators would be briefed on the business group's activities and would often indicate which senators might be approachable.

Senators joined the core group for a variety of reasons. Bill Bradley was a natural reformer; Mitchell also had leaned toward reform for some time. Chafee was Packwood's best friend and stood behind him in his hour of need.

Moynihan supported reform as long as it retained the state and local tax deductions. Danforth offered his support in return for a concession worth about $8 billion. This was the retention of the completed contract method of accounting, which was important to his Defense constituents. Wallop liked the low rates and was willing to participate as long as oil and gas provisions were protected. Later, Durenberger announced that he belonged to the group, although his presence was somewhat baffling to the staff. Roth joined the group because he wanted to be included in the Joint Conference Committee, so that he might get the IRAs reinstated. Long was not part of the core group and refrained from articulating his position on reform until the end. But Senator Packwood kept Long informed about everything that happened in order to maintain goodwill.

A movement led by Bentsen and Dole to revoke the passive loss changes almost succeeded in scuttling the bill but lost by one vote. The real estate industry felt that Roth had "sold out, trading a chicken coop amendment for passive losses." A real estate lobbyist reported that, after the Senate Finance bill was marked up, Packwood refused to meet with representatives of that industry.[121]

The last item to be resolved was the petroleum industry's packet of issues. Senator Long arranged a caucus of oil industry lobbyists and concerned senators: Bentsen, Boren, Dole, and Wallop. The lobbyists pushed to have oil excluded from the passive loss provisions, arguing that it would undermine risk capital and consequently exploratory drilling. As defined, passive investors would include individuals who do full-time work in the industry: "geologists and engineers whose full time occupation is putting deals together, even though they aren't the 'operator of record.' " The senators felt that the lobbyists were exaggerating the negative consequences. But the industry prevailed, and the senators agreed to support the exemption of oil producers from the passive loss provisions.[122]

Upon completion of the gas and oil negotiations, Long finally endorsed the bill. The day before the final markup vote Long called many Democratic members, saying that this was the best bill they could produce and that Packwood needed to be strong with Rostenkowski. Packwood garnered other votes in a final "orgy of vote buying": each vote cost $50 to $100 million in tax expenditures. Besides the oil and gas concessions, Symms (R–ID) was given an amendment to exclude mining exploration and development costs from the minimum tax base. Heinz (R–PA) and Durenberger (R–MN) won a shorter depreciation period for residential rental real estate. These concessions made it possible for the committee to deliver a unanimous vote for tax reform, increasing the chance for success on the Senate floor.

At the end the low rates could no longer sustain the cashing in of investment tax credits, since the measure cost $3 billion. Diefenderfer called John Meaghar and offered $500 million: how should they use it? When Meaghar requested a transition rule for the steel industry, six major steel companies got a transition rule worth about $500 million. Some other members of the Basic Industries Coalition, such as mining representatives, were bitter. Liberal use of transition rules greatly greased the wheels of legislation in the final days. Cabbage Patch magnate, Xavier Roberts, received a tax break designed for a "taxpayer who incorporated on Sept. 7, 1978, which is engaged in the business of manufacturing dolls and accessories." [123]

After Senator Packwood offered his low-rate proposal, relations with the original business reform supporters greatly improved. William Ris went to work for Packwood to organize a private sector coalition, which met for the first time on May 13 and was entitled 15/27/33. [124] In order to belong to the coalition members had to refrain from supporting amendments which would increase rates. Packwood made the following statement to the coalition:

> We have a chance to make a difference for a generation in America if we can pass on the Senate floor the tax bill as it came out of the Finance Committee.
>
> To the extent that you can get everyone to resist amendments to increase the rates, I think we can accomplish that task. Every time an amendment comes up to raise the individual rate one percent to pay for something, or to raise the corporate rate one or two percent to pay for something, we must defeat that amendment. We can then go to conference with the House with the best bill for Americans—both individuals and businesses—that we have had in a decade, and maybe a generation.
>
> I'm sorry I can't be there—we desperately need your help. Thanks so much for coming on board to help in what is probably the most critical economic decision we can make for America in this Congress. [125]

The coalition behind reform greatly expanded with the rate reductions to include about seven hundred members. Mary McAuliffe was brought in from the Commerce Department to mobilize and coordinate private sector support. The 15/27/33 coalition at this point consisted of two kinds of groups: business associations and the do-gooders, or public-interest groups such as the League of Women Voters. Members were required to make a commitment: if they lobbied against the bill, they had to leave the group. Each group was to recruit seven people to join; finding participants at this point was easy, since "everyone wanted to be a part of it." McAuliffe held daily briefings on the progress of the committee and gave participants assignments to contact senators. Usually a do-gooder and a business representative would be sent together. In order to lobby effectively, staff would come to the briefings and educate participants about both sides of the argument. McAuliffe and the group kept a count on every major vote. The business participants helped out by trying to ascertain each senator's position. [126]

After the low-rate proposal passed, the reform effort took on aspects of a mass social movement for participants in both government and business. One staff person remarked: "When it came back to life it was an exciting time . . . There was this sense that this would really qualify for true reform, so people were real enthusiastic about it." A lobbyist agreed: "Tax reform was all consuming for many of us."

Packwood decided that a no-amendment strategy was needed for tax reform to survive the Senate floor. Packwood and Long wrote a bipartisan letter to their colleagues urging acceptance of the tax reform package as a whole.

> Each of us will receive enormous pressure from many interest groups to make concessions. The trade-off for many of these concessions would have to be increased rates. We ask you to keep an open mind and reserve your commitments until you have had an opportunity to review the committee's bill in its entirety.[127]

The strategy worked, and the bill passed the Senate on June 24, 1986. During the conference committee participants negotiated a trade-off between the two bills. The low rates from the Senate bill were exchanged for the corporate loophole provisions and base broadeners in the House bill.

Business Participation in the Alliance

> Tax Reform in 1986 was an oddball thing: it shifted the tax burden back onto business, but business was a core support for the '86 act.
> Senate Finance Committee staff

Contrary to the prevailing wisdom on the Tax Reform Act of 1986, private sector pressure groups were important allies in the legislative process. First, business groups played a fairly large role building support for the new order and laying the groundwork for the policy changes.

Second, business groups worked to build support for the legislation using the broadcast media and the press. TRAC staged a variety of events to try to influence public opinion. Just before the final vote, TRAC met with Rostenkowski and presented him with a sledgehammer "gavel." This gesture alluded to a session in which Rostenkowski had broken his gavel while calling the committee to order. TRAC's Lee Williams said that he hoped the gavel would help Rostenkowski "hammer out a fair and equitable tax reform bill."[128] T-shirts and balloon drops were other media props.

Third, business groups helped state actors negotiate the intricacies of the legislative process with an elaborate vote-counting operation and intense lobbying at key junctures. TRAC had a boiler room operation where vote counts were kept of members of Congress. These were tabulated according to a one–five range. One meant that the member was firmly on their side; five, that the member was firmly opposed. Members of Congress generally offer varying answers to where they stand on complex issues. Therefore, the group tried to develop top-quality contacts, individuals with personal ties to the member, in order to find out how the member really felt. Generally a member was approached by a variety of individuals. "If the member was wishy-washy, we would have to get in there and work him." Many TRAC member firms also had action networks that could match members of the association with congressional members. The NAW Washington Action Network polled all forty-five thousand member companies to determine who the members knew and how well they knew them.

Finally, business allies worked to discipline legislators. In the tax reform battle business allies spent much of their time in the final days before passage urging business groups and congressmen to refrain from particularistic demands. At several points in 1986 TRAC staged an all-out mobilization effort. Getting the bill reported out by the Committee on Ways and Means was one such effort. When Tip O'Neill requested fifty Republican votes for the bill, TRAC identified the fifty Republicans most likely to support reform, "on the basis that 'Sam' wants this, so we will give him this or we won't screw him on that."

The role of business in gaining passage of the tax reform act has often been understated. Yet, as one participant explained, "For most of the period of tax reform there was no other support than that element of the business community." [129]

Conclusion

The peculiarities surrounding passage of the tax reform act can be attributed to a fundamental change in the perception of economic growth and investment. The legislation greatly reduced individual and corporate rates; simultaneously, it repealed many loopholes, the selective tax incentives used to further social and economic goals. There was also a significant redistribution of the tax burden, shifts from the individual to the corporate sphere, and among industrial sectors. The distribution of the corporate tax burden in 1986 reflected entirely different assumptions about how to invest in our economic future.

Contrary to the often-heard assertions of business exclusion, I argue that private sector interests were critical to this process. Business groups came to view their interests in terms of the new investment strategy. Jack Albertine argued, "The rage in the late 1970s had been the problem of inflation and effective depreciation reform. All bought on to the depreciation reform idea. Yet after the passage of the Economic Recovery Act of 1981, many business groups discovered that their gains were small in comparison to those of their business allies." (see table 7.1).

Table 7.1. Divisions in State and Society over Tax Options

Goals	Business	State	Policy
Equity neutral investment	High tech, small business, service	House Democrats, Reagan supply-siders	Repeal ITC, reduce ACRS, lower rates
Protect investment incentives	Manufacturing	House GOP, originally Senate Finance	Limited individual tax reform, no corporate
Reduce deficits	Finance	The Fed	Raise taxes, not reform them

The primary beneficiaries of the new order worked to make postindustrial taxation a reality. The predecessor to the Tax Reform Action Coalition began in 1982 to support a more neutral investment strategy. Participants sought to convert others in the business community, lobbied vigorously throughout the legislative process, and worked to limit their own particularistic demands to create the conditions for reform. Once again a new growth order was achieved through a state-society partnership.

Appendix 7.1

Fifty Firms Receiving Refunds or Paying Net Zero Tax, 1981–84
(thousands of dollars)

Company	Profit	1981–84 Refund	Profit Share
Boeing	$2,099.0	$285.0	13.6%
Dow Chemical	972.0	180.0	18.5
IT&T	815.0	177.7	21.8
Tenneco	3,401.0	166.0	4.9
PepsiCo	1,798.7	135.8	7.6
Santa Fe Southern Pacific	2,309.0	133.4	5.8
General Dynamics	1,579.5	103.8	6.6
General Electric	9,577.0	98.0	1.0
Transamerica	748.6	93.6	12.5
Texaco	1,819.0	68.0	3.7
Ashland Oil	336.1	62.0	18.5
E. F. Hutton Group	372.5	59.6	16.0
Weyerhaeuser	929.2	59.1	6.4
Georgia-Pacific	783.0	59.0	7.5
IC Industries	534.7	55.4	10.4
Northrup	416.8	46.4	11.1
First Executive	444.2	44.2	10.0
International Minerals	371.6	43.7	11.8
Mitchell Energy & Dev.	458.7	41.1	9.0
E. I. du Pont de Nemours	4,075.0	40.0	1.0
Mellon Bank	544.7	32.8	6.0
International Paper	1,136.3	32.6	2.9
Ohio Edison	1,524.4	31.8	2.1
Scott Paper	594.6	30.5	5.1
Philadelphia Electric	1,892.5	30.3	1.6
Panhandle Eastern	1,220.7	28.8	2.4
Union Carbide	892.0	26.0	2.9
Piedmont Aviation	169.0	25.4	15.0
Tesoro Petroleum	124.3	22.5	18.1
Harris	307.6	19.5	6.3
Allied	693.0	17.0	2.5
Columbia Gas	1,147.1	15.9	1.4
Northern Indiana Public	792.5	14.6	1.8
Arizona Public Service	1,278.4	14.1	1.1
Singer	194.2	11.6	6.0
Sun Chemical	103.2	10.4	10.1
Greyhound	419.9	10.4	2.5
Centex	264.4	10.2	3.9
Pennsylvania Power & Light	1,362.9	10.0	0.7
Xerox	1,122.7	9.2	0.8
Southwest Airlines	213.0	8.1	3.8
Comerica	135.3	7.1	5.3
Dun & Bradstreet	967.0	6.7	0.7

Company	Profit	1981–84 Refund	Profit Share
Ogden	251.5	5.6	2.2
Jim Walter	361.7	4.1	1.1
International Multifoods	43.9	3.2	7.3
Burlington Northern	2,799.2	1.1	0.0
Tyson Foods	69.1	1.0	1.4
Grumman	653.4	0.0	0.0
Lockheed	1,670.9	0.0	0.0

Source: Timothy Clark, "Big Profits and Tax Refunds Can Go Together," *National Journal,* September 7, 1985, p. 1994.

Appendix 7.2

Membership of Steering Committee, Tax Reform Action
Coalition (TRAC)

American Business Conference
American Electronics Association
American Frozen Food Institute
American Home Products Corporation
American Retail Federation
American Textile Manufacturers Institute
American Trucking Associations
Amway Corporation
Apple Computer, Inc.
Beneficial Management Corporation of America
BP America, Inc.
Bristol-Myers Company
Citizens for a Sound Economy
Computer & Business Equipment Manufacturers Association
Consolidated Freightways Incorporated
Dairy and Food Industries Supply Association, Inc.
Digital Equipment Corporation
Edison Electric Institute
Eli Lilly & Company
Emerson Electric Company
E-Systems, Inc.
Food Marketing Institute
Foodservice and Lodging Institute
General Motors Corporation
Georgia-Pacific Corporation
Greyhound Corporation
Grocery Manufacturers of America
Hershey Foods Corporation
Hospital Corporation of America
Household International
IBM Corporation
International Banana Association
International Mass Retailing Association
Levi Strauss & Company
McDonald's Corporation
McGraw-Hill, Inc.
Merrill Lynch & Company
National Association of Chain Drug Stores
National Association of Manufacturers
National Association of Tobacco Distributors
National Association of Wholesaler-Distributors
National Federation of Independent Business
National Pasta Association
National Restaurant Association
National Retail Merchants Association

National Soft Drink Association
Nestle Enterprises, Inc.
PepsiCo
Pharmaceutical Manufacturers Association
Philip Morris Incorporated
Pillsbury Company
Primerica Corporation
Procter & Gamble Manufacturing Company
Quaker Oats Company
Ralston Purina Company
RJR Nabisco, Inc.
Roadway Services, Inc.
Sara Lee Corporation
3M
U.S. Tobacco
Wine & Spirits Wholesalers of America
Winn-Dixie Stores Incorporated

Conclusion: Implications for State, Society, and Policy Outcomes

The corporate tax cases detail episodes in a serial monogamy between the state and business beneficiaries of the regime. This is a story of divorce from capital-intensive manufacturing and flirtation with postindustrial sectors. New directions in corporate taxation have been the offspring of these successive liaisons.

Why did this fiscal infidelity come about? I have argued that changes in corporate taxation reflect successive investment subsystems, or public/private coalitions organized around growth strategies. In chapter 1, I posit multiple paths to economic development and illustrate how corporate taxation has alternately followed various paths. For example, Kennedy's tax initiatives were constructed around a very different investment strategy from that guiding the Tax Reform Act of 1986. Chapter 2 investigates the political mechanism by which all this occurred: state actors building coalitions with business allies around a chosen strategy. The present chapter concludes with a discussion of the implications of the model for business, government, and the course of corporate taxation.

Implications for Business

Investment subsystems describe a world where business interests are less fixed and more susceptible to state intermediation than we often think of them; nonetheless, corporate influence is extremely influential. This more fluid reading of business interests differs from the standard view, which sees those interests as a product of the economic structure. Where labor interests are thought to be partially defined by ideas, social networks, and identity, business groups derive their interests solely from material circumstances. Offe writes that the organization of labor and the organization of business have two separate logics:

> Differences in the position of a group in the class structure . . . not only lead to differences in power that the organizations can acquire, but also lead to differences in the associational practices, or logics of collective action, by which organizations of capital and labor try to improve their respective position vis-à-vis each other.[1]

Yet there are good theoretical reasons for thinking that business interests are open to interpretation, and thus amenable to molding by ideas.[2] Plotke points out that the factional capitalist class can assume several objective positions; therefore, businessmen identify their interests through discourse.[3] Quinn suggests that preferences for macroeconomic growth strategies reflect ideology and image politics.[4] Since the economy is constantly in flux, interests change over time. There may be a lag time between socioeconomic change and the recognition of new interests. A rejection of economic determinism also enhances the power of ideas. Multiple investment strategies compete for hegemony, and the power of these ideas is a factor in the contest.

The history of corporate tax policy illustrates how ideas are transforming, bringing business to construct interests differently over time. For example, two ideas prompted business groups to redefine their interests and support tax reform in 1986. McIntyre's study of effective tax rates reframed the debate as an equity issue. New arguments about the competitiveness of U.S. industry changed elite and public perceptions of growth. One lobbyist reflected:

> Every once in a while an insight comes along which can be transforming. In 1981 everyone in the business community was supportive of accelerated cost recovery. In retrospect it was heavily oriented toward capital-intensive industries. The capital-intensive guys realized this, but the bulk of the business community never thought of it that way. The general notion prior to 1982 was that the corporate tax structure uniformly affected business. Some time in 1982 the notion of disparities between different business sectors began to creep into the debate.[5]

Noneconomic, social factors may influence the adoption of ideas. Sometimes an idea seems to take on a life of its own, creating a business issue attention cycle dynamic. In the case of taxes, successive ideas gained popular acceptance far beyond their initial set of supporters and beyond those who benefited from them the most. Business groups work to convince other business groups (and key government leaders) to move in their desired direction. One TRAC steering committee member explained, "Some coalition members opposed to tax reform concluded that the movement had reached a point where they couldn't stop it, so they decided to jump on the bandwagon."[6] Robert Ragland (NAM assistant vice-president for taxation) explained the dilemma: "The business community is the one paying the bill here—we represent 85 percent of the nation's manufacturers, and some of them are going to be hurt . . . But the matter went to our tax committee in May and was approved by a near-unanimous vote, 44–3."[7]

Small group dynamics, relationships among the various actors, and personal attachments also affect the process. Some whose interests were ultimately hurt by the legislation supported it "because we had been involved with it for such a long time, and just couldn't pull out." Commitment to the president kept many business groups neutral or favorable to TEFRA despite its unfavorable impact on their narrowly defined interests.

The coalition strategy suggests that the state actively organizes business interests. The concept of emerging growth strategies provides us with a way to reconcile the changes in the policy positions of state technicians and the expressed interests of business groups. The same economic transformations or crises which worsen the fit of ideas to objective reality make a parallel assault on economic interests. This is not to say there is a one-to-one relationship between economic development and either policy change or interest redefinition. Rather, by focusing on sectoral change and possible emerging orders, we see that business groups and experts who support a new strategy are natural allies. Ideas and interests are both working definitions of reality that change as new growth regimes emerge.

Thus, business interests are constrained in certain predictable ways. Often, no clear growth mandate exists: business sectors are divided over the best vehicle for economic development. State actors influence, organize, and mobilize their private sector allies.

Yet in asserting the limits of corporate influence we can go too far in the other direction. Although what it takes to grow is disputable, economic growth remains central to state and society. Lindblom has argued that shared economic interests provide a basis for the structural relationship between the state and the capitalist class in an industrial democracy, the "privileged position of business."[8] I argue here that at the individual level of analysis, shared political interests also link factions of the state and dominant groups in the private economy. The struggle over corporate growth in America has been led by industrialists and bankers. Even when manipulated by politicians for political ends, the business presence is a force to be dealt with.

The limits on business influence in this story partially reflect the setting. As during the Eighteenth Brumaire, the tax cases present a point of transformation when interests are less clear than usual: this heightens the sense of state autonomy.[9] When business is unified and clear about its interests, it usually gets what it wants.[10] The focus here is on the broad outlines of corporate taxation; however, a nitty-gritty view reveals a system of deals and politics. Many substantive details of the tax legislation were enacted to satisfy private interests. The revolving door between state and the corporate world also gives weight to corporate actors. Rust-belt congressmen, oil senators, and Atari Democrats inhabit the hallowed halls of Congress.

Increasing use of the public/private coalition has strengthened business influence and capacity. Single-sector trade associations seem better organized, have more resources, and devote more of those resources to policy-making. Many of the association spokespeople interviewed reported that their government relations departments have increased in size dramatically. Trade association staff often come from congressional committees and have an intricate knowledge of policy issues. Government officials recognize trade associations as the legitimate representatives of their sectoral interests.

The rise of business participation in American politics during the 1970s has been widely noted. Yet most other analysts view business mobilization as a cause rather than an effect of the coalition strategy. Generally it is argued that the rise of business participation was a spontaneous action by the corporate community to counter the reformist legislation of the period.[11] This heightened politicization of business in turn motivated presidents to systematize their ties with business.[12] Some have noted that bureaucrats recognized the potential of private sector allies. Walker argues that many not-for-profit groups were formed in response to the urging of federal officials who desired regular contact clientele agency administrators.[13] Pika recognizes that the change in the national policy agenda influenced the presidential mobilization of private interests. But this was initiated by business itself. The new policies inspired greater business lobbying; presidents were forced to respond to the groups. Pika denies that JFK and LBJ saw business as a resource, and argues that they did little to orchestrate contacts in pursuit of administration goals.[14] Generally, then, presidential mobilization of business interests has been viewed as a defensive posture.

A related argument is that the decline in traditional channels of authority motivated presidents to cultivate interest groups in order to secure the allegiance of key congressmen and senators. Thus, congressional reforms and the decline of party discipline precipitated coalition building.[15]

The case studies suggest a somewhat different scenario: the process happened the other way around. Presidents began using the coalition strategy before the burst of liberal legislation and antibusiness sentiment, in order to build electoral and policy support. The strategy grew out of the dictates of the new regime of governmental activism, and the inability of presidents to win fellow government players over to this activism.

Rather than a response to the decline of congressional and party leaders, presidential mobilization of business was a strategy for side-stepping the autonomous authority of other political figures. Special interests had already come to play an important role in the 1960s, before the post-1968 party reforms and the post-Watergate congressional reforms. The Ways and Means Committee was celebrated for its norms of caution and consensus. Yet the Kennedy and Johnson administrations perceived Wilbur Mills and his committee as a stronghold of conservatism and an obstacle to the presidential agenda. Both administrations mobilized business interests to discipline a reluctant Mills and his fellow conservative legislators. Thus, executive branch officials encouraged the expansion of interest groups as political organizations even before structural changes in Congress took place. This process was not a response to the structural changes in Congress but rather a mechanism for emasculating Congress. The further decline of congressional power in turn reinforced the executive branch tendency to use external interests.

Mobilization by the state has also accelerated the business community's own use of ad hoc coalitions to pursue policy objectives. Trade associations worked together to establish a cross-class consensus on ERTA before the legislative process had even begun. The Basic Industries Coalition grew out of the group which organized to prevent the repeal of safe harbor leasing. The Coalition to Reduce High Effective Tax Rates formed to prevent the surtax from being chosen as a vehicle for increasing taxes.

Technological changes in political pressure techniques, especially changes in information processing, have enhanced the political capacity of business. Many trade associations now have computerized listings of their members' affiliations with legislators. During key votes, associations send out mailograms specifying action strategies for their members. Associations publish ratings of congressmen and use these to distribute PAC money.

Increasing use of the public/private coalition seems to have altered the balance of power among groups in the business community. The change in lobbying techniques has given a competitive advantage to labor-intensive sectors with broad-based constituencies, such as small business and high technology. Channels of influence have become more pluralistic as groups which had little visibility in the 1960s emerged as powerful lobby forces by the 1980s. In the 1960s small business associations, apart from the Chamber of Commerce, were thought to have limited power and parochial policy interests. By the 1980s the National Federation of Independent Business, the National Association of Wholesaler-Distributors, and the American Business Conference were being included with the National Association of Manufacturers and the Business Roundtable when Washington observers discussed important lobbying trade associations.

The development of mass mobilization political strategies has enhanced the power of sectors with a large and diverse membership conducive to grass roots efforts. One trade association representative explained that capital-intensive manufacturing has suffered from the lack of a large clientele and must rely instead on the older method of hiring well-paid Washington lobbyists. Technological political developments seem to shift political power among sectors just as technological innovation leads to a change in the hierarchy of economic power.

Implications for Government

The use of the public/private coalition has also affected the institutional capacity of the state. Private sector groups have begun to take on state functions: drafting legislation, acting as legislative liaison, and generating legitimation or at least the appearance of it.

In the 1960s business groups participated in proposal development through advisory boards and private forums such as the Business Council and the Chamber of Commerce. By the 1980s trade association representatives were drafting the sections of the bills which affected their industries. For example, oil lobbyists joined congressional staff in drafting the oil provisions in Conable-Hance II, which became ERTA. Business support can be used as a mechanism for legitimation: a unified business community demonstrates widespread support for the political agenda. Industrial support works as a legitimation mechanism when the multisector political groups appear to come spontaneously from business itself.

The importance of business in the policy process is also demonstrated by the trade associations' active role in securing legislation. Business lobbying campaigns to pass specific provisions are an integral and familiar part of politics. Yet, with the decline of party discipline, trade associations have transcended their traditional role and have increasingly acted as liaisons between party leaders and members: business concessions are the medium of exchange. This was most dramatic in 1981, when partisan conflict was at its height. Incremental concessions to industry groups were made by both sides in order to swing important blocks of congressmen. Thus, changes in oil and estate taxes were used by both sides to appeal to southern Democrats. Safe harbor leasing developed as a mechanism to secure support from rust-belt congressmen.

Just as an artificial limb becomes almost a part of the living organism, interest groups as an institution have become almost a part of the state apparatus. As private groups take on more state tasks it may become increasingly difficult for normal channels to function without them.

If the coalition model best explains the tax policy process, the debate over state autonomy may be the wrong way to approach the relationship between state and society. The concept of state autonomy misrepresents the complex reality that emerges from the case studies in three ways. First, the autonomy debate fails to capture the mutuality of interests. It suggests an unfortunate polarization: action must either be state-directed or a response to special interests. Yet the case studies demonstrate that a third alternative lies outside the logic of capture and insulation.

Second, the autonomy debate shifts attention away from the reciprocity of influence. Either the state mobilizes business interests, or business defines state policy. In fact the tax case suggests that the two events occur simultaneously. State actors are catalysts in mobilizing interests and coalitions between groups. But business groups also help politicians define their own interests. Actors on both sides struggle to construct the public agenda.

Finally, the notion of "autonomy" fails to capture the blurring of the boundaries between public and private. Interaction between public and private professionals has become extremely important in the definition and formulation of policy. Private sector groups have assumed many policy-making functions. This tendency is reinforced by the staffing patterns of public and private institutions. Many private trade associations employ individuals who have had experience on "the Hill." The relationship appears symbiotic and enmeshed, a challenge to the best family therapist. The boundaries surrounding coalitions may come to replace in importance the boundaries between the state and civil society.

Corporate Taxation and Investment Subsystems

Investment subsystems have contributed to the peculiar development of U.S. corporate taxation. The coalition strategy has required expensive concessions to private partners: the long-term decline of the tax burden reflects this high cost. But the lack of consensus among business groups makes it very hard to get enduring political compromise, or a set of tax preferences with widespread enduring political support. This contributes to the desultory nature of corporate taxation: the inconsistency of tax initiatives reflects contradictory business pulls. Outcomes become to a large extent dependent on the particular political coalitions put together by policy entrepreneurs. Inconsistent corporate taxation is the policy manifestation of fragmented institutional structures in state and society.

What predictions can we make about the policy future? Historical extrapolation permits two somewhat contradictory predictions. The first prediction is that we are likely to continue to get major (and inconsistent) tax acts every few years. The unpredictable, contingent nature of the making of tax policy does not bode well for future efforts. The stop-go nature of corporate taxation has been due largely to divergent business interests and contradictory macroeconomic requisites. The recent tax reform benefited one segment of business; already other groups are clamoring to have the investment incentives and the differential treatment of capital gains reinstated. As Charls Walker warned, "This is not the last chapter in tax reform." [16]

During the 1980s the course of corporate taxation meandered through many meadows. No consensus emerged to replace the Keynesian consensus which loosely regulated economic policy throughout much of the postwar period. Yet we are unlikely to see a stable consensus within the business community until a new general growth strategy has been definitively established. The 1986 Tax Reform Act represents the most significant deviation from the earlier status quo. There is no guarantee, however, that the current position represents a new plateau in economic policy. We are in transition to a new order, but what that order will be remains to be seen. [17]

The second prediction is more sanguine. Under the new conditions of fiscal austerity and declining faith in government economic intervention, political leaders will continue to search for mechanisms to reduce the postwar dependence on sectoral interests. Economic prosperity permitted the costly coalition strategy. Economic decline and the budget deficit have made the coalition strategy politically more difficult to afford. Tax acts are now required to be revenue-neutral; this has instilled a new zero-sum dynamic into the process. The desire to avoid leakage to special interests prompted a new bipartisanship during the Reagan years, achieved largely by secret meetings between party leaders in forums far removed from the normal political process. Will this new bipartisan effort replace the coalition strategy? Will the politics of the Tax Reform Act of 1986 become the new paradigm in economic policy-making? Despite the initial problems of the Bush administration in achieving similar bipartisan unity, political leaders on both sides may continue to try to resolve their disputes away from private interests. The positive side of this type of secret negotiation is that more consistent, rational policy-making may be possible. The negative side is that the policy process retreats further from the legitimate channels of government.

Notes

Introduction

1. This statement is not inconsistent with Stein's conception of a series of fiscal revolutions. Herbert Stein, *Presidential Economics* (New York: Simon & Schuster, 1984).

2. Robert Collins, *The Business Response to Keynes* (New York: Columbia University Press, 1981).

3. Martin Feldstein, "Fiscal Policy for the 1980s," in Charls Walker and Mark Bloomfield, eds., *New Directions in Federal Tax Policy for the 1980s* (Cambridge, MA: Ballinger, 1983), pp. 23–34. Norman Ture and B. Kenneth Sanden, *The Effects of Tax Policy on Capital Formation* (New York: Financial Executives Research Foundation, 1977). Stein, *Presidential Economics*.

4. Ironically, the ultimate embodiment of the hyper-accumulation strategy rejoined accumulation and consumption. The Economic Recovery Tax Act of 1981 combined huge rate cuts with extensive investment incentives.

5. Stephen Skowronek, "Presidential Leadership in Political Time," in Michael Nelson, ed., *The Presidency and the Political System* (Washington, DC: Congressional Quarterly Press, 1984), pp. 87–132.

6. Stephen Weatherford, "Macroeconomic Policy Making beyond the Electoral Constraint," in George C. Edwards III et al., eds., *The Presidency and Public Policy Making* (Pittsburgh: University of Pittsburgh Press, 1985). William Keech, "Elections and Macroeconomic Policy," in James Pfiffner, ed., *The President and Economic Policy* (Philadelphia: Institute for the Study of Human Issues, 1986).

7. A point also made by Kim McQuaid, *Presidential Power and Big Business* (New York: Morrow, 1982).

8. Herbert Stein, *The Fiscal Revolution in America* (Chicago: University of Chicago Press, 1969).

9. Stephen Weatherford, "The President and the Political Business Cycle," in James Pfiffner, ed., *The President and Economic Policy* (Philadelphia: Institute for the Study of Human Issues, 1986), pp. 36–59.

10. Nicos Poulantzas, *Political Power and Social Classes*, trans. Timothy O'Hagan (London: Verso, 1978).

11. Jurgen Habermas, *Legitimation Crisis*, trans. Thomas McCarthy (Boston: Beacon Press, 1973).

12. James O'Connor, *The Fiscal Crisis of the State* (New York: St. Martin's Press, 1973).

13. Ronald King, "From Redistributive to Hegemonic Logic: The Transformation of American Tax Politics, 1894–1963," *Politics and Society* 12, no. 1 (1983): 46–47.

14. Thomas Reese, *The Politics of Taxation* (Westport, CT: Quorum Books, 1980).

15. John Witte, *The Politics and Development of the Federal Income Tax* (Madison: University of Wisconsin Press, 1985).

16. Theodore Lowi, "American Business, Public Policy, Case Studies, and Public Theory," *World Politics* 16 (July 1964): 677–715.

Chapter 1

1. "Federal Administration Budget Receipts by Major Source," *Statistical Abstract of the United States* (Washington, DC: U.S. Government Printing Office, 1966), table 539, p. 391; "Federal Budget Receipts by Major Source: 1960 to 1984," *Statistical Abstract of the United States* (Washington, DC: U.S. Government Printing Office, 1985), table 488, p. 307.

2. "Federal Administration Budget Receipts by Major Source," *Statistical Abstract of the United States* (Washington, DC: U.S. Government Printing Office, 1966), table 539, p. 391; "Federal Budget Receipts by Major Source," *Statistical Abstract of the United States* (Washington, DC: U.S. Government Printing Office, 1983), table 503, p. 318.

3. Pechman calculates that, even under the most progressive assumptions, effective tax rates in 1980 went from about 20 percent for those with the lowest incomes to 27 percent for those with the highest. Joseph Pechman, *Who Paid the Taxes, 1966–1985?* (Washington, DC: Brookings Institution, 1985), p. 35.

The Income Tax and Net Adjusted Family Income, 1966

Before-Tax Income Groups	Before Tax	After Tax	Mean Income before Tax	Effective Tax Rate
Top 1%	9.2%	8.3%	$92,425	18.0%
Next 4%	11.7	11.5	29,340	10.6
Rest of top quintile	25.8	25.6	17,257	9.8
Fourth quintile	23.2	23.4	11,638	8.3
Third quintile	16.1	16.4	8,076	7.2
Second quintile	10.0	10.5	5,016	5.1
Lowest quintile	4.0	4.3	2,006	2.5

Source: Richard Goode, *The Individual Income Tax*, rev. ed. (Washington, DC: Brookings Institution, 1976), p. 250.

4. Benjamin Page, *Who Gets What from Government?* (Berkeley: University of California Press, 1983), p. 35.

5. *Revenue Statistics of OECD Countries 1965–1980* (Paris: OECD, 1981).

6. Ibid; note the OECD figure for the U.S. differs slightly from Pechman's figure in note 3.

7. Sven Steinmo, "Political Institutions and Tax Policy in the United States, Sweden, and Britain," *World Politics* 41, no. 4 (July 1989): 510.

8. Michael Luger, "Federal Tax Incentives as Industrial and Urban Policy," in William Tabb and Larry Sawers, eds., *Sunbelt-Frostbelt: Urban Development and Regional Restructuring* (New York: Oxford University Press, 1984), pp. 204–5.

9. Alan Feld, *Tax Policy and Corporate Concentration* (Lexington, MA: Lexington Books, 1982).

10. Michael Luger, "Tax Incentives and Tax Inequities," *Journal of Contemporary Studies*, Spring 1982, pp. 36–37.

11. Tax Analysts, *Effective Corporate Tax Rates in 1980,* a special supplement to *Tax Notes* (Arlington, VA, 1981); Tax Analysts, *Effective Corporate Tax Rates in 1981,* a special supplement to *Tax Notes* (Arlington, VA: 1982), p. 639.

It should be mentioned that there are several problems with calculating effective tax rates. First, until recently the SEC did not require corporations to state domestic and foreign income separately on the 10-K forms. Therefore, if one were to try to divide total world income by U.S. taxes paid, one would have a grossly underestimated effective tax rate. *Tax Notes* petitioned the SEC to change this practice, which it recently did. However, for this reason one cannot calculate domestic effective tax rates before the late 1970s. Tax Analysts, 1982, p. 568.

Second, inflation poses a problem for calculating effective tax rates. Income is generally reported in current dollars whereas costs are often allocated on the basis of prior-year expenses and therefore are stated in previous-year dollars. This means that income tends to be overstated, again inflating the effective tax rates. Victor Bernard, "Inflation and the Distribution of the Corporate Income Tax Burden," working paper (Ann Arbor: University of Michigan, 1984).

Finally, offsetting this tendency to overstate income is the understating of income caused by deferred taxes. Companies count deferred income taxes as liabilities; however, very often these taxes will never be paid. For example, although companies use accelerated depreciation in writing off capital assets, they calculate these write-offs as straight-line depreciation on their balance sheets. They are thus able to defer more tax than is reflected. As long as companies keep acquiring new assets, they keep deferring taxes. Therefore, their incomes and net worth are greatly understated. Dennis Beresford of the Ernst and Whinney Accounting firm found that 26 of the 250 largest industrial companies in the United States had deferred taxes that valued more than 20 percent of their stockholders' equity. In 1971 such companies' deferred taxes were only about 10 percent of equity. Tax Analysts, 1982, pp. 15–16.

12. GNP figures for 1960–79 based on Council of Economic Advisers, "Gross National Product by Industry, 1947–81," table B-10, *Economic Report of the President* (Washington, DC: U.S. Government Printing Office, 1983), p. 174; GNP figures for 1981 and 1982 based on U.S. Bureau of the Census, "Gross National Product—Summary: 1929 to 1984," *Statistical Abstract of the United States* (Washington, DC: U.S. Government Printing Office, 1986), table 718, p. 431. Revenue estimates based on Council of Economic Advisers, "Federal Receipts by Source and Outlays by Function: 1970 to 1985," *Statistical Abstract of the United States* (1986) table 493, p. 306; and *Statistical Abstract of the United States* (Washington, DC: U.S. Government Printing Office, 1972), table 61, p. 386.

13. Joint Committee on Taxation, *General Explanation of the Economic Recovery Tax Act of 1981* (Washington, DC: U.S. Government Printing Office, 1981), p. 380.

14. Joint Committee on Taxation, *General Explanation of the Revenue Provisions of the Tax Equity and Fiscal Responsibility Act of 1982* (Washington, DC: U.S. Government Printing Office, 1982), p. 455.

15. Interview.

16. "Federal Receipts by Source and Outlays by Function: 1970 to 1987," *Statistical Abstract of the United States* (Washington, DC: U.S. Government Printing Office, 1988), table 471, p. 292.

17. David Rosenbaum, "Senate, 74–23, Votes Tax Bill; Widest Revisions in 40 Years Cut Rates, Curb Deductions," *New York Times,* September 28, 1986, pp. 1, 34.

18. Nicos Poulantzas, *Political Power and Social Classes,* trans. Timothy O'Hagan (London: Verso, 1978). Adam Przeworski and Michael Wallerstein, "Democratic Capitalism at the Crossroads," *Democracy,* July 1982. Roger Benjamin and Stephen Elkin, *The Democratic State* (Lawrence: University Press of Kansas, 1985).

19. Ronald King, "From Redistributive to Hegemonic Logic," 46–47.

20. James O'Connor, *The Fiscal Crisis of the State* (New York: St. Martin's Press, 1973).

21. The motivation for the regime of accumulation and the structural problems which lead to a new regime are related to maintaining the demand necessary for continued accumulation. Thus, the regime of accumulation must address the conditions of both production and reproduction of wage labor. Alain Lipietz, *Mirages and Miracles* (New York: Verso, 1987), p. 14.

22. Bob Jessop, "Conservative Regimes and the Transition to Post-Fordism: The Cases of Great Britain and West Germany," paper delivered at the Conference on the State, Copenhagen.

23. Michel Aglietta, *A Theory of Capitalist Regulation* (New York: Verso, 1987), pp. 71–93. See also Dennis Quinn, "The End of the End of Ideology: The Reemergence of Ideology in Economic Policy," paper presented at the annual meeting of the American Political Science Association, Atlanta, GA, 1989.

24. These procedures, rules, laws, and institutions are called modes of regulation. Aglietta, *A Theory of Capitalist Regulation,* pp. 12–14.

25. Jessop suggests that elites in society reach agreement on an "accumulation strategy" which unites factions of capital around a "growth model." The accumulation strategy is sold to the general public as a "hegemonic project," or an ideological package presenting this model of growth as a policy for the public good. Jessop, *Capitalist State.*

26. Lipietz, *Mirages and Miracles,* p. 48.

27. Fordism is charactertized by mass production and mass consumption.

28. John Bellamy Foster, "The Fetish of Fordism," *Monthly Review,* March 1988.

29. Karel Williams, Tony Cutler, John Williams, and Colin Haslam, "The End of Mass Production?" *Economy and Society* 16, no. 3 (August 1987): 404–39.

30. See, for example, Samuel Bowles, David Gordon, and Thomas Weisskopf, *Beyond the Waste Land* (Garden City, NY: Anchor Press, 1983); David Calleo, *The Imperious Economy* (Cambridge, MA: Harvard University Press, 1982); Charles Maier, "The Politics of Productivity: Foundations of American International Economic Policy after World War II," in Peter Katzenstein, ed., *Between Power and Plenty* (Madison: University of Wisconsin Press, 1978); Mike Davis, *Prisoners of the American Dream* (New York: Verso, 1986); Bennett Harrison and Barry Bluestone, *The Great U-Turn* (New York: Basic Books, 1988); Alan Wolfe, *America's Impasse* (Boston: South End Press, 1981); Kenneth Dolbeare, *Democracy at Risk: The Politics of Economic Renewal* (Chatham, NJ: Chatham House, 1986); Edward Greenberg, *Capitalism and the American Political Ideal* (Armonk, NY: M. E. Sharpe, 1985).

31. Michael Piore and Charles Sabel, *The Second Industrial Divide* (New York: Basic Books, 1984), p. 4.

32. Ibid., p. 49.

33. Barry Bosworth, *Tax Incentives and Economic Growth* (Washington, DC: Brookings Institution, 1984), p. 3.

34. This is reinforced by a tendency toward unemployment as production becomes

more capital-intensive, since fewer workers are needed as machines are integrated into the production process. Poverty constrains the full demand potential of an economy. John M. Keynes, *The General Theory* (New York: Harcourt Brace Jovanovich, 1964).

35. Herbert Stein, *The Fiscal Revolution in America* (Chicago: University of Chicago Press, 1969), pp. 160–61.

36. Collins, *Business Response to Keynes,* pp. 17–19.

37. Bosworth, *Tax Incentives and Economic Growth,* p. 5.

38. Two other incentives, the depletion allowance and favorable treatment of capital gains, had long been included in the tax code. The mineral depletion allowance was designed to compensate for unfruitful drilling and inspire industry toward risky undertakings. Favorable treatment of capital gains was developed as an equitable way of dealing with long-term investment.

39. The tax system constitutes a built-in stabilizer. During recessions, incomes fall, individuals pay in lower marginal brackets, and the government collects less from tax revenues, thereby injecting resources into the private economy and cushioning the bust. During booms, incomes rise, individuals move into higher brackets, and government coffers bulge, thereby withdrawing resources from the private economy and counteracting the boom. Another automatic feature of the income tax is that tax revenues tend to grow (the "fiscal dividend") and individuals move into higher brackets ("bracket creep") with growth in the economy. This has historically been a way for governments to raise revenues without increasing tax rates. Joseph Pechman, *Federal Tax Policy* (Washington, DC: Brookings Institution, 1983), pp. 16–18.

40. Ibid., p. 5.

41. Walter Blum and Harry Kalven, Jr., *The Uneasy Case for Progressive Taxation* (Chicago: University of Chicago Press, 1953), pp. 64, 36–37.

42. A. G. Pigou, *Studies in Public Finance* (London: Macmillan & Company, 1975), pp. 40–45.

43. Milton Friedman, *Capitalism and Freedom* (Chicago: University of Chicago Press, 1962).

44. Short-run shifting is based on a question of how prices are set. The classical view is that prices and output will be set in a way that will maximize a firm's profits, whether or not taxes are imposed. Output and prices will remain the same regardless of a tax, and the tax will be taken out of profits rather than passed on to the consumer. The other side argues that taxes are treated as a cost and that firms set prices at a level covering costs plus a profit margin or achieving an after-tax rate of return on capital. Here the tax is passed on to the consumer. In the long run the tax can reduce the rate of return and thereby decrease investment in capital equity. The incidence of the corporate income tax greatly affects the assumed progressivity of the measure. If as much as one-half is shifted to consumers, the tax looks somewhat regressive among lower-income taxpayers. If none of the tax is shifted, it is a fairly progressive measure. Pechman, *Federal Tax Policy,* pp. 136–41.

45. Gerald Epstein, "Domestic Stagflation and Monetary Policy: The Federal Reserve and the Hidden Election," in Tom Ferguson and Joel Rogers, eds., *The Hidden Election* (New York: Pantheon Books, 1981), p. 145.

46. Lance LeLoup, "Congress and the Dilemma of Economic Policy," in Allen Shick, ed., *Making Economic Policy in Congress* (Washington, DC: American Enterprise Institute, 1983), p. 9.

47. Fiscal and monetary policy can sometimes cancel one another out. For ex-

ample, the government could reduce taxes to stimulate the economy but at the same time reduce the level of resources available for increased investment through a contractionary monetary policy. Competition for existing money and credit would drive up interest rates, which would constrain business spending. The depressing effect of the monetary intervention would cancel out the stimulating effect of the fiscal intervention, which is what happened in 1981. Pechman, *Federal Tax Policy,* pp. 24–26.

48. E. Ray Canterbury, *Economics on a New Frontier* (Belmont, CA: Wadsworth Publishing Company, 1968).

49. Ibid., p. 158.

50. Memo, Paul Samuelson and Robert Solow to JFK, "The Changed Mid-Year Outlook," Kennedy Library, Presidential Office Files, Box 74, CEA 6/1/62–6/15/62.

51. Memo, Walter Heller to LBJ, "That Tax Increase Again," 5/13/66, CF FI11–4, Income Tax (1964–66), LBJ (Johnson Presidential Library).

52. Memo, Gardner Ackley to LBJ, "The Case for Higher Taxes," 5/10/66, p. 1, EX FI11, 3/17/66–8/20/66, LBJ.

53. Ibid., p. 2.

54. Another $14 billion in obligational authority was also to be eliminated from the budget.

55. Bowles, Gordon, and Weisskopf, *Beyond the Waste Land,* p. 26.

56. Edward Wolff, "The Magnitude and Causes of the Recent Productivity Slowdown in the United States: A Survey of Recent Studies," in William Baumol and Kenneth McLennan, eds., *Productivity Growth and U.S. Competitiveness* (Oxford: Oxford University Press, 1985), p. 32.

57. President's Commission on Industrial Competitiveness, *Global Competition: The New Reality* (Washington, DC: U.S. Government Printing Office, January 1985), p. 11.

58. John Kendrick, "International Comparisons of Recent Productivity Trends," in Japan Productivity Center, ed., *Measuring Productivity Trends and Comparisons from the First International Productivity Symposium* (New York: UNIPUB, 1984), p. 98.

59. President's Commission on Industrial Competitiveness, *Global Competition,* p. 13.

60. Harrison and Bluestone, *Great U-Turn,* p. 7.

61. Taking 1977 as an index, wages and benefits were 75.5 percent of the 1977 level in 1964. Yet in 1983 real compensation was back down to 98.2 percent of the 1977 figure. President's Commission on Industrial Competitiveness, *Global Competition,* pp. 12–13.

62. Harrison and Bluestone, *Great U-Turn,* p. 115.

63. During the golden age the split between Keynesian and neoclassical thinking was less pronounced. A rebirth of conflict between paradigms broke out with the crisis. The system of labor-management relations, collective bargaining with built-in wage and benefit increases, allegedly contributed to cost-push inflation. Critics charged that government regulation was imposing huge costs on the private sector. Murray Weidenbaum, chair of Reagan's Council of Economic Advisers, estimated the cost of regulation to be over $100 billion. Business Week Team, *The Reindustrialization of America* (New York: McGraw-Hill, 1982), p. 32.

64. See also Thomas Ferguson and Joel Rogers, *Right Turn* (New York: Hill & Wang, 1986); Thomas Edsall, *The New Politics of Inequality* (New York: Norton, 1984); Harrison and Bluestone, *Great U-Turn.*

65. Ture and Sanden, *Effects of Tax Policy on Capital Formation.*

66. Bosworth, *Tax Incentives and Economic Growth*, pp. 11–12.

67. Robert Eisner, "Tax Incentives for Investment," *National Tax Journal* 26, no. 3: 399.

68. Michael Boskin, "Saving Incentives: The Role of Tax Policy," in Walker and Bloomfield, *New Directions in Federal Tax Policy for the 1980s*, pp. 94–97.

69. Increases in the after-tax rate of return on capital may actually erode savings by increasing consumption. E. Philip Howry and Saul H. Hymans, "The Measurement and Determination of Lonable Funds Savings," *BPEA* 3 (1978): 655–705.

70. It is generally accepted that corporate taxation perversely encourages debt over equity financing, since interest payments but not dividends can be deducted. Pechman, *Federal Tax Policy*, pp. 143–45.

71. Feldstein, "Fiscal Policy for the 1980s," in Walker and Bloomfield, *New Directions in Federal Tax Policy for the 1980s*, p. 33.

72. Volcker worried that the deficit problem would be circumvented with a looser monetary policy. Paul Volcker, "Monetary Policy for the 1980s," in Walker and Bloomfield, *New Directions in Federal Tax Policy for the 1980s*, p. 39.

73. Martin Neil Bailey, "What Has Happened to Productivity Growth?" *Science* 234, no. 4775 (10/24/86): 447.

74. Carl Thor, George Sadler, and Elliot Grossman, "Comparison of Total Factor Productivity in Japan and the United States," in Japan Productivity Center, *Measuring Productivity Trends and Comparisons from the First International Productivity Symposium*, p. 61.

75. Wolff, "Magnitude and Causes of the Recent Productivity Slowdown in the United States," in Baumol and McLennan, *Productivity Growth and U.S. Competitiveness*, p. 36.

76. Ibid., p. 36.

77. Alan Auerbach and Dale Jorgensen, "Inflation-Proof Depreciation of Assets," *Harvard Business Review*, September–October 1980, p. 113.

78. Business Week Team, *Reindustrialization of America*, p. 43.

79. Kendrick, "International Comparisons of Recent Productivity Trends," in Japan Productivity Center, *Measuring Productivity Trends and Comparisons from the First International Productivity Symposium*, p. 111.

80. Bosworth, *Tax Incentives and Economic Growth*, pp. 53–55.

81. Edward F. Denison, *Accounting for Slower Economic Growth: The United States in the 1970s* (Washington, DC: Brookings Institution, 1979).

82. True economic depreciation, or the "loss in real value of productive assets," is very hard to determine; therefore, depreciation is calculated according to either a "profits" or a "cash flow" method of accounting.

83. Julian Alworth, "Piecemeal Corporation Tax Reform: A Survey," in Alan Peacock and Francesco Forte, eds., *The Political Economy of Taxation* (New York: St Martin's Press, 1981), pp. 64–69.

84. Business Week Team, *Reindustrialization of America*, p. 119.

85. Michael Barker and Michael Kieschnick, "Taxes and Growth," *Tax Notes*, special report, May 7, 1984, p. 635.

86. Eugene Seskin and David Sullivan, "Revised Estimates of New Plant and Equipment Expenditures in the United States, 1947–83," *Survey of Current Business* 65, no. 2 (February 1985): 33; Eugene Seskin and David Sullivan, "Plant and Equip-

ment Expenditures, First and Second Quarters and Second Half of 1985," *Survey of Current Business* 65, no. 4 (April 1985): 21.

87. Maggie McComas, "Did Supply-Side Incentives Work?" *Fortune* 110 (November 26, 1984): 53–54.

88. Ibid.

89. See Luger, "Tax Incentives and Tax Inequities," pp. 33–47; Emil Sunley, Jr., "Towards a More Neutral Investment Tax Credit," *National Tax Journal* 36, no. 2: 209–20; Robert Eisner and M. I. Nadiri, "Investment Behavior and Neo-Classical Theory," *Review of Economics and Statistics* 50:369–83.

90. Lee Sheppard, "Corporate Tax Said to Encourage Investment in Equipment, Not Structures," *Tax Notes,* February 20, 1984, p. 655.

91. Advisory Commission on Intergovernmental Relations, "Changing Public Attitudes on Governments and Taxes" (Washington, DC, 1985), p. 1.

92. Harrison and Bluestone, *Great U-Turn,* p. 9.

93. Scott Lash and John Urry, *The End of Organized Capitalism* (Oxford: Polity Press, 1987), p. 202.

94. Charles Alexander, "That Threatening Trade Gap," *Time,* July 9, 1984, p. 63.

95. George Silvestri and John Lukasiewicz, "A Look at Occupational Employment Trends to the Year 2000," *Monthly Labor Review,* U.S. Department of Labor Statistics, September 1987, pp. 49–50.

96. For a discussion of the postindustrial strategy see Piore and Sabel, *Second Industrial Divide.*

97. Bailey, "What Has Happened to Productivity Growth?" p. 446.

Investment in computers and other office machines to increase white collar productivity is one area in which overinvestment seems to have contributed to the decline in the growth rate. Stephen Roach, "America's Technology Dilemma: A Profile of the Information Economy," Morgan Stanley Special Economic Study, April 22, 1987, pp. 1–2.

See also Robert Brenner, "The International Crisis and U.S. Decline," paper presented at Seminar on the State and Capitalism since 1800, Center for European Studies, Cambridge, MA, October 2, 1990, pp. 2–3.

98. Service employees have discovered that "sophisticated machines in many cases have been hampering their work." The productivity growth rate of workers in industries such as health care, law, and accounting has actually declined. Keith Schneider, "Services Hurt by Technology," *New York Times,* June 29, 1987, pp. D1, 6.

99. The productivity crisis is a problem of "how to compete": managers who focus on a "narrow product mix for a particular market niche" will achieve higher performance rates than their conventional competitors. Wickham Skinner, "The Focused Factory," *Harvard Business Review* 52, no. 3 (May–June 1974): 113–14.

100. C. F. Pratten, *Labor Productivity Differential within International Companies* (Cambridge: Cambridge University Press, 1976), pp. 55–56.

101. Ramchandran Jaikumar, "Postindustrial Manufacturing," *Harvard Business Review,* November–December 1986, p. 69.

102. Piore and Sabel, *Second Industrial Divide.*

103. Business Week Team, "What Tax Reform Really Means," *Business Week,* June 17, 1985, p. 129.

104. Kenneth McLennan, "The Case for a Non-targeted Approach to Industrial

Strategy," in F. Stevens Redburn, Terry Buss, and Larry Ledebur, eds., *Revitalizing the U.S. Economy* (New York: Praeger, 1986), pp. 46–47.

105. Appendix source: Joseph Pechman, *Federal Tax Policy* (Washington, DC: Brookings Institution, 1983), pp. 132–35.

Chapter 2

1. Much of the literature concerns which interests get organized and represented. Marxists, elite theorists, and some pluralists argue that the political system limits by class and wealth the interests which can be expressed. C. Wright Mills, *The Power Elite* (New York: Oxford University Press, 1956); G. William Domhoff, *Who Really Rules?* (New Brunswick, NJ: Transaction Books, 1978); E. S. Schattschneider, *The Semisovereign People* (New York: Holt, Rinehart & Winston, 1960); Mancur Olson, *The Logic of Collective Action* (Cambridge, MA: Harvard University Press, 1965); Page, *Who Gets What from Government?* (Berkeley: University of California Press, 1983).

The traditional pluralists believe interests throughout the socioeconomic spectrum are permitted. David Truman, *The Governmental Process* (New York: Knopf, 1951); Earl Latham, *The Group Basis of Politics* (Ithaca, NY: Cornell University Press, 1952); Robert Dahl, *Who Governs?* (New Haven: Yale University Press, 1961).

2. Anthony Downs, *An Economic Theory of Democracy* (New York: Harper, 1957). Fiorina applies this model to congressional decision making. Morris Fiorina, *Congress: Keystone of the Washington Establishment* (New Haven: Yale University Press, 1977).

3. James Q. Wilson, "The Rise of the Bureaucratic State," *Public Interest* 41 (Fall 1975): 77–103. Wilson conceptualized a more indeterminate relationship between actors in state and society in his later work. See James Q. Wilson, *The Politics of Regulation* (New York: Basic Books, 1980).

4. Joseph Schumpeter, "The Crisis of the Tax State," *International Economic Papers*, translations prepared for the International Economic Association, no. 4 (London: Macmillan & Company, 1954), p. 7.

5. Randall Bartlett, *Economic Foundations of Political Power* (New York: Free Press, 1973).

6. Lester Salamon and John Siegfried, "Economic Power and Political Influence: The Impact of Industry Structure on Public Policy," *American Political Science Review* 71, no. 4 (December 1974): 1026–43; David Jacobs, "Corporate Economic Power and the State: A Longitudinal Assessment of Two Explanations," *American Journal of Sociology* 93, no. 4 (January 1988): 852–81.

7. John Zysman, *Governments, Markets and Growth* (Ithaca, NY: Cornell University Press, 1983).

8. Gerald Epstein and Juliet Schor, "Macropolicy in the Rise and Fall of the Golden Age," table 2, "Connections between Finance and Industry," based on OECD Financial Statistics.

9. Piore and Sabel, *Second Industrial Divide*, pp. 71–71.

10. Zysman, *Governments, Markets and Growth*, p. 18.

11. Ian Maitland, "House Divided: Business Lobbying and the 1981 Budget," *Corporate Social Performance and Policy*, vol. 5, (Greenwich, CT: JAI Press, 1983), pp. 1–25.

12. Thomas Ferguson, "From Normalcy to New Deal: Industrial Structure, Party Competition, and American Public Policy in the Great Depression," *International Organization* 38, no. 1 (Winter 1984): 41–94.

13. Becker argues that taxation in colonial America was constructed so as to minimize its impact on dominant industry groups. Robert Becker, *Revolution, Reform and the Politics of American Taxation, 1768–1783* (Baton Rouge: Louisiana State University Press, 1980). Ferguson describes how different industrial sectors favored diverse tax policies in postrevolutionary America. E. James Ferguson, *The Power of the Purse* (Chapel Hill: University of North Carolina Press, 1961).

14. The industrial sector approach is a fairly sophisticated society-centered explanation. Analysts using this approach recognize historical complexity and often include a discussion of state participants in accounts of policy development. In this way society-based and state-based explanations seem to converge on one another, each holding constant what the other seeks to explain. Yet the industrial sector approach and the sophisticated state-centered models still accord causal primacy to one sphere over another. Consequently, they fail to explore systematically the interconnections between state and society.

See James Kurth, "The Political Consequences of the Product Cycle: Industrial History and Political Outcomes," *International Organization* 33, no. 1 (Winter 1979): 33. Peter Gourevitch, "International Trade, Domestic Coalitions and Liberty: Comparative Responses to the Crisis of 1873–1896," *Journal of Interdisciplinary History,* Autumn 1977. Tom Ferguson, "Party Realignment and American Industrial Structure: The Investment Theory of Political Parties in Historical Perspective," in Paul Zarembka, ed., *Research in Political Economy* (Greenwich, CT: JAI Press, 1983).

15. Drawn from J. R. Moroney, table 6.1, "Wage Rates and Capital-Labor Ratios: South, New England, and Rest of U.S., 1957," *The Structure of Production in American Manufacturing* (Chapel Hill: University of North Carolina Press, 1972), p. 132.

16. Kurth, "Political Consequences of the Product Cycle," p. 33.

17. The most reductionist version of pluralism all but removes rationality as a motivation in favor of political self-interest. The institutional responsibility for promoting a healthy economy, maintaining control and domestic order, and interacting with transnational structures all focus the attention of the politician on concerns beyond immediate constituent demands. Theda Skocpol, "Bringing the State Back In: Strategies of Analysis in Current Research," in Peter Evans, Dietrich Rueschemeyer, and Theda Skocpol, eds., *Bringing the State Back In* (New York: Cambridge University Press, 1985).

18. It should be noted that most state-centered analyses differentiate between bureaucrats and elected officials, granting much more autonomy to the former.

19. Margaret Levi, *Of Rule and Revenue* (Berkeley: University of California Press, 1988), p. 3.

20. Charles Bright and Susan Harding, "Process of State Making and Popular Protest," in Charles Bright and Susan Harding, eds., *Statemaking and Social Movements* (Ann Arbor: University of Michigan Press, 1984), p. 4.

21. Eric Nordlinger, *On the Autonomy of the Democratic State* (Cambridge, MA: Harvard University Press, 1981).

22. John Manley, *The Politics of Finance* (Boston: Little, Brown & Company, 1970), pp. 246, 279. Also see Richard Fenno, *Congressmen in Committees* (Boston: Little, Brown & Company, 1973), pp. 3–5.

23. Sven Steinmo, "Shaping Policy Preferences: Political Institutions and Tax Policy Outcomes in the United States, Sweden and Britain," paper presented at the annual meeting of the American Political Science Association, Washington, DC, September 1988.

24. Witte, *Politics and Development of the Federal Income Tax,* p. 22.

25. Peter Hall, *Governing the Economy: The Politics of State Intervention in Britain and France* (New York: Oxford University Press, 1986), p. 18.

26. C. Herman Pritchett, "The President's Constitutional Position," in Thomas Cronin, ed., *Rethinking the Presidency* (Boston: Little, Brown & Company, 1982).

27. James Sundquist, *The Decline and Resurgence of Congress* (Washington, DC: Brookings Institution, 1981), pp. 16–18.

28. Weatherford, "Macroeconomic Policy Making beyond the Electoral Constraint," in Edwards et al., *The Presidency and Public Policy Making.*

29. James Anderson, "Developing Fiscal Policy," in Pfiffner, *The President and Economic Policy,* p. 91.

30. Ibid., pp. 91–93.

31. Roger Porter, "The President and Economic Policy: Problems, Patterns, and Alternatives," in Hugh Heclo and Lester Salamon, eds., *The Illusion of Presidential Government* (Boulder, CO: Westview Press, 1981), p. 204.
The Keynesian consensus made economic policy questions seem amenable to technical resolution; therefore, separate policy bodies were likely to come up with similar analyses. Greater ideological uncertainty has paralleled the proliferation of policy planning units, adding to the level of institutional conflict. Anderson, "Developing Fiscal Policy," in Pfiffner, *The President and Economic Policy,* pp. 99–100.

32. Porter, "President and Economic Policy," in Heclo and Salamon, eds., *Illusion of Presidential Government,* pp. 211–13.

33. Walter Dean Burnham, "The Changing Shape of the American Political Universe," *American Political Science Review* 59, no. 1 (March 1965): 7–28.

34. Significant reforms in Congress included the revocation of Ways and Means' right to assign members to committees, modification of the closed-rule system whereby the committee bill was considered on the House floor without amendment, enlargement of the committee by one-third, a different recruitment whereby members from unsafe districts were routinely assigned to Ways and Means, and the creation of subcommittees. Catherine Rudder, "Tax Policy: Structure and Choice," in Allen Schick, ed., *Making Economic Policy in Congress* (Washington, DC: American Enterprise Institute, 1983), p. 202.
The main party changes had to do with the nominating and financing of candidates, which shifted power away from the old power elite. This, combined with an increase in primaries, greatly decreased the party's control over nomination practices, thus reducing subsequent party loyalty. Austin Ranney, "The Political Parties: Reform and Decline," in Anthony King, ed., *The New American Political System* (Washington, DC: American Enterprise Institute, 1978), pp. 230, 242.

35. Rudder, "Tax Policy," in Schick, *Making Economic Policy in Congress,* pp. 203–4.

36. Thomas Reese, "The Politics of Tax Reform," from the Laurence N. Woodworth Memorial Symposium, *National Tax Journal* 32, no. 3 (September 1979): 249–50.

37. Randall Strahan, *New Ways and Means: Reform and Change in a Congressional Committee* (Chapel Hill: University of North Carolina Press, 1990).

38. Hugh Heclo, "Issue Networks and the Executive Establishment," in Anthony King, *The New American Political System,* pp. 87–125.

39. Hall, *Governing the Economy.*

40. Charles Lindblom, *Politics and Markets* (New York: Basic Books, 1977).

41. Katzenstein, "Introduction: Domestic and International Forces and Strategies of Foreign Economic Policy," *Between Power and Plenty,* pp. 17, 19. The corporatist literature puts forth that state actors organize societal interests to achieve policy legislation and implementation. See Suzanne Berger, "Introduction," in Berger, ed., *Organizing Interests in Western Europe* (Cambridge: Cambridge University Press, 1981); Peter Hall, *Governing the Economy;* Richard Samuels, *The Business of the Japanese State* (Ithaca: Cornell University Press, 1987). It is usually assumed, however, that the fragmentation of the U.S. political system has prevented corporatism from emerging in America. Philippe Schmitter, "Interest Intermediation and Regime Governability in Contemporary Western Europe and North America," in Suzanne Berger, ed., *Organizing Interests in Western Europe,* pp. 285–327.

42. Joseph Pika, "Interest Groups and the Executive: Presidential Intervention," in Allan Cigler and Burdett Loomis, eds., *Interest Group Politics* (Washington, D.C.: Congressional Quarterly Press, 1983), pp. 298–323. Martha Joynt Kumar and Michael Baruch Grossman, "The Presidency and Interest Groups," in Michael Nelson, ed., *The Presidency and the Political System* (Washington, DC: Congressional Quarterly Press, 1984), p. 287.

43. Heclo, "Issue Networks and the Executive Establishment," in Anthony King, *The New American Political System,* p. 169. McQuaid, *Big Business and Presidential Power.*

44. Early relations with business were disastrous, and the president's attempts at activist economic intervention met with considerable business resistance.

45. Memo, Henry Fowler to JFK, 9/23/63, Presidential Office Files, Box 90, Treasury 9/63, JFK (Kennedy Presidential Library).

46. Ibid.

47. Ibid.

48. Memo, Joseph Califano to LBJ, 5/2/68, EX LE/FI11–4, 5/1/68–5/15/68, LBJ.

49. "Notes of the Luncheon Meeting of the President with Business Leaders," 8/10/67, Meeting Notes File, August 10, 1967, Luncheon Meeting with Business Leaders, attached to memo, George Christian to LBJ, 8/15/67, LBJ.

50. Interview with a senior Ways and Means staff.

51. Interview with a high-ranking member of the administration.

52. Ways and Means Committee Hearings, *Administration's Fiscal Year 1983 Economic Program,* part 1, 2/18/82–5/5/82.

53. H. Brand, "Not Much Reform in 'Tax Reform,' " *Dissent* 33 (Fall 1986): 389–93.

54. The bill was to transfer about $120 billion from individuals to corporations.

55. Gerald Boyd, "Claiming the Credit in 1988," *New York Times,* October 23, 1986, p. D18.

56. David Rosenbaum, "Sweeping Tax Bill Is Voted by House; Senate Acts Next," *New York Times,* September 26, 1986, pp. D1, 17.

57. Eileen Shanahan, "New, Diverse Coalition Works to Pass Tax Bill," *Congressional Quarterly,* May 24, 1986, p. 1147.

Chapter 3

1. Stein, *The Fiscal Revolution in America,* p. 3.

2. Collins, *Business Response to Keynes.*

3. Stein, *The Fiscal Revolution in America.*

4. For a very good example of Eisenhower revisionism see Fred Greenstein, *The Hidden-Hand Presidency* (New York: Basic Books, 1982).

5. Stephen Weatherford, "The President and the Political Business Cycle," in James Pfiffner, ed., *The President and Economic Policy* (Philadelphia: Institute for the Study of Human Issues, 1986), pp. 49–52.

6. Memo, Council of Economic Advisers to JFK, "A Second Look at Economic Policy in 1961," 3/17/61, Presidential Office Files, Box 73, CEA 1/61–3/61, JFK.

7. Memo, CEA to JFK, "Highlights of the Current Economic Expansion," 5/29/62, Presidential Office Files, Box 74, CEA 6/1/62–6/15/62, JFK.

8. Memo, Samuelson and Solow to JFK, "The Changed Mid-Year Outlook."

9. Canterbury, *Economics on a New Frontier,* p. 90. Data from the Department of Commerce, Office of Business Economists.

10. Canterbury, *Economics on a New Frontier,* p. 89.

11. Joel Krieger, *Reagan, Thatcher and the Politics of Decline* (New York: Oxford University Press, 1986), pp. 22–23.

12. Collins, *Business Response to Keynes.*

13. Heller described the differences between the conventional budget and the "income-and-product-account" budget and argued that the latter is a more accurate measure of the effect of government activity on the economy. The conventional budget is calculated on a cash rather than an accrual basis so that taxes are included when the government actually receives the funds. The income-and-product-account budget uses the accrual method and includes only transactions which have a real income-generating effect rather than all balance sheet changes. The difference between the two is that the conventional budget tends to understate the deficit during downturns and overstate it during upturns. Speech, "Remarks of Walter Heller, Chairman of Economic Advisers before the American Life Convention," Chicago, October 13, 1961, Presidential Office Files, Box 73, CEA 10/61, JFK.

14. Memo, Walter Heller to JFK, "The Balance-of-Payments Dilemma," 11/28/61, Presidential Office Files, Box 73, CEA 11/61, JFK.

15. Business Week Team, "To Bring Two Deficits under Control," *Business Week,* March 4, 1962, pp. 30–32.

16. Memo, Heller to JFK, "The Balance-of-Payments Dilemma," 11/28/61, Presidential Office Files, Box 73, CEA 11/61, JFK.

17. Stein, *The Fiscal Revolution in America,* p. 335.

18. Memo, Walter Heller to JFK, "The Case for Flexible Tax Authority," 12/23/61, Presidential Office Files, Box 73, CEA 12/61, JFK.

19. "Report of the Bank for International Settlement in Baisle," Presidential Office Files, Box 89, Treasury 6/62, JFK.

20. Canterbury, *Economics on a New Frontier,* p. 82.

21. Memo, Joseph Barr to Douglas Dillon, "White House Regional Congerences," 11-24-61, Presidential Office Files, 11-7-21-1961, JFK.

22. Memo, Walter Heller to JFK, "Highlights of Paris-Bonn-Frankfurt Consultations," Presidential Office Files, Box 73, 6/16/62–6/30/62, JFK.

23. Memo, "Protecting the Dollar from the New York (and Swiss) Bankers," 10/16/61, Presidential Office Files, Box 73, CEA 10/61, JFK.

24. "What for Taxes?" *New York Times*, December 17, 1962, p. 10.

25. Memo, Walter Heller to JFK, "Business Views on the Economic Outlook and Tax Cuts," 11/10/62, Presidential Office Files, Box 75, CEA 11/7/62–11/14/62, JFK.

26. The Chamber of Commerce was the only trade association actively representing small business at the national level in the early 1960s. Since the Chamber of Commerce included many large concerns, its use as a representative of small business must be qualified.

27. "Chamber Renews Tax Plan Attack," *New York Times*, April 12, 1963, p. 12.

28. Richard Mooney, "Two Business Groups Oppose Tax Program at Senate Hearing," *New York Times*, April 4, 1962, p. A1.

29. "You May Think the Corporate Profit Tax is 'Bad,' but . . . ," *Fortune*, April, 1963, p. 230.

30. A 6 percent credit was available for purchases constituting 50 to 100 percent of depreciation accounts.

31. John Morris, "Text of President's Message and Budget Analysis," *New York Times*, January 19, 1962, p. 14.

32. Business Week Team, "Tax Plan Draws More Brickbats," *Business Week*, May 20, 1961, p. 36.

33. Arthur Krock, "In the Nation an Unexpected Variation of Divide and Conquer," *New York Times*, April 5, 1962, p. 32.

34. Letter, Douglas Dillon to Wilbur Mills, 8/2/61, Presidential Office Files, Box 89, Treasury 7/61–8/61, JFK.

35. Ellison contacted James O'Brien. Letter, George Ellison to James O'Brien, 4/2/62, White House Staff Files, O'Brien, Mill, Wilbur D., Arkansas D, Folder 1, JFK.

36. Memo, Larry O'Brien to Ken O'Donnell, 4/6/62, and memo, Claude Desautels to Larry O'Brien, 9/17/62, White House Staff Files, O'Brien, Mills Folder 1, JFK.

37. Assets with useful lives of four to five years could have the credit applied to one-third of their value; credits could be applied to two-thirds of the value of assets with six- to seven-year lives. Equipment with useful lives of at least eight years was eligible for the entire credit. "Tax Credit a Spur to Capital Outlays," *Outlook*, February 26, 1962, p. 920.

38. Robert Metz, "Tax Aid for Expansion," *New York Times*, April 2, 1962, p. 39.

39. Robert Metz, "Chamber Opposes Parts of Tax Bill," *New York Times*, June 8, 1962, p. 39.

40. Senate Finance Committee, "Hearings on the Revenue Act of 1962," on H.R. 10650, 87th Congress, 2d Session, Item 1038 (Washington, DC: Government Printing Office, 4/2/62–7/3/62), p. 1798.

41. Walker further criticized those who resisted the tax credit in favor of corporate rate cuts. Walker feared that rate cut demands would mobilize "organized labor's passive resistance to the tax credit into active and effective resistance. Stated bluntly, an over-all cut in the corporate income tax rate is simply not in the cards at this time." "ABA Backs Plan on Plant Outlays," *New York Times*, May 9, 1962, p. 69.

42. Letter, William Butler, Chase Manhattan Bank, to Walter Heller, 2/14/61, Heller Personal Papers, Box 47, Block-B, JFK.

43. "Senate Coalition to Fight Kennedy on Tax Proposal," *New York Times*, April 1, 1962, p. 1.

44. The Machinery and Allied Products Institute and the utilities industry were early allies. Richard Mooney, "Two Liberals Voice Tax Plan Qualms," *New York Times*, April 5, 1962, p. 54; "Utility Head Asks Rise in Tax Credit," *New York Times*, April 10, 1962, p. 26. By the time the legislation reached the Senate floor the administration had persuaded trade associations from the following sectors to personally call legislators: coal, railroads, aerospace, cotton, petroleum, chemical, electronics, small business, and utilities. "Industry Support of H.R. 10650," Presidential Office Files, Box 89A, Treasury 8/1/62–8/20/62, JFK.

45. "Congress Enacts Major Tax Law Provisions," *Congressional Quarterly Almanac* (Washington, DC: Congressional Quarterly Service, 1962), p. 484.

46. When United States Steel rescinded the price increases, proponents of the tax credit had a new argument. "Kennedy's Steel Victory Viewed as Spur to His Economic Policies," *New York Times*, April 15, 1962, pp. 1, 55.

47. Memo, Fowler to JFK, "Business Council Meeting," 5/15/62, Presidential Office Files, Box 89, Treasury 5/62, JFK.

48. Memo, "Memorandum of Discussion at President Kennedy's Luncheon of July 12, 1962," 7/17/62, Presidential Office Files, Box 89A, Treasury 7/16/62–7/31/62, JFK.

49. Immediately after the steel battle, Douglas Dillon recommended making the depreciation plans known without delay. Walter Heller advised against such an announcement as staff members were preoccupied with the revenue act, the benefits would be realized at the same time anyway, and "one carrot for passage of the tax bill will be removed." Finally, the administration decided to announce at the May Business Council meeting that the new guidelines would be released by July. Memo, Walter Heller to JFK, "Douglas Dillon on Depreciation Revision Speed-up," 4/18/62, Presidential Office Files, Box 74, CEA 4/62, JFK.

50. Memo, Fowler to JFK, "Business Council Meeting," 5/15/62, Presidential Office Files, Box 89, Treasury 5/62, JFK.

51. The rationale for this was that it would generate funds for companies during recessions when earnings and taxes paid were lower. Richard Mooney, "Dillon Modifies Tax Bill Stand," *New York Times*, May 11, 1962, p. A1.

52. Business Week Team, "Winning on Taxes," *Business Week*, September 1, 1962, p. 25.

53. The original proposal allowed no exemptions; the revised version excluded withholding on interest income from savings institutions for children under eighteen and elderly over sixty-five who filed for the necessary certificate. Under both versions, individuals could request quarterly refunds. Robert Metz, "Withholding Bill Gaining," *New York Times*, January 28, 1962, pp. F1, 11; "House Unit for 20 percent Withholding on Dividends, Savings Interest," *New York Times*, January 26, 1962, p. 15.

54. Senate Finance Committee, "Hearings on the Revenue Act of 1962," pp. 2054–57, 2030. The industry groups argued that many individuals would have too much withheld from their income on interest and dividends since marital and dependency status would not be taken into account. Senate Finance Committee, "Hearings on the Revenue Act of 1962," p. 2169. Mutual funds companies claimed

that withholding would prevent them from meeting their legal obligation to distribute 90 percent of their earnings each year in order to avoid corporate income tax. Robert Metz, "Tax and Mutual Funds," *New York Times,* May 28, 1962, p. 41.

55. Senate Finance Committee, "Hearings on the Revenue Act of 1962," p. 2248. The Pennsylvania Bankers Association recommended "more effective enforcement of tax laws and active prosecution of offenders," "revision of tax forms to more clearly emphasize tax payers' obligations," and continuing the "taxpayer educational program" that enlightens people to their responsibilities. Ibid., p. 2115.

56. Senate Finance Committee, "Hearings on the Revenue Act of 1962," p. 2181.

57. Memo, Walter Heller to JFK, "Interest and Dividend Withholding," 5/8/62, Presidential Office Files, Box 74, CEA 5/6/62–5/15/62, JFK. The Treasury claimed that, for 50 percent of the 2 million suffering from overwithholding, the excess would total no more than $10. "Drive against Tax Boomerangs in the Senate," *New York Times,* May 6, 1962, p. 42.

58. Senate Finance Committee, "Hearings on the Revenue Act of 1962," pp. 2213–16.

59. Robert Metz, "Tax Debate Intensifies," *New York Times,* April 30, 1962, p. 39.

60. Gene Smith, "Mutual Funds: Drive against Tax Bill of U.S.," *New York Times,* May 7, 1962, p. 50.

61. "Drive against Tax Boomerangs in the Senate," *New York Times,* May 6, 1962, p. 42.

62. "The Tax Bill Battle: Withhold—Or Not?," *Newsweek,* June 4, 1962, pp. 78–83.

63. Kennedy claimed that the public suffered four misconceptions: that the provision involved a new tax, that it took money unjustly, that it created red tape, and that it hurt the elderly. A tax evasion of $800 million yearly had to be eradicated. In fact, 80 percent of dividend income went to less than 7 percent of taxpayers, those having incomes of over $10,000. "President Charges Deceit by Withholding-Tax Foes," *New York Times,* May 10, 1962, p. 1.

64. John Morris, "Savings Members Drop Fight to Prevent Tax Withholding," *New York Times,* June 10, 1962, pp. A1, 32.

65. Mooney, "Dillon Modifies Tax Bill Stand," pp. A1, 16.

66. Joseph Loftus, "Withholding Turned Down by Senate Finance Group," *New York Times,* July 12, 1962, pp. A1, 15.

67. Edward O'Toole, "Financial Battle Nearing a Climax," *New York Times,* February 18, 1962, p. F1.

68. The change was to be implemented over a five-year transition period, to provide for minimal disruption to housing markets and interest rates. "Tax Plan Backed on Mutual Banks," *New York Times,* January 31, 1962, p. 14.

69. "Pro and Con: What's Back of a Growing Tax Fight," *U.S. News and World Report,* May 7, 1962, p. 113.

70. Ibid., p. 114.

71. "Savings Group Fight Tax Plan," *New York Times,* February 7, 1962, p. A1.

72. "Tax Plan Backed on Mutual Banks," *New York Times,* January 31, 1962, p. 14.

73. Industry representatives proposed a compromise of a 5 percent debt ratio. Ways and Means responded with three alternatives. The mutuals could either deduct 3 percent of any increase in outstanding loans from their annual taxable income, deduct "whatever amount their experience indicates is necessary to assure them an adequate

reserve against losses," or pay tax on 40 percent of their income and set the other 60 percent aside for reserves. John Morris, "New Taxes Eased for Savings Units," *New York Times,* February 23, 1962.

74. Memo, Henry Fowler to JFK, "Editorial in the Wall Street Journal of November 13," 11/15/61, Presidential Office Files, Box 89, Treasury 10/61–12/61, JFK.

75. Business Week Team, "Why the Tax Bill Scares Businessmen," *Business Week,* May 5, 1962, p. 92.

76. "U.S. Subsidiaries Pick Swiss Haven," *New York Times,* April 15, 1962, p. 42.

77. Robert Metz, "Tax Relief Sought by Mining Industry for Expropriation," *New York Times,* February 18, 1962, pp. F1, 5.

78. IT&T testified that in the past ten years (1952–1961) American firms in Western Europe brought in $444 million more in repatriated earnings than was invested abroad in direct investments. Only in 1956 and 1960 did new direct investment exceed earnings returned to the United States. Senate Finance Committee, "Hearings on the Revenue Act of 1962," p. 2407. To some extent the question of the impact of direct foreign investment depended on the time frame used. Commerce pointed out that the "new inflow of dividends over and above capital outflow for the decade 1950–1960 was $7.6 billion." The Treasury Department was concerned about the marginal increases in capital outflows in recent years: from 1957 through 1960 the net outflow over dividend inflow was $655 million, $421 million of this in Western Europe. Ibid., p. 2552.

79. Companies included American Machine & Foundry, Armco International, Cabot, Continental Can, Corn Products, Eastman Kodak, General Electric, Goodyear International, H. J. Heinz, Merck Sharp & Dohme, Monsanto Chemical, Otis Elevator, Pfaudler Permutit, Pfizer International, Ritter, Taylor Instrument, Texas Butadiene Chemical, Proctor & Gamble, and Union Carbide. Robert Metz, "Business Fights Kennedy on Tax," *New York Times,* May 20, 1962, p. E1.

80. Senate Finance Committee, "Hearings on the Revenue Act of 1962," p. 5242.

81. Robert Metz, "Tax Bill Scored by Businessmen," *New York Times,* June 10, 1962, p. III 9.

82. "Gore Says Tax Plan Faces 'Blackmail,'" *New York Times,* February 13, 1962, p. 38.

83. Senate Finance Committee, "Hearings on the Revenue Act of 1962," pp. 2369–70. Tektronix Inc. pointed out that foreign countries could "retaliate with higher tax rates to counteract this country's attempt to tax earnings of foreign subsidiaries of U.S. companies before the earnings are remitted." Ibid., p. 3210.

84. IT&T pointed out that only a small portion of European taxes could be deducted as foreign taxes paid. Three IT&T subsidiaries in France paid taxes of 78 percent, 82 percent, and 78 percent, respectively; yet the IRS only allowed deductions of 20 percent, 19 percent, and 16 percent, respectively. Senate Finance Committee, "Hearings on the Revenue Act of 1962," p. 2404.

85. Robert Metz, "Tax Experts Map Strategy on Bill," *New York Times,* June 14, 1962, pp. 43, 51.

86. For example, the administration had proposed taxing all foreign income generated in developed countries whether or not it had been repatriated. Ways and Means amended this provision to allow income reinvested in the subsidiary or another foreign enterprise to escape taxation. John Morris, "House Unit Backs Foreign Tax Curb," *New York Times,* February 2, 1962, p. 12. Pressure from organized labor and from

the administration ultimately forced the Ways and Means Committee to amend its revisions. It revoked the deferral privilege (except where funds were reinvested in underdeveloped countries), passed the gross-up requirement, and passed the anti–tax haven measures. Robert Metz, "Status of Tax Bill," *New York Times,* March 5, 1962, p. 33. But the Senate moved the proposal back toward the industry's position. Business Week Team, "Tax Credit Gets Push in Senate," *Business Week,* July 21, 1962, pp. 29–30.

87. John Morris, "Democrats Draft Tax Bill Revision to Save Revenues," *New York Times,* March 18, 1962, p. A1.

88. "House GOP Moves to Weaken Tax Bill," *New York Times,* March 29, 1962, p. 15.

89. "G.O.P. Says Tax Bill Aids Bars but Hurts Millions with Savings," *New York Times,* March 28, 1962, p. 15.

90. John Morris, "Kennedy Praises Revised Tax Bill; Business Aid Cut," *New York Times,* March 23, 1962, p. 1.

91. "Congress Enacts Major Tax Law Provisions," *Congressional Quarterly Almanac* (Washington, DC: Congressional Quarterly Service, 1962), p. 478.

92. Mooney, "Two Business Groups Oppose Tax Program at Senate Hearing."

93. John Morris, "Senate Approves Tax Bill in Diluted Form, 59 to 24," *New York Times,* September 7, 1962, pp. 1, 15.

94. "Congress Enacts Major Tax Law Provisions," p. 504.

95. Richard Mooney, "Income Tax Cuts Planned for 1963, Dillon Declares," *New York Times,* June 5, 1962, p. 1.

96. Council of Economic Advisers, "Proposals for Tax Reduction," 6/5/62, Presidential Office Files, Box 74, CEA 6/1/62–6/15/62, JFK.

97. Memo, Council of Economic Advisers to JFK, "What It Takes to Get to Full Employment," Presidential Office Files, Box 74, CEA 3/3/62–3/15/62, JFK.

98. Memo, Arthur Okun to Council of Economic Advisers, "Must We Have a 1963 Recession?," 9/1/61, attached to memo, Heller to JFK, "The Political Economy of the Next Recession," Presidential Office Files, Box 73, CEA 9/61, JFK.

99. Memo, Paul Samuelson and Robert Solow to JFK, "The Changed Mid-Year Outlook," 6/6/62, Presidential Office Files, Box 74, CEA 6/1/62–6/15/62, JFK.

100. Memo, Arthur Schlesinger, Jr., to JFK, "Tax Cut," 7/17/62, Presidential Office Files, Box 89A, Treasury 7/16/62–7/31/62, JFK.

101. Memo, Seymour Harris to JFK, 6/7/62, Presidential Office Files, Box 89, Treasury 6/62, JFK.

102. Letter, Fowler to JFK, 11/13/61, Presidential Office Files, Box 89, Treasury 10/61–12/61, JFK.

103. Memo, Arthur Okun to Walter Heller, "Another Myth for Our List," 6/30/62, Presidential Office Files, Box 74, CEA 6/16/62–6/30/62, JFK.

104. Cabell Phillips, "Senate Test Near on Tax Measure; Reforms Deleted," *New York Times,* July 23, 1962, p. A1.

105. Memo, Douglas Dillon to JFK, "Visit with New York Bankers," 7/27/62, Presidential Office Files, Box 89A, Treasury 7/16/62–7/31/62, JFK.

106. Richard Mooney, "U.S. Chamber Asks for Tax Cut Now; Accepts a Deficit," *New York Times,* June 30, 1962, pp. 1, 47.

107. Memo, Walter Heller to JFK, "Report from Scattered Sectors—Economic and Tax Front," 7/20/62, Presidential Office Files, Box 74, CEA 7/16/62–7/25/62, JFK.

108. Joseph Loftus, "Kennedy Accepts a Tax Plan Delay to Aid Trade Bill," *New York Times,* July 4, 1962, pp. 1, 22.

109. "Summary of Hearings on the Status of the Economy before the House Committee on Ways and Means," Presidential Office Files, Box 75, CEA 8/1/62–8/7/62, JFK.

110. Joseph Loftus, "Kennedy Delays Tax-Cut Decision," *New York Times,* July 14, 1962, pp. A1, 10; Joseph Loftus, "Senators Clear Tax Revision Bill," *New York Times,* August 1, 1962, pp. A1, 35.

111. Tape transcript, "Off-the-Record Meeting with Wilbur Mills," 8/6/62, 6:00–6:42 P.M., Presidential Office Files, Presidential Recording Transcripts, Tax Cut Proposals, vol. 1, audiotape 7, items .0B-1, JFK.

112. John Finney, "Byrd Denounces Chamber's Call for Cut in Taxes," *New York Times,* July 9, 1962, p. A1.

113. John Pomfret, "Output Estimate Reduced by U.S.; Lag Is Accented," *New York Times,* July 21, 1962, pp. A1, 8.

114. Business Week Team, "So No Tax Cut," *Business Week,* August 11, 1962, pp. 29–31.

115. Business Week Team, "Hopes for Tax Cut Take Setback," *Business Week,* August 4, 1962, pp. 27–28.

116. Robert Metz, "Clamor for a Tax Cut," *New York Times,* July 5, 1962, p. 35.

117. Business Week Team, "Frowning Mildly on a Tax Cut," *Business Week,* August 11, 1962, p. 32.

118. Loftus, "Kennedy Delays Tax-Cut Decision," pp. A1, 10.

119. Richard Mooney, "Kennedy Bars Tax Cuts Now, Citing Upturn," *New York Times,* August 14, 1962, pp. A1, 20.

120. *New York Times,* January 11, 1962, p. A3.

121. Mooney, "U.S. Chamber Asks for Tax Cut Now; Accepts a Deficit," pp. 1, 47.

122. Richard Mooney, "Labor Presents Its Tax Cut Plan," *New York Times,* December 24, 1962, pp. A1, 3.

123. Memo, Walter Heller to JFK, "CEA Meeting with AFL-CIO Staff," 10/18/62, Presidential Office Files, Box 75, CEA 10/10/62–10/31/62, JFK.

124. Memo, Walter Heller to JFK, "AFL-CIO Rumblings," 10/17/62, Presidential Office Files, Box 75, CEA 10/10/62–10/31/62, JFK.

125. Memo, Douglas Dillon to JFK, "Visit with New York Bankers," 7/27/62, Presidential Office Files, Box 89A, Treasury 7/16/62–7/31/62, JFK.

126. Memo, Douglas Dillon to JFK, 7/12/63, "Use of the Recession Argument in Connection with the Tax Bill," Presidential Office Files, Box 90, Treasury 7/63, JFK.

127. This action was taken at the Conference on Fiscal and Monetary Policy. Business Week Team, "Juggling Deficit and Tax Cuts," *Business Week,* November 17, 1962, p. 44.

128. Charls Walker, "A Federal Tax Cut This Summer—Some Neglected Considerations," *Commercial and Financial Chronicle* 196, no. 6178 (7/19/62): 1, 20.

129. Memo, Douglas Dillon to JFK, 7/12/62, Presidential Office Files, Box 89, Treasury 7/1/62–7/15/62, JFK.

130. Business Week Team, "Washington Outlook," *Business Week,* June 16, 1962, pp. 43–44.

131. Memo, Douglas Dillon to JFK, 3/5/63, Presidential Office Files, Box 90, Treasury 3/63, JFK.

132. "House Votes $11.2 Billion Tax Cut," *Congressional Quarterly Almanac* (Washington, DC: Congressional Quarterly Service, 1963), p. 497.

133. "CEA Meeting with the AFL-CIO Economic Policy Committee, November 1, 1962," Presidential Office Files, Box 75, CEA 11/1/62–11/6/62, JFK.

134. Memo, Walter Heller to JFK, 6/7/63, Presidential Office Files, Box 76, CEA 6/1/63–6/13/63, JFK.

135. Richard Mooney, "Ten-Billion Tax Cut Urged by Labor-Business Panel," *New York Times,* November 20, 1962, pp. A1, 22.

136. "Chances Now of a Tax Cut," *U.S. News and World Report,* May 6, 1963, pp. 109–13.

137. "Kennedy Advised to Make Tax Deal," *New York Times,* August 12, 1963, p. 17.

138. "House Votes $11.2 Billion Tax Cut," *Congressional Quarterly Almanac,* pp. 470, 472.

139. In February, Secretary Dillon found that the reforms would only total $3.3 billion; thus, the total tax cut equaled $10.3 billion. "House Votes $11.2 Billion Tax Cut," *Congressional Quarterly Almanac,* pp. 473–74.

140. Ibid., p. 473.

141. "Tax Reduction Survey," Presidential Office Files, Box 90, Treasury 1/63, JFK.

142. Richard Mooney, "Tax Cut Debate: How Much; For Whom?" *New York Times,* November 25, 1962, p. E10.

143. Richard Mooney, "A Tax Cut, Yes, but What Kind?" *New York Times,* March 4, 1963, p. 16.

144. Business Week Team, "Business Gives It a Sour Reception," *Business Week,* February 2, 1963, pp. 26–27.

145. "A Change in Signals on Tax Cuts," *U.S. News and World Report,* December 17, 1962, pp. 97–100.

146. Business Week Team, "Tax Cut Drive Is On," *Business Week,* December 22, 1962, p. 15.

147. Memo, Fowler to Files, "Conference with Chairman Wilbur Mills re Tax Program," Presidential Office Files, Box 90, Treasury 11/62–12/62, JFK.

148. "An Idea on the March," *Time,* January 11, 1963, pp. 19–21.

149. M. J. Rossant, "Tax Psychology Scare," *New York Times,* February 18, 1963, p. 15.

150. "Tax Cuts," *New York Times,* March 4, 1963, p. 14.

151. Eileen Shanahan, "Kennedy Decides to Renew Effort for Tax Reform," *New York Times,* May 26, 63, p. 1.

152. Letter, Gabriel Hauge to JFK, Presidential Office Files, Box 76, CEA 6/14/63–6/30/63, JFK.

153. "Congress 1963—The Year in Review," *Congressional Quarterly Almanac* (Washington, DC: Congressional Quarterly Service, 1963), p. 77.

154. "An Idea on the March," *Time,* January 11, 1963, pp. 19–21.

155. John Morris, "Funston Critical of Tax Reforms," *New York Times,* March 6, 1963, p. 5.

156. John Morris, "House Unit Votes Capital Gain Cut," *New York Times,* August 10, 1963, p. 15.

157. John Morris, "House Panel Backs Smaller Reduction in Capital Gain Tax," *New York Times,* August 8, 1963, pp. A1, 32.

158. Memo, Walter Heller to Theodore Sorensen, "Slippage in Content of the Tax Bill," Presidential Office Files, Box 76, CEA 7/1/63–7/16/63, JFK.

159. John Morris, "House Panel Due to Back Stiffer Dividend Tax Plan," *New York Times,* August 2, 1963, pp. 1, 13.

160. "House Votes $11.2 Billion Tax Cut," *Congressional Quarterly Almanac,* p. 484.

161. Richard Mooney, "Omissions in Bill Stir Tax Debate," *New York Times,* February 4, 1963, p. A13.

162. "House Votes $11.2 Billion Tax Cut," *Congressional Quarterly Almanac,* p. 483.

163. The industry argued that current U.S. reserves would only last twenty years, mandating continued exploration. "Coal, Oil Officials Protest Tax Plan," *New York Times,* March 26, 1963, pp. 11, 17.

164. Business Week Team, "Even the Hearings Are under Fire," *Business Week,* April 20, 1963, p. 35–6.

165. This was to disallow the grouping for tax purposes of oil and gas properties together. Eileen Shanahan, "House Group Limits Rise in Tax on Oil-Gas Industry," *New York Times,* August 6, 1963, pp. A1, 39.

166. The individual and corporate rate cuts would total about $11 billion. John Morris, "Treasury Agrees to Tax Cut Plan," *New York Times,* August 9, 1963, pp. 1, 20.

167. Eileen Shanahan, "President Offers Two-Year Program for Tax Cutting," *New York Times,* August 13, 1963, pp. A1, 16.

168. John Morris, "Tax Cut Assailed in GOP Report," *New York Times,* September 14, 1963, p. 26.

169. Byrnes submitted an amendment to tie the revenue reductions to spending controls. The amendment was subsequently defeated with solid Democratic opposition. "Congress 1963—The Year in Review," *Congressional Quarterly Almanac* (Washington, DC: Congressional Quarterly Service, 1963), p. 77.

170. Memo, Henry Fowler to JFK, "Tax Bill Strategy and Tactics," no date, Presidential Office Files, Box 90, Treasury 9/63, JFK.

171. Ibid.

172. "Lower Taxes, Higher Revenue—Can LBJ Do It?," *U.S. News and World Report,* January 20, 1964, pp. 84–85.

173. "Taxes and Economic Policy," *Congressional Quarterly Almanac* (Washington, DC: Congressional Quarterly Service, 1964), pp. 518–27.

174. "House Votes $11.2 Billion Tax Cut," *Congressional Quarterly Almanac,* p. 497.

175. Memo, Henry Fowler to JFK, "Organizing Procedure for the Business and Finance Committee for Tax Reduction in 1963," Presidential Office Files, Box 90, Treasury 4/63, JFK.

176. Ibid.

177. Memo, Henry Fowler to JFK, 5/24/63, Presidential Office Files, Box 90, Treasury 5/63, JFK.

178. "Tax Cut Committee Picks Co-Chairmen," *New York Times,* May 4, 1963, p. 34.

179. *National Conference on Tax Reduction,* 9/63, p. 3, Presidential Office Files, Box 90, Treasury Tax Reduction Business Committee 9/63, JFK.

180. John Morris, "Business Group to Push Tax Cut," *New York Times,* April 14, 1963, p. 55.

181. Memo, Henry Fowler to JFK, 9/23/63, Presidential Office Files, Box 90, Treasury 9/63, JFK.

182. Ibid.

183. These associations included among others the National Association of Railroads, American Textile Manufacturing Association, American Petroleum Institute, Independent Petroleum Association, National Coal Association, National Association of Electrical Companies, Electronics Manufacturers Association, Aerospace Industries, Chamber of Commerce, National Association of Auto Dealers, American Retail Federation, National Association of Independent Business, American Trucking Association, National Association of Home Builders, National League of Insured Savings Associations, National Association of Real Estate Boards, and the U.S. Savings and Loan League.

184. Memo, Henry Fowler to JFK, 9/23/63, Presidential Office Files, Box 90, Treasury 9/63, JFK.

185. Ibid.

Chapter 4

1. Memo, Arthur Okun to LBJ, "Commerce–SEC Survey," 5/28/66, p. 1, CF BE5, National Economy (May 1966), LBJ.

2. Memo, Walter Heller to LBJ, "That Tax Increase Again," 5/13/66, CF FI11–4, Income Tax (1964–66), LBJ.

3. "Notes on Suspension of Investment Credit and Accelerated Depreciation," CEA, 9/8/66, EX LE/FI11–4, 4/7/66–9/15/66, LBJ.

4. Memo, Wirtz to LBJ, EX FI11–4, 6/11/67–7/15/67, attached to memo, Califano to LBJ, 7/11/67, LBJ.

5. Memo, Fowler to LBJ, 7/11/67, EX FI11–4, 6/11/67–7/15/67, attached to memo, Califano to LBJ, 7/11/67, LBJ.

6. Memo, Martin to LBJ, EX FI11–4, 6/11/67–7/15/56, attached to memo, Califano to LBJ, 7/11/67, LBJ.

7. Memo, Ackley to LBJ, "The Case for Higher Taxes," 5/10/66, p. 1, EX FI11, 3/17/66–8/20/66, LBJ.

8. Ibid.

9. Memo, Secretary of Labor to LBJ, "The Economy and the Government," 3/17/66, CF FI11, Taxation, LBJ.

10. Memo, Heller to LBJ, "Boost Taxes, Cut Interest Rates," 11/23/66, EX BE5, 9/27/66–11/27/66, LBJ.

11. Memo, Martin to LBJ, 12/13/66, EX FI11–4, 10/11/66–12/15/66, attached to note, Martin to LBJ, 12/13/66, LBJ. Memo, Fowler to LBJ, "Economic and Financial Policy Mix for 1967," 12/10/66, EX BE5, 12/1/66–12/15/66, attached to memo, Califano to LBJ, 12/11/66, LBJ.

12. Memo, Ackley to LBJ, "Tax Policy and Deficits," 12/13/66, EX FI11–4, 10/11/66–12/15/66, LBJ.

13. Memo, Martin to LBJ, 12/13/66, EX FI11–4, 10/11/66–12/15/66, attached to note, Martin to LBJ, 12/13/66, LBJ.

14. Memo, Ackley to LBJ, "Tax Policy and Deficits," 12/13/66, EX FI11–4, 10/11/66–12/15/66, LBJ.

15. Memo, Califano to LBJ, "Your FY1968 Tax Decision," 12/21/66, CF FI11–4, Income Tax (1964–66), LBJ.

16. Memo, Gardner Ackley to LBJ, "Effect of a Tax Increase on Government Revenues," 12/11/66, EX FI11–4, 10/11/66–12/15/66, LBJ.

17. Memo, Fowler to LBJ, "A Proposed Economic Program and Rationale," 12/23/66, CF FI11–4, Income Tax (1964–66), LBJ.

18. Memo, Fowler to LBJ, "The Need for Tax Restraint," 5/11/66, EX FI11, 3/17/66–8/20/66, LBJ.

19. Ibid., p. 3.

20. Memo, Ackley to LBJ, "The Case for Higher Taxes," 5/10/66, LBJ.

21. Memo, Joe Califano to LBJ, 5/2/68, EX LE/FI11–4, 5/1/68–5/15/68, LBJ.

22. Memo, Louis Martin to Joe Califano, 3/29/68, EX LE/FI11 4, 2/1/68–4/30/68, LBJ.

23. Memo, Joseph Barr to LBJ, "Tax Bill and the Fate of Antipoverty Programs," EX FI11–4, 3/28/68–5/20/68, LBJ.

24. "Patsy Mink," Papers of Barefoot Sanders, Tax Increase Headcount 1967, LBJ.

25. "Congressional Comments on Tax Proposal," Barefoot Sanders Personal Papers, Tax Bill 1967, LBJ.

26. Ibid.

27. Memo, Charles Schultze to LBJ, "Wilbur Mills and the Tax Bill," 9/16/67, EX LE/FI11–4, 9/1/67–10/15/67, LBJ. Much later, the executive advisers were inclined to think that Mills was trying to "torpedo the tax bill." Memo, Califano to LBJ, 5/2/68, EX LE/FI11–4, 5/1/68–5/15/68, LBJ.

28. Memo, Barefoot Sanders to LBJ, 11/28/67, EX FI11–4, 10/16/67–12/13/67, LBJ.

29. Memo, Marvin Watson to LBJ, 10/3/67, EX LE/FI11–4, 9/1/67–10/15/67, LBJ.

30. Memo, Charles Roche to LBJ, 10/2/67, EX LE/FI11–4, 9/1/67–10/15/67, LBJ.

31. Memo, Barefoot Sanders to LBJ, 5/23/68, CF LE/FI8-CF/FI11–3, CF LE/FI11–4, LBJ.

32. *President's Proposal on Suspension of the Investment Credit and Application of Accelerated Depreciation,* Hearings before the Committee on Ways and Means (Washington, DC: U.S. Government Printing Office, 1966), p. 253.

33. Ways and Means Hearings, 1966, p. 245.

34. Letter, Hervey Machen to LBJ, 10/4/66, EX BE5, 9/27/66–11/31/66, LBJ.

35. "Are Tax Increases Always Necessary?" *Banking,* November 1967, pp. 51–52.

36. The American Bankers Association was the one exception to this: they endorsed a surtax after tax credits and contingent on spending cuts. Ways and Means Hearings, 1967, p. 393.

37. Memo to LBJ, author unnamed, "The Business Economists' View of 1976," 10/26/66, EX BE5, 9/27/66–11/31/66, LBJ.

38. The National Association of Manufacturers found that most top executives were

not opposed to the reinstatement of the 52 percent corporate tax rate, although suspension of the investment tax credit was considered impractical. The Gallagher President's Report, 9/7/66, WHCF EX BE5, 8/25/66–9/26/66, LBJ. By October 1967, 75 percent of the National Association of Business Economists were for the surtax including many who "were opposed or on the fence a couple of months ago." The main reason for the shift in expert opinion was the strengthening of third-quarter GNP, the "fifth largest quarterly advance ever." Memo, Ackley to LBJ, 10/13/67, EX FI11–4, 9/26/67–12/13/67, LBJ.

39. Memo, Trowbridge to LBJ, "Business Support for Tax Message," 8/3/67, EX LE/FI11–4, 7/1/67–8/31/67, attached to memo, Califano to LBJ, 8/18/67, LBJ.

40. Ways and Means Hearings, 1966, pp. 235–37.

41. Memo, Trowbridge to LBJ, "Meeting with Executives of the Retail Industry, November 9, 1967," 11/10/67, EX FI11–4, 9/26/67–12/13/67, LBJ.

42. Memo, Fowler to LBJ, 5/11/66, EX FI11, 3/17/66–8/20/66, LBJ.

43. Memo plus attachments, Fowler to LBJ, 3/29/66, CF BE, Business Economics 1966, LBJ. The Business Council's Treasury Consultant Group met regularly with Secretary Fowler and was composed primarily of businessmen from the manufacturing sector. Only Sidney Weinberg (Goldman, Sachs) was from a financial firm.

44. Memo, Jack Valenti to LBJ, 3/25/66, EX SO2/3-30-66, 3/1/66–3/26/66, LBJ. Of the 120 businessmen who attended the meeting only 3 were from financial institutions: Sidney Weinberg (Goldman, Sachs), Howard Clark (American Express), and Thomas Gates (Morgan Guaranty Trust). Four guests were from major retail concerns: Crowdus Baker (Sears, Roebuck & Company), William Batten (J. C. Penney), Justin Dart (Rexall Drug), and Fred Lazarus (Federated Department Stores). With a few exceptions, such as Kermit Gordon from the Brookings Institution, the rest of the guests were from manufacturing concerns. Guest list, "Dinner at the White House," 3/30/66, EX SO2/3-30-66, 3/1/66–3/26/66, LBJ.

45. "Summary of Response to the President's Request for Restraint in Business Capital Spending," EX BE5, 3/22/66–4/29/66, LBJ.

46. Letter, Charles Allen Thomas, Monsanto Chemical Co, to LBJ, 4/6/66, EX SO2/3-30-66, 4/13/66–4/22/66, LBJ.

47. Letter, Langborne Williams, Freeport Sulphur Company, to LBJ, 4/20/66, EX FI11–4, 4/20/66–7/6/66, attached to memo, Califano to Williams, LBJ.

48. Memo, Jack Connor to LBJ, 4/4/66, EX SO2/3-30-66, 3/27/66–4/12/66, LBJ.

49. The committee was chaired by David Rockefeller; six of its nine private sector members were from finance. Memo, Otto Eckstein to LBJ, "The Tax Question and the Business Leadership," 4/29/66, EX BE5, 4/30/66–5/21/66, attached to memo, Califano to LBJ, 5/2/66, LBJ.

50. Letter, David Rockefeller to LBJ, 4/4/66, EX BE5, 3/22/66–4/29/66, attached to letter, Califano to David Rockefeller, 4/25, LBJ.

51. Memo, Marvin Watson to LBJ, 4/11/66, EX BE4, 3/22/66–4/29/66, LBJ.

52. Letter, Robert Gerholz to LBJ, 4/19/66, EX SO2/3-30-66, 4/13/66–4/22/66, LBJ.

53. "Report to the President by Secretary of Commerce John T. Connor on Business Cooperation in the Stabilization Effort," EX BE5, 6/1/66–7/14/66, LBJ, attached to memo, Kintner to Morton.

54. Memo, "A Program to Insure Stable Prosperity," 8/29/66, CF BE5, National Economy (August 1966), attached to memo, Califano to LBJ, 8/29/66, LBJ.

55. Memo, Ackley to LBJ, "An Immediate Tax Program," 8/9/66, EX FI11, 3/17/66–8/20/66, LBJ.

56. Memo, Okun to LBJ, "The Case for Suspending Accelerated Depreciation on Buildings," 9/3/66, EX FI11–4, 7/7/66–10/10/66, LBJ.

57. Memo, Fowler to LBJ, EX FI11–4, 12/16/66–1/15/67, LBJ. Kermit Gordon (CEA) used balance-of-payment arguments to promote suspension. Memo, Gordon to LBJ, "Secretary Fowler's Memorandum on a Tax Increase Program," 8/22/66, EX FI11, 8/21/66–1/2/67, attached to memo, Ackley to LBJ, "Comments on Joe Fowler's "Tax Increase Program," 8/22/66, LBJ.

58. Fowler, "Economic Pros and Cons on the Advisability of an Administration Request to Suspend the Investment Credit in This Session of Congress," EX FI11–4, 7/7/66–10/10/66, attached to memo, Fowler to LBJ, 8/23/66, LBJ.

59. Memo, Fowler, "Memorandum on September 1966 Program," CF BE5, National Economy (August 1966), attached to memo, Califano to LBJ, 8/29/66, LBJ.

60. Wire, Robert Roosa to LBJ, 8/31/66, WHCF EX BE5, 8/22/66–9/26/66, LBJ.

61. Memo, Ackley to LBJ, "Financial Markets," 8/26/66, EX BE5, 8/25/66–9/26/66, LBJ.

62. These included groups such as the National Association of Real Estate Boards, National Association of Home Builders, and Realty Committee on Taxation. Ways and Means Hearings, 1966, pp. 245–47.

63. Letter, William Biggs to Hubert Humphrey, 9/6/66, EX FI11–4, 7/7/66–10/10/66, attached to memo, Humphrey to Califano, 9/7/66, LBJ.

64. Ways and Means Hearings, 1966, pp. 273, 285, 167.

65. Ibid., pp. 281, 273.

66. Ibid., pp. 344–45, 293, 285.

67. Memo, Califano to LBJ, 9/8/66, 5:30 P.M.; memo, Califano to LBJ, 9/8/66, 6:30 P.M., both in EX BE5, 8/25/66–9/26/66, LBJ.

68. Letter, William Verity to LBJ, 9/7/66, EX LE/FI11–4, 4/7/66–9/15/66, LBJ.

69. Interview with congressman. Memo, Walter Heller to LBJ, 8/20/66, EX BE5, 7/15/66–8/24/66, LBJ.

70. Memo, Fowler to LBJ, "Talking Paper for Telephone Conversation with Congressman Mills," 9/16/66, EX LE/FI11–4, 9/16/66–10/31/66, LBJ.

71. Memo, Gardner Ackley to Joe Califano, 9/19/66, CF BE, National Economy (September December 1966), LBJ.

72. Saunders supported the suspension but asked that exemptions be granted to railroad equipment, airlines, and steel. Ways and Means Hearings, 1966, pp. 147–52.

73. Memo, Fowler to LBJ, 9/20/66, EX LE/FI11, 4/3/66–, LBJ.

74. Memo, Joseph Barr to Marvin Watson, 9/26/66, EX LE/FI11–4, 9/16/66–10/31/66, LBJ.

75. The airline industry also lobbied for sweeteners to be obtained after the suspension period was over: an increase in the amount of tax liability that could be offset by the investment tax credit and an extension of the carryover period for unused credits. Memo, Charlie Murphy to Califano, 9/9/66, WHCF EX LE/FI11–4, 4/7/66–9/15/66; memo, Fowler to LBJ, "HR17607—Suspension of the Investment Credit and Accelerated Depreciation," 9/15/66, WHCF EX LE/FI11–4, 9/16/66–10/31/66, attached to Fowler memo, "Talking Paper for Telephone Conversation with Congressman Mills," LBJ.

76. Memo, Ackley to LBJ, "Implications of the Plant and Equipment Survey," 3/7/67, EX FI11–4, 2/24/67–3/15/67, LBJ.

77. Telegrams arrived from individuals and trade associations in many sectors: railroads, machine tools, chemicals, oil, airlines, and lumber, among others. See EX FI11–4, 2/24/67–4/24/67, LBJ.

78. Republicans also wanted to increase the limit on the credit to 50 percent on March 10 instead of waiting until January 1, 1968, as the original legislation specified. They also pushed for a very flexible cancellation rule which would allow firms to cancel contracts made during the six-month period and then reinstate the orders. Memo, Henry Wilson to LBJ, 3/15/67, EX LE/FI11–4, 11/1/66–6/30/67, LBJ.

79. The president's bill would lose $605 million in revenue; the House version would lose $1.28 billion. Rolling the effective date back to October 10 would push the loss to $1.53 billion. Memo, Fowler to LBJ, 3/21/67, EX LE/FI11–4, 11/1/66–6/30/66, LBJ.

80. Memo, Ackley to LBJ, "Briefing Paper on Economic Policy for 1967," 1/4/67, CF BE5, National Economy (1967–1968), emphasis in the original, LBJ.

81. Memo, Fowler to LBJ, 7/11/67, EX FI11–4, 6/11/67–7/15/67, attached to memo, Califano to LBJ, 7/11/67, LBJ.

82. Deficit reduction in and of itself was not cause enough to take the leap. Memo, Ackley to LBJ, "Reactions to Your Economic Policy Program," 2/25/67, EX BE5, 12/16/66–3/15/67, LBJ.

83. Memo, Fowler to LBJ, 2/20/67, EX FI11–4, 1/25/67–2/23/67, LBJ.

84. Memo, Ackley to LBJ, "Economic Situation and Strategy," 5/22/67,, EX BE5, 3/16/67–7/15/67, LBJ.

85. First National City Bank urged caution in its monthly newsletter. Monthly Economic Letter, EX FI11–4, 10/11/66–12/15/66, LBJ. Goldman, Sachs economists, on the other hand, supported the president's package, calling it "a notable achievement" combining "maximum budgetary benefit with minimum adverse effect on income flows." Statement, Goldman, Sachs, "Implications of the Tax Proposal," 1/11/67, EX FI11–4, 1/16/67–1/24/67, attached to memo, Fowler to LBJ, 1/16/67, LBJ.

86. Memo, Ackley to LBJ, "Quotable Quotes on the Economy and Your Fiscal Program," 8/29/67, Barefoot Sanders Personal Papers, Tax Bill (1967), LBJ.

87. Memo, Fowler to LBJ, "Views of New York Bankers," 7/26/67, CF FI11, "Taxation," attached to memo, Califano to LBJ, 7/26/67, LBJ.

88. *President's 1967 Tax Proposals,* Hearings before the Committee on Ways and Means (Washington, DC: U.S. Government Printing Office, 1967), p. 389.

89. Ways and Means Hearings, 1967, pp. 327, 307.

90. Memo, Trowbridge, "Summary of Business Opinion Survey on Tax Increase," 7/26/67, CF FI11, "Taxation," attached to memo, Califano to LBJ, 7/26/67, LBJ.

91. The single most frequently cited reason against a surtax was a prefernce for expenditure cuts. Memo, Ackley to LBJ, "More on Economists' Support for the Tax Increase," 9/11/67, EX FI11–4, 8/15/67–9/21/67, LBJ.

92. Ways and Means Hearings, 1967, p. 416.

93. Memo, Trowbridge, "Summary of Business Opinion Survey on Tax Increase," 7/26/67, CF FI11, "Taxation," attached to Memo, Califano to LBJ, 7/26/67, LBJ.

94. Memo, Fowler to LBJ, "Views of New York Bankers," 7/26/67, CF FI11, "Taxation," attached to memo, Califano to LBJ, 7/26/67, LBJ.

95. In the administration's original proposal, the surtax was to be applied before

the investment credit was subtracted from net taxes. First, precedent demanded it: prior surtaxes and percentage tax cuts were applied before credits were taken. Second, if the investment tax credit were taken before the surtax, the credit proportion of total tax liability would increase from 7 to 7.7 percent. Also, if corporations were allowed to take credits first, they would have lower effective surtax rates than individuals. The financial community did not object to the administration's proposal; they were scarcely affected by the distinction. Memo, Fowler to LBJ, "Surcharge and Tax Credits," 8/21/67, EX LE/FI11–4, 7/1/67–8/31/67, attached to memo, Califano to LBJ, 8/21/67, LBJ.

96. Letter, Henry Ford II to LBJ, 8/11/67, EX FI11–4, 8/15/67–9/21/67, attached to letter, Califano to Ford, 8/22/67, LBJ.

97. Ways and Means Hearings, 1967, pp. 239–41.

98. Letter, Joe Califano to Allan Shivers, 8/28/67, GEN BE, 12/9/65–5/3/66, LBJ.

99. Ways and Means Hearings, 1967, pp. 257–58.

100. Memo, Wirtz to LBJ, EX FI11–4, 6/11/67–7/15/67, attached to memo, Califano to LBJ, 7/11/67, LBJ.

101. Memo, Schultze to LBJ, 7/11/67, EX FI11–4, 6/11/67–7/15/67, attached to memo, Califano to LBJ, 7/11/67, LBJ.

102. Memo, Schultze to LBJ, "Can the Economy Stand a Tax Increase?" 7/17/67, EX BE5, 7/16/67–10/20/67, LBJ.

103. Memo, Trowbridge to LBJ, 7/11/67, EX FI11–4, 6/11/67–7/15/67, LBJ.

104. Memo, Fowler to LBJ, 7/11/67, EX FI11–4, 6/11/67–7/15/67, attached to memo, Califano to LBJ, 7/11/67, LBJ.

105. Memo, Ackley to LBJ, "Cost of Not Increasing Taxes," 10/4/67, EX FI11–4, 9/26/67–12/13/67, LBJ.

106. Stocks had been overpriced due to expectations of inflation. Memo, Gardner Ackley to LBJ, "Reaction of Financial Markets to Your Tax Message," 8/3/67, EX LE/FI11–4, 7/1/67–8/31/67, LBJ.

107. Memo, Sanders to LBJ, 1/24/68, EX LE/FI11–4, 1/1/68–1/31/68, LBJ.

108. Memo, James Jones to the president, "Congressional Leadership Breakfast," 9/19/67, Meeting Notes File, 9/19/67, 8:36 A.M., LBJ.

109. Memo, Stanley Surrey, "Memo on Conversations with Congressmen Ullman and Bush on the Tax Surcharge," LE/FI11–4, 9/1/67–10/15/67, attached to memo, Fowler to LBJ, "Ways and Means Committee and Tax Bill," 9/20/67, LBJ.

110. Also, the administration wanted to make it known that it had done all it could to get the tax increase; should the effort end in failure, blame should be pinned on the Republicans. Memo, Schultze to LBJ, "Impasse on the Tax Increase," 10/13/67, EX LE/FI11–4, 9/1/67–10/15/67, LBJ.

111. Memo, Fowler to LBJ, "Situation Report as of November 5," EX BE5, 6/1/68–, LBJ.

112. Memo, Joe Califano to LBJ, 10/7/67, CF LE/FI11–4, LBJ.

113. Memo, Califano to LBJ, 11/27/67, EX LE/FI11–4, 10/16/67–12/31/67, LBJ.

114. Press Release, "Summary of Announcement by Chairman Mills," 11/20/67, Barefoot Sanders Personal Papers, Tax Bill (1967), LBJ.

115. Memo, Califano to LBJ, 11/27/67, 3:15 P.M., EX FI11–4, 9/26/67–12/13/67, LBJ.

116. Memo, Califano to LBJ, 11/27/67, 5:15 P.M., EX LE/FI11–4, 10/16/67–12/31/67, LBJ.

117. "What Sank the Tax Bill," *Business Week,* January 27, 1968, pp. 27–29.

118. Memo, Barefoot Sanders to LBJ, 2/24/68, EX LE/FI11–4, 2/1/68–4/30/68, LBJ.

119. "Gold Rush Dusts Off the Tax Bill," *Business Week,* March 28, 1968, p. 33.

120. Memo, Sanders to LBJ, 3/15/68, EX LE/FI11–4, 2/1/68–4/30/68, LBJ.

121. "Tax Hike Gets Its First O.K.," *Business Week,* April 6, 1968, pp. 28–29.

122. Memo, Fowler to LBJ, "Tax Bill," 3/22/68, CF LE/FI11–4, LBJ.

123. "Tax Hike Gets Its First O.K.," pp. 28–29.

124. Memo, Sanders to LBJ, 4/4/68, EX LE/FI11–4, 2/1/68–4/30/68, LBJ.

125. Memo, Califano to LBJ, 4/30/68, EX LE/FI11–4, 2/1/68–4/30/68, attached to memo, Zwick to LBJ, "Conversations with Richard Stoner," 4/30/68, LBJ.

126. Memo, Zwick to LBJ, "Tax Conference," 5/2/68, EX LE/FI11–4, 5/1/68–5/15/68, LBJ.

127. Memo, Sanders to LBJ, 5/2/68, EX LE/FI11–4, 5/1/68–5/15/68, LBJ.

128. Memo, Califano to LBJ, 5/2/68, EX LE/FI11–4, 5/1/68–5/15/68, LBJ.

129. Memo, DeVier Pierson, 5/3/68, EX LE/FI11–4, 5/1/68–5/15/68, LBJ.

130. Memo, Fowler to LBJ, "Conferees' Action on the Tax Bill," 5/9/68, EX LE/FI11–4, 5/1/68–5/15/68, LBJ.

131. Memo, Sanders to LBJ, 5/9/68, EX LE/FI11–4, 5/1/68–5/15/68, LBJ, emphasis in the original.

132. Private individuals attending included C. Douglas Dillon, Henry Ford II, Thomas Gates, Jr., Werner Gullander, Frederick Kappel, William Murphy, Albert Nickerson, Rudolph Peterson, David Rockefeller, Stuart Saunders, Allan Shivers, Harris Ward, Sidney Weinberg, Frazar Wilde, and Walter Wriston.

133. "Notes of the Luncheon Meeting of the President with Business Leaders," 8/10/67, Meeting Notes File, August 10, 1967, Luncheon Meeting with Business Leaders, attached to memo, George Christian to LBJ, 8/15/67, LBJ.

134. "Press Release," 8/24/67, EX LE/FI11, 11/22/63–12/20/63, attached to memo, Califano to LBJ, 8/24/67, LBJ.

135. Press Release, W. A. Lashley, 9/13/67, EX LE/FI11–4, 9/1/67–10/15/67, attached to memo, Ackley to LBJ, "The Growing Consensus on Tax Policy," LBJ.

136. Memo, "Work on Tax Bill," Fowler to LBJ, 8/18/67, "Attachment B," EX LE/FI11–4, 7/1/67–8/31/67, LBJ.

137. Ibid.

138. Memo, John Horne to Henry Fowler, 8/29/67, EX LE/FI11–4, 7/1/67–8/31/67, LBJ.

139. Memo, Larry Levinson to Joe Califano, 8/7/67, EX LE/FI11–4, 7/1/67–8/31/67, LBJ.

140. Memo, Marvin Watson to LBJ, 9/16/67, EX FI11–4, 8/15/67–9/21/67, LBJ.

141. Memo, Ackley to LBJ, "Report on a Dinner," 8/27/67, LE/FI11–4, 9/26/67–12/13/67, LBJ.

Chapter 5

1. See Lester Thurow's *The Zero-Sum Society: Distribution and the Possibilities for Economic Change* (New York: Basic Books, 1980).

2. Krieger, *Reagan, Thatcher, and the Politics of Decline,* p. 26.

3. See Ferguson and Rogers, *Right Turn;* and Edsall, *New Politics of Inequality.*

4. Although the 1973 oil crisis is often given as the starting point of the crisis, signs of weakening in the economy were apparent in the late 1960s. Bowles, Gordon, and Weisskopf, *Beyond the Waste Land.*

5. Epstein, "Domestic Stagflation and Monetary Policy," in Ferguson and Rogers, *The Hidden Election,* pp. 141–95.

6. Bosworth, *Tax Incentives and Economic Growth,* p. 7.

7. Wolff, "Magnitude and Causes of the Recent Productivity Slowdown in the United States," in Baumol and McLennan, *Productivity Growth and U.S. Competitiveness,* p. 32.

8. President's Commission on Industrial Competitiveness, *Global Competition,* p. 11.

9. Ibid., p. 12.

10. The Federal Reserve can control inflation in two ways: through manipulation of interest rates and through buying and selling Treasury notes to control the expansion and contraction of bank reserves. Beginning in October of 1979 the Federal Reserve under the leadership of Paul Volcker began a monetarist approach, controlling the money supply through reserve requirements and allowing interest rates to respond to the market. The technique used has an effect on how the economy functions. If changes in credit demand occur, the Federal Reserve must expand the bank reserves and the money supply in order to keep interest rates at the same level. Yet, if one is determined to keep bank reserves at a certain level, credit demand increases will push interest rates up instead. Joseph Pechman and Barry Bosworth, in Joseph Pechman, ed., *Setting National Priorities: The 1983 Budget* (Washington, DC: Brookings Institution, 1982), p. 45. "The Fed Is Likely to Stick to Its Guns," *Business Week,* July 14, 1980, p. 37.

11. Epstein, "Domestic Stagflation and Monetary Policy," in Ferguson and Rogers, *The Hidden Election,* p. 143.

12. James Fallow, "The Reagan Variety Show," *New York Review of Books,* April 12, 1984, p. 10.

13. Stein, *Presidential Economics,* pp. 255–56.

14. Paul Craig Roberts, *The Supply-Side Revolution* (Cambridge, MA: Harvard University Press, 1984), pp. 94–96.

15. In the 1960s fiscal policy was used to eradicate the natural lows of the business cycle; an expansionary monetary policy was pursued to pay for the deficits created by these fiscal interventions. This strategy culminated in inflation and ultimately stagflation and a confusing stop-go policy which alternatively tried to reduce inflation by a tight monetary policy and stimulate growth by the relaxation of that policy.

16. The monetarist revolution elevates the concept of economic expectations and reopens questions about the long-run. Stein, *Presidential Economics,* pp. 223, 294–96.

17. Alan Greenspan, "Statement," Hearings before the Committee on Ways and Means, *Tax Aspects of the President's Economic Program,* Serial 97–10 (Washington, DC: U.S. Government Printing Office, March 5, 1981), pp. 496–500.

18. Roberts, *Supply-Side Revolution,* pp. 94–95.

19. Stephen Rattner, "Top Officials Clash on Tax Cut Timing," *New York Times,* January 28, 1981, pp. D1, 4.

20. Roberts, *Supply-Side Revolution,* p. 116.

21. Although Treasury was home to the supply-siders, not all Treasury staff shared

the faith. Deputy Secretary McNamar and Buck Chapotan, Assistant Secretary for Tax Policy, were viewed by the supply-siders as enemies to the cause. Ibid., p. 183.

22. Ibid., pp. 91–92.

23. "Democrats Draw a Battle Line over Tax Cuts," *Business Week,* April 13, 1981, p. 135.

24. Edward Cowan, "Dole Cites Panel Doubt on Tax Cut," *New York Times,* May 12, 1981, p. D1.

25. "Conservative Southerners Are Enjoying Their Wooing as Key to Tax Bill Success," *Congressional Quarterly,* June 13, 1981, pp. 1023–24.

26. "Democrats Draw a Battle Line over Tax Cuts," p. 135.

27. Interviews with Ways and Means staff.

28. Interview with congressman; Gerald Rosen, "The Key to Reagan's Program," *Dun's Review,* March 1981, pp. 54–57.

29. Ferguson and Rogers, *Right Turn.*

30. Edsall, *New Politics of Inequality,* p. 31.

31. Interview with Ways and Means staff.

32. Banks and savings and loans would be able to issue these one-year, tax-exempt savings certificates at 70 percent of the interest rate on current one-year Treasury bills. It was argued that the costs of these mortgages would go down since the interest rates were lower than the normal taxable rates. Since new money market accounts could offer much higher returns on savings than saving and loan institutions, the latter were having difficulty attracting savers and remaining solvent. The "all savers" provision, therefore, would put the failing mortgage institutions on a more competitive basis.

33. "'All-Savers' Plan: Some Second Thoughts," *Congressional Quarterly,* July 11, 1981, p. 1214.

34. Included were the American Bankers Association, Mortgage Bankers Association of America, National Association of Mutual Savings Banks, U.S. League of Savings Institutions, National Association of Realtors, and National Association of Home Builders. The realtors wanted 5 percent across-the-board individual tax cuts for each of the three years instead of the annual 10 percent formula. House Ways and Means Committee Hearings, *Tax Aspects of the President's Economic Program,* part 2, 2/24/81–4/7/81 (Washington DC: U.S. Government Printing Office, 1981), pp. 699–700, 720.

35. The industry associations tried to meet these objections, endorsing the Financial Accounting Standards Board's definition of research and development, making the tax credit apply only to incremental increases, and increasing the credit to 25 percent. American Electronics Association, "Not By Accident: Heros of the 1981 Tax Bill," internal document.

36. Under the existing law the options would be taxed as ordinary income at the time they were received. The industry wanted the stock options taxed only when the employee sells the stock, with the profits treated as a capital gain. Lloyd Schwartz, "Industry-backed Tax Measure Appears in Senate Panel's Bill," *Electronic News,* September 15, 1980, p. Q.

37. American Electronics Association, *Not by Accident.* 38. As it then stood, the corporate tax rate was graduated only up to the first $100,000 of income. Michael Thoryn, "It's Taxes' Turn," *Nation's Business,* December 1980, p. 38.

38. As it then stood, the corporate tax rate was graduated only up to the first

$100,000 of income, Michael Thoryn, "It's Taxes' Turn," *Nation's Business*, December 1980, p. 38.

39. The system in use until 1979 classified steel plant equipment as having eighteen-year asset lives. In 1979 the depreciation life was changed to fifteen years. Ways and Means Hearings, 1981, p. 1430.

40. The paper industry also requested that depreciation schedules be flexible to allow for longer-range planning and cyclical profitability. The industry also wanted as much first-year depreciation as possible and requested double declining balance in the five-year category. In the paper and timber industry, sales are considered capital gains rather than ordinary income. Periodically, reformers question this categorization; however, 1981 was not such a year.

41. Ways and Means Hearings, 1981, p. 1433.

42. Two men have been given credit for developing the actual safe harbor leasing concept: a Chicago lawyer named Fred Hickman who represented a large railroad car manufacturer and a Treasury lawyer, Bill McKee, who had worked with leasebacks in a Wall Street firm. Hickman and John Meaghar of LTD contacted Bill McKee at the Treasury and pointed out that cyclical industries had been accumulating unearned investment tax credits since 1978. The creation of ACRS would only compound this problem. McKee was sympathetic and went to work on the concept. Treasury staff were initially skeptical, worried as they were about the relative benefits made available to the buyers and sellers. Yet the provision was included as a bid for the support of basic industries.

43. Interview with a lobbyist.

44. The depletion allowance had been scheduled under the Windfall Profit Tax Act to decrease to 18 percent. The stripper well provision was the most crucial of the demands, followed by the exemption for royalty owners. From the beginning, the independents doubted they would be able to freeze the depletion allowance; however, they included it as a bargaining tool. *Petroleum Independent*, October 1981, p. 15.

45. Edsall, *New Politics of Inequality*.

46. Ibid., pp. 121–29.

47. Interview with industry participant.

48. Interview.

49. A. F. Ehrbar, "The Battle over Taxes," *Fortune*, April 19, 1982, p. 62.

50. Interviews.

51. Interview with oil trade representative.

52. Ann Reilly, "What Business Wants from Reagan," *Dun's Review*, March 1981, p. 47.

53. *Business and Public Affairs Fortnightly*, vol. 6, no. 13 (September 1, 1984).

54. In the original Carlton Group, expensing had been NFIB's policy of choice; however, the National Association of Manufacturers resisted expensing as a policy option. The National Association of Manufacturers, instrumental in devising accelerated cost recovery, was reluctant to abandon its brainchild.

55. Edward Knight, *The Reagan Strategy: Implications for Small Business* (Washington, DC: Congressional Research Service, October 2, 1981), p. 13.

56. Interview.

57. "No Big Breaks for Small Business in the Tax Cuts," *Business Week*, August 24, 1981, p. 100.

58. House Ways and Means Hearings, part 2, 1981, p. 1137.

59. The president defended his position and deflected criticism of the projected deficits by endorsing the Laffer curve. This was an attempt to reconcile the top priorities of both the supply-siders and the traditional economists. Roberts has criticized this early promise as unrealistic and as making later compromise on the tax cuts inevitable. Roberts, *Supply-Side Revolution,* pp. 95–96.

60. Interview with high-ranking administration official.

61. Interview with industry representative.

62. Dale Tate, "Tax Cut Compromise Barred as Committee Markups Near," *Congressional Quarterly,* April 18, 1981, pp. 670–71.

63. "The Emerging Deal on Taxes," *Business Week,* June 1, 1981, p. 28.

64. Lee Walczak, "Reagan's New Flexibility on Taxes," *Business Week,* April 20, 1981, p. 131.

65. Interview; Bill Keller, "Democrats and Republicans Try to Outbid Each Other in Cutting Taxes for Business," *Congressional Quarterly,* June 27, 1981, p. 1136.

66. Interview with congressman.

67. Dale Tate, "Tax Cut Proves Elusive," *Congressional Quarterly,* May 30, 1981, p. 937.

68. Ibid.

69. Interview with congressman.

70. Dale Tate, "Reagan and Rostenkowski Modify Tax Cut Proposals to Woo Conservative Votes," *Congressional Quarterly,* June 6, 1981, p. 979.

71. Ibid.

72. Interview with congressman.

73. Tate, "Reagan and Rostenkowski Modify Tax Cut Proposals to Woo Conservative Votes," p. 979. When Reagan presented his modified program on June 4, 1981, he scaled back some of the benefits for the retailing industry. Most upsetting was the change in the depreciation schedules from ten to fifteen years with 150 percent declining balance. "Tax Bill Amendment Changes Retail Supported Provision," *Federation Report* 8, no. 29 (July 27, 1981): p. 1.

74. Interviews with various industry and administration participants.

75. Interview with industry lobbyist.

76. "Less Help than Expected," *Business Week,* June 22, 1981, p. 31.

77. Keller, "Democrats and Republicans Try to Outbid Each Other in Cutting Taxes for Business," p. 1136.

78. "Tax Council Plans Seminar," Electronics Industry Association Executive Report, September–October 1981, p. 3.

79. Interview.

80. American Electronics Association, "Not by Accident."

81. Interview. There were some divisions between the trade associations here. Although the American Electronics Association, a group of small West Coast firms, worked with the Democrats, the Electronics Industry Association, the big multinationals, supported the Republicans.

82. Keller, "Democrats and Republicans Try to Outbid Each Other in Cutting Taxes for Business," p. 1136.

83. "Coming: Tax Incentives to Stimulate Research and Development," *Business Week,* July 6, 1981, p. 76.

84. The industry persuaded John Glenn to propose an amendment on the Senate floor to include the comprehensive credit in the Senate bill as well.

85. Jack Robertson, "Industry Applauds Both Democratic and GOP Tax Cut Bills," *Electronic News*, July 27, 1981, p. 8.

86. Pamela Fessler, "Swift Passage Sought for Senate Tax Bill," *Congressional Quarterly*, July 11, 1981, p. 1211.

87. *Petroleum Independent*, October 1981, pp. 10–13.

88. Interview.

89. *Petroleum Independent*, October 1981, p. 14.

90. *Petroleum Independent*, August 1981, p. 31.

91. *Petroleum Independent*, October 1981, pp. 14–15.

92. Pamela Fessler, "Senate Backs Tax Indexing; House Bill Gels," *Congressional Quarterly*, July 18, 1981, p. 1307.

93. *Petroleum Independent*, October 1981, p. 15.

94. Interview with industry lobbyist.

95. Interviews. Tim Carrington, "Sold Short? Many Wall Streeters Regret They Helped Reagan Pass Tax Bill," *Wall Street Journal*, September 11, 1981, pp. 1, 20.

96. "Reagan Economic Plan Nears Enactment," *Congressional Quarterly*, August 1, 1981, p. 1371.

97. Interview.

98. Keller, "Democrats and Republicans Try to Outbid Each Other in Cutting Taxes for Business," p. 1137.

99. Elisabeth Wehr, "Reagan May Try to Block August Recess . . . If Work Unfinished on Tax Measure," *Congressional Quarterly*, June 27, 1981, p. 1135.

100. Interviews with individuals in business and government.

101. Ann Reilly, with Joe Weber, "How Reagan Did It," *Dun's Business Month*, September 1981, p. 53.

Chapter 6

1. Ways and Means Committee Hearings, *Administration's Fiscal Year 1983 Economic Program*, part 1, 2/18/82–5/5/82 (Washington, DC: U.S. Government Printing Office, 1982).

2. Pechman and Bosworth, in Pechman, *Setting National Priorities*, pp. 30–31.

3. *Economic Report of the President, February 1983* (Washington, DC: U.S. Government Printing Office, 1983), pp. 124–30.

4. John Palmer and Isabel Sawhill, *The Reagan Record*, an Urban Institute Study (Cambridge, MA: Ballinger, 1984).

5. Pechman, in Pechman, *Setting National Priorities*, p. 5.

6. Kenneth Bacon, "The Outlook: The President Fights for Credibility," *Wall Street Journal*, August 31, 1981, p. 1.

7. Kenneth Bacon, "Steady on Course," *Wall Street Journal*, September 17, 1981, p. 1.

8. John Leger, "Losing Friends: Reagan Program Stirs Worries in New Area, the Currency Markets," *Wall Street Journal*, September 18, 1981, p. 1.

9. Senate Finance Committee Hearings, *Administration's Fiscal Year 1983 Budget Proposal*, part 4, 2/23/81–3/19/81 (Washington, DC: U.S. Government Printing Office, 1982), pp. 217–20.

10. Interview.

11. Interview.

12. The other two sectors hit hardest by the minimum tax would have much lower increases: petroleum taxes would go up by 27 percent; utilities, by 15 percent.

13. Senate Finance Hearings, part 4, 1982, p. 220.

14. Interview.

15. Interview.

16. Senate Finance Hearings, part 5, 1982, p. 3.

17. Interviews.

18. Senate Finance Hearings, part 5, 1982, p. 7.

19. Senate Finance Hearings, part 4, 1982, pp. 260–64.

20. House Ways and Means Hearings, part 1, 1982, pp. 7–8.

21. The National Federation of Independent Business, the National Association of Wholesaler-Distributors, the Chamber of Commerce, and the Independent Petroleum Association of America.

22. Interviews.

23. Stanford Jacobs, "Leasing Breaks Limited for Small Firms," *Wall Street Journal,* February 8, 1982, p. 29.

24. Interview.

25. House Ways and Means Hearings, 1982, p. 6.

26. Interview.

27. Bill Keller, "With Tax Hikes in Prospect, Lobbyists Revert to Form: 'Don't Tax Me, Tax Thee,' " *Congressional Quarterly,* June 5, 1982, p. 1328.

28. Kenneth Bacon, "Cloudier Outlook: Reaganites Are at Odds over How Far to Trim 1982 Economic Forecast," *Wall Street Journal,* October 27, 1981, p. 1.

29. Bacon, "The Outlook," p. 1.

30. Roberts, *Supply-Side Revolution,* pp. 168–69.

31. "Tax Increases May Be Needed, Volcker Warns," *Wall Street Journal,* November 12, 1981, p. 3.

32. Bacon, "Steady on Course," p. 1.

33. Kenneth Bacon and Rich Jaroslovsky, "Reagan Asks 'Firm Steady Course' of Fiscal Austerity and Further Budget Cuts of $13 Billion for Fiscal 1982," *Wall Street Journal,* September 25, 1981, p. 3.

34. Kenneth Bacon, "Regan Says Economic Plan Is Working but Sees Difficulties in Next Few Months," *Wall Street Journal,* November 11, 1981, p. 3.

35. Interview.

36. Elisabeth Drew, "A Reporter in Washington: First Year," *New Yorker,* January 4, 1982, p. 38.

37. "Safe Harbor Leasing a Stormy Future," *Business Week,* December 21, 1981, pp. 104, 107; also pp. 36–37.

38. Interview.

39. Dennis Farney, "O'Neill Says Reagan Must Admit Failure on Economy before Democrats Offer Plan," *Wall Street Journal,* October 28, 1981, p. 4.

40. Elisabeth Drew, *Politics and Money* (New York: Macmillan, 1983), pp. 38–45.

41. Interview.

42. Dale Tate, "Reagan Budgets 1983 Deficit of $91.5 Billion," *Congressional Quarterly,* February 13, 1982, pp. 225–27.

43. Interview.

44. "1982 Tax Increase," National Association of Realtors internal document.

45. Robert Merry, "Reagan's Plan Could Allow for Tax Boost of $35 Billion, Dole and Others Assert," *Wall Street Journal*, February 2, 1982, p. 3.

46. Pamela Fessler, "Cool Reception for Reagan Tax Proposals," *Congressional Quarterly*, February 27, 1982, p. 460.

47. Interview.

48. Pamela Fessler, "Pressure Mounting to Modify the Tax Cuts Passed Last Year," *Congressional Quarterly*, February 20, 1982, p. 315.

49. Rich Jaroslovsky, "GOP Members Grouse about Reagan Plan, Doubt Passage of Some Tax Measures," *Wall Street Journal*, February 26, 1982, p. 10.

50. Interview.

51. "Business Roundtable Proposes Changes in Tax Cuts, Spending to Shrink Deficits," *Wall Street Journal*, March 5, 1982, p. 3.

52. "Regan Censures Business Leaders for Lack of Faith," *Wall Street Journal*, March 12, 1985, p. 5.

53. Keller, "With Tax Hikes in Prospect, Lobbyists Revert to Form," p. 1329.

54. Lindley Clark, Jr., "How Businessmen Became So Disillusioned," *Wall Street Journal*, March 9, 1982, p. 31.

55. Keller, "With Tax Hikes in Prospect, Lobbyists Revert to Form," pp. 1328–30.

56. Ibid., p. 1330.

57. "Firms Battling Uncertainties, Midnight Deadline in Drive for Tax Gains on Leasing," *Wall Street Journal*, November 13, 1981, p. 56.

58. John Emshwiller, "New Tax Rules on Leasing Spark GENERAL ELECTRIC Unit," *Wall Street Journal*, October 16, 1981, p. 29.

59. Leonard Apcar, "Law Permitting Trading of Tax Benefits to Be Repealed or Tightened, Dole Says," *Wall Street Journal*, February 22, 1982, p. 2.

60. Interview with industry representative.

61. "1982 Tax Bill," industry document.

62. Interview with White House staff person.

63. "Thirteen GOP Senators Pledge to Protect Tax Cuts, Complicating Work on Budget," *Wall Street Journal*, March 24, 1982, p. 3.

64. Interviews with members of the White House staff.

65. Leonard Apcar and Robert Merry, "Reagan Backs Plan in Senate for Tax Boost," *Wall Street Journal*, May 6, 1982, p. 3.

66. Pamela Fessler, "Spending Cuts, Record Tax Hike Pass Senate," *Congressional Quarterly*, July 24, 1982, pp. 1747–48.

67. Pamela Fessler, "Handling of Tax Bill Upsets Democrats on Finance Panel," *Congressional Quarterly*, July 15, 1982, pp. 1705–6.

68. Interview with participating congressman.

69. Interviews with congressman and congressial aides.

70. Dale Tate, "Congress Clears $98.3 Billion Tax Increase," *Congressional Quarterly*, August 21, 1982, p. 2035.

71. Dale Tate, "Members' Mixed Motives Obscure Message of Tax Bill," *Congressional Quarterly*, August 28, 1982, p. 2121.

72. William Miller, "Get Ready for Higher Business Taxes," *Industry Week*, May 17, 1982, p. 19.

73. Interview with White House staff person.

74. Interview with industry representative.

75. Ibid.

76. Ibid.

77. Interviews with public and private sector participants.

78. Interviews with public and private sector participants.

Chapter 7

1. A transition rate of 33 percent for upper-income taxpayers was phased out in 1988. Rosenbaum, "Sweeping Tax Bill Is Voted by House; Senate Acts Next," pp. D1, 17.

2. Rosenbaum, "Senate, 74–23, Votes Tax Bill; Widest Revisions in 40 Years Cut Rates, Curb Deductions," pp. 1, 34.

3. Andrew B. Lyon, "Tax Reform and Economic Productivity: An Overview of the Goals and Results of the Tax Reform Act of 1986," *National Productivity Review,* Autumn 1987, p. 360.

4. Emil Sunley, "Federal Tax Policy and the Budget," in in Ralph Landau and Dale Jorgenson, eds., *Technology and Economic Policy* (Cambridge, MA: Ballinger, 1986), p. 93.

5. All but Bradley were unlikely tax reformers; their commitment to the issue seemed based partly on their own reputations. Their perseverance, however, was responsible for its success. Jeffrey Birnbaum and Alan Murray, *Showdown at Gucci Gulch* (New York: Random House, 1987), pp. 17–22.

6. Timothy Conlan, David Beam, and Margaret Wrightson, "Tax Reform Legislation and the New Politics of Reform," paper delivered at the 1988 annual meeting of the American Political Science Association, Washington, DC, September 1988, pp. 19–20.

7. Birnbaum and Murray, *Showdown at Gucci Gulch,* p. 285.

8. Robert Kuttner, *The Economic Illusion: False Choices between Prosperity and Social Justice* (Boston: Houghton Mifflin, 1984). Critical realignments occur when an issue rivets public attention and divides the electorate along new fault lines, redefining partisan commitments and making radical policy possible. See, for example, Walter Dean Burnham, *Critical Elections and the Mainsprings of American Politics* (New York: Norton, 1970).

9. Martin Shefter and Benjamin Ginsberg, "Institutionalizing the Reagan Regime," in Benjamin Ginsberg and Alan Stone, eds., *Do Elections Matter?* (New York: M. E. Sharpe, 1986), p. 193; also see *New York Times,* May 29, 1985, p. A17.

10. See Brand, "Not Much Reform in 'Tax Reform,' " pp. 389–93. The "simplicity" accomplished by the reform act has also been questioned. See Ellen Benoit, "Tax Follies," *Financial World,* March 8, 1988, p. 100.

11. Interview with a high-technology industry representative, November 1989.

12. "Study Faults Tax Incentives," *Federation Report* 12, no. 4 (February 4, 1985): 2.

13. Edward G. Jefferson, "Tax Policy for the Eighties," in Landau and Jorgenson, *Technology and Economic Policy,* p. 62.

14. Harrison and Bluestone, *Great U-Turn,* p. 9.

15. Robert Lawrence, *Can America Compete?* (Washington, DC: Brookings Institution, 1984).

16. Bailey, "What Has Happened to Productivity Growth?" p. 446.

17. Schneider, "Services Hurt by Technology," pp. D1, 6.

18. The system of industrial relations affects productivity levels in a variety of ways. Less antagonistic systems allow for smoother introduction of technological improvements and minimize disruptive strikes and lockouts. Pratten, *Labor Productivity Differential within International Companies,* pp. 55–56.

19. Skinner, "Focused Factory," pp. 113–14.

20. Robert Hayes and Kim Clark, "Explaining Observed Productivity Differential between Plants: Implications for Operations Research," *Interfaces* 15, no. 6 (November–December 1985): 10. See also Robert Hayes and William Abernathy, "Managing Our Way to Economic Decline," *Harvard Business Review,* July–August 1980, pp. 76–77, and Steven Wheelwright and Robert Hayes, "Competing through Manufacturing," *Harvard Business Review,* January–February 1985, pp. 99–109.

21. See Lugar, "Tax Incentives and Tax Inequities," pp. 33–47; Sunley, "Towards a More Neutral Investment Tax Credit," pp. 209–20; Eisner and Nadiri, "Investment Behavior and Neo-Classical Theory," pp. 369–83.

22. Sheppard, "Corporate Tax Said to Encourage Investment in Equipment, Not Structures," p. 655.

23. John Zysman, *Manufacturing Matters: The Myth of the Post-Industrial Economy* (New York: Basic Books, 1987).

24. Although the Japanese corporate rate is higher, three aspects of the revenue code greatly decrease the tax burden on capital: First, capital gains on corporate securities are not taxed but capital gains on other transactions are fully taxed; this funnels investment into the corporate sector. Second, about one-fifth of corporate dividends are tax deductible, lowering equity costs. Finally, the Japanese tax code has a looser definition of interest-bearing debt, giving Japanese firms greater access to low-cost funds. George Hatsopoulos and Stephen Brooks, "The Gap in the Cost of Capital: Causes, Effects, and Remedies," in Landau and Jorgenson, *Technology and Economic Policy,* p. 245.

25. Ralph Landau, "Technology, Economics, and Public Policy," in Landau and Jorgenson, *Technology and Economic Policy,* p. 62.

26. "International Competitiveness Could Be Hurt by Ways and Means Plan," *Tax Notes,* October 14, 1985, p. 124.

27. Landau, "Technology, Economics, and Public Policy," in Landau and Jorgenson, *Technology and Economic Policy,* pp. 59–60.

28. Business Week Team, "What Tax Reform Really Means," p. 129.

29. Eileen Shanahan, "Tax Debate Keys on Economic Consequences," *Congressional Quarterly,* May 17, 1986, p. 1093.

30. J. Gregory Ballentine, "Life after Tax Reform," *World,* January 1987, pp. 31–32.

31. To reduce the variation in effective tax rates across industries, policymakers should equalize credits and depreciation allowances, and broaden the tax base by reducing the number of tax deductions. The commission also included the more traditional policy recommendations of reducing the bias against savings and investment and encouraging risk (through more favorable treatment of capital losses). President's Commission on Industrial Competitiveness, *Global Competition,* pp. 28, 35.

32. Lyon, "Tax Reform and Economic Productivity," p. 360.

33. Business Week Team, "What Tax Reform Really Means," p. 129.

34. The authors weighted the effective tax rate for each of the four assets by the percentage of the total capital stock accounted for by that asset in order to calculate

the total effective tax rate for the corporate sector. Don Fullerton, Yolanda Henderson, and James Mackie, "Investment Allocation and Growth under the Tax Reform Act of 1986," in *Compendium of Tax Research 1987* (Washington, DC: U.S. Government Printing Office, 1987).

35. Bill Liebtag, "Capital Formation by Small Business," *Journal of Accountancy,* June 1987, p. 91.

36. Anna Cifelli Isgro, "The Tax Upheaval: What It Means for Business," *Fortune,* June 9, 1986, p. 18.

37. Ann Reilly, "A Tax Bill That Hits Investment," *Fortune,* December 23, 1985, p. 106.

38. Interview with participant, November 1989.

39. Birnbaum and Murray, *Showdown at Gucci Gulch,* pp. 36–39.

40. Alan Murray, "With an Eye on '84 Elections, Democrats Lay Foundations for National Industrial Policy," *Congressional Quarterly,* August 20, 1983, pp. 1679–81. I am indebted to Jim Shoch for clarifying the connection between the Democrat's industrial policy agenda and tax reform.

41. Felix Rohatyn, *The Twenty-Year Century* (New York: Random House, 1983), pp. 129–33.

42. Alan Murray, "With an Eye on '84 Elections," p. 1679.

43. His recommendation is simply to do away with the corporate income tax and replace it with a value-added tax. Lester Thurow, *The Zero-Sum Solution* (New York: Simon & Schuster, 1985), pp. 225–28.

44. Bruce Stokes, "Conservatives Eyeing Tax Reform as Step to Pro-Business Federal Economic Role," *National Journal,* December 1, 1984, pp. 2298–2301.

45. McLennan, "The Case for a Non-targeted Approach to Industrial Strategy," in Redburn, Buss, and Ledebur, *Revitalizing the U.S. Economy,* pp. 52–54.

46. Stokes, "Conservatives Eyeing Tax Reform as Step to Pro-Business Federal Economic Role," pp. 2298–2301.

47. McLennan, "The Case for a Non-targeted Approach to Industrial Strategy," in Redburn, Buss, and Ledebur, *Revitalizing the U.S. Economy,* pp. 46–47.

48. The question reads: "Here are a few statements people make about the income tax system. For each, tell me if you agree or disagree, or if perhaps you have no opinion on it . . . The present tax system benefits the rich and is unfair to the ordinary working man or woman." Survey by ABC News/*Washington Post,* January 11–16, 1985 (*Public Opinion,* February–March 1985, p. 23).

49. Taxes include the federal income, state income, state sales, and local property taxes. Advisory Commission on Intergovernmental Relations, "Changing Public Attitudes on Governments and Taxes," p. 1.

50. The question was: "We'd like to know about the federal taxes you or your family paid last year and whether you think everyone in the United States pays his or her fair share. Do you think our system of federal taxes is basically fair, or not?" Survey by the *Los Angeles Times,* January 19–24, 1985 ("Opinion Roundup," *Public Opinion,* February–March 1985, p. 22).

51. The first poll asked the question: "Have you heard or read anything about the Treasury Department's proposal to simplify the tax system by reducing the tax rate and eliminating most deductions?" Poll taken by ABC News/*Washington Post,* January 11–16, 1985.

The second poll asked the question: "The current federal income tax has 14 or 15 different tax rates starting at 11 percent and going all the way up to 50 percent. The poorest people pay the lowest tax rates, and the richest people pay the highest rates. But the administration wants to pare down the tax brackets to just three rates: 15%, 25%, and 30%.

"Do you think it's better if a lot of people pay the same rate of tax or do you think it's better if a few people pay very different rates depending on their incomes?"

Both polls found in "Opinion Roundup," *Public Opinion,* February–March 1985, p. 28.

52. Susan Hansen, *The Politics of Taxation: Revenue without Representation* (New York: Praeger, 1983), pp. 72, 273.

53. Timothy Clark, "Democrats Say: Reduce Deficit, Not Tax Rates," *National Journal,* September 21, 1985, p. 2143.

54. Birnbaum and Murray, *Showdown at Gucci Gulch,* p. 26.

55. Ibid., p. 31.

56. Randall Strahan, "Members' Goals and Coalition-building Strategies in the U.S. House: The Case of Tax Reform," *Journal of Politics* 51, no. 2 (May 1989): 378.

57. Interview with Ways and Means staff, November and December 1989.

58. Gerald Boyd, "Claiming the Credit in 1988," p. D18.

59. Interview, November 1989.

60. Kent Weaver, *Automatic Government: The Politics of Indexation* (Washington, DC: Brookings Institution, 1988), pp. 18, 28.

61. Interview with Senate Finance staff.

62. Ann Cooper, "New Business Coalition Wants to Keep the Ball Rolling on Reagan's Tax Reform Plan," *National Journal,* July 20, 1985, p. 1675.

63. Interview with major industry lobbyist, November 1989.

64. For a discussion of business concerns about competitiveness, see Kevin Phillips, *Staying on Top* (New York: Random House, 1984).

65. American Electronics Association, "A Perspective on the 1986 Tax Reform Act," internal document, October 10, 1986.

66. American Retail Federation, "President Reagan Unveils Tax Reform; Retailing Supports Major Features," *Federation Report* 12, no. 21 (June 3, 1985): 1.

67. By the mid-1980s members included the American Business Conference, American Trucking Association, Armstrong World Industries, Beatrice, Dart & Kraft, General Mills, General Motors, IBM, Levi Strauss, National Association of Wholesaler-Distributors, National Federation of Independent Business, National Retail Merchants Association, Pillsbury, Procter & Gamble, RJR Nabisco, and 3M (Minnesota Mining and Manufacturing). (List from industry source.)

68. "A Self-Promoter or Skilled Communicator?" *National Journal,* July 20, 1985, p. 1676.

69. Interview with industry representative, November 1989.

70. Companies included Allied, American Can, Beneficial, Dart & Kraft, Dayton-Hudson, Emerson Electric, Federated Department Stores, General Foods, General Motors, Hallmark Cards, Hewlett-Packard, IBM, Levi Strauss, Merck & Company, 3M (Minnesota, Mining and Manufacturing), J.C. Penney, Pepsico, Procter & Gamble, Pillsbury, and Sara Lee.

71. Cooper, "New Business Coalition Wants to Keep the Ball Rolling on Reagan's Tax Reform Plan," p. 1678.

72. Timothy B. Clark, "Divided They Stand," *National Journal*, April 19, 1986, p. 932.

73. Included were AT&T, Goodyear, Commonwealth Edison, Inland Steel, and Weyerhaeuser. Isgro, "The Tax Upheaval," p. 20.

74. Birnbaum and Murray, *Showdown at Gucci Gulch*, p. 111.

75. National Association of Home Builders, "Political Update," internal document, May 14, 1986.

76. "Knights of the Roundtable," *Business Week*, October 21, 1988, p. 39.

77. Timothy Conlan, Margaret Wrightson, and David Beam, *Taxing Choices: The Politics of Tax Reform* (Washington, DC: Congressional Quarterly Press, 1990), pp. 57–58.

78. Birnbaum and Murray, *Showdown at Gucci Gulch*, p. 60.

79. Ibid., pp. 49–51.

80. Pamela Fessler, "Treasury Tax Overhaul Excites Little Interest," *Congressional Quarterly*, December 1, 1984, p. 3016.

81. Laurie McGinley and Alan Murray, "High-Tech Firms Cool on Tax Plan," *Wall Street Journal*, December 6, 1984, p. 64.

82. Interviews with industry representatives.

83. Interview with industry representative, November 1989.

84. Interview with a high-technology industry representative, November 1989.

85. Birnbaum and Murray, *Showdown at Gucci Gulch*, pp. 84, 87.

86. Interviews with individuals in industry and government, November 1989.

87. Conlan, Wrightson, and Beam, *Taxing Choices*, p. 91.

88. Interview with Ways and Means staff, November 1989.

89. Conlan, Wrightson, and Beam, *Taxing Choices*, p. 92.

90. Interview with Ways and Means staff, November 1989.

91. Birnbaum and Murray, *Showdown at Gucci Gulch*, p. 122.

92. Ibid., p. 124.

93. Ibid., p. 113.

94. Interview with Ways and Means staff, November 1989.

95. Ann Reilly, "Tax Reform Faces the Lobbyists' Best," *Fortune*, June 24, 1985, p. 87.

96. Anna Cifelli Isgro, "Congress Reshapes Reagan's Tax Plan," *Fortune*, September 30, 1985, p. 113.

97. Richard Harris, "Chamber of Commerce Directors Reject Ways and Means Tax Reform Effort," *Tax Notes*, November 18, 1985, p. 672.

98. Richard Harris, "House Republicans Mount Tax Reform Insurgency," *Tax Notes*, November 11, 1985, p. 563.

99. "Ways and Means Marks Up Insurance Provisions; Rostenkowski on the Defensive," *Tax Notes*, November 18, 1985, p. 669.

100. "Ways and Means Reports Out Tax Bill, Bucking Republican Alternative," *Tax Notes*, December 9, 1985, p. 989.

101. American Retail Federation, "Reagan's Efforts Result in House Tax Action," *Federation Report* 12, no. 58 (December 23, 1985): 2.

102. Interview with industry participants, November 1989.

103. "Ways and Means Reports Out Tax Bill, Bucking Republican Alternative," p. 991.

104. Birnbaum and Murray, *Showdown at Gucci Gulch*, p. 182.

105. Interview with Senate Finance staff, November 1989.

106. One TRAC supporter included in Packwood's informal coalition was the National Federation of Independent Business. NFIB has a very heterogeneous membership, including capital-intensive manufacturers and construction firms along with other labor-intensive small business firms. Therefore, NFIB's position on reform was more complicated that that of groups with a more homogeneous membership. As one leader in the organization put it: "From an overall standpoint, the Tax Reform Act of 1986 was most difficult and frustrating because there were so many issues that affected our membership. It has hard to prioritize." Interview with industry representative, November 1989.

107. American Retail Federation, "Packwood Takes Aim at Tax Provisions Impacting Retailers," *Federation Report* 13, no. 12 (March 31, 1986): 1.

108. American Retail Federation, "Packwood Provisions Disturb Industry, Retailers Urged to Contact Members," *Federation Report* 13, no. 10 (March 17, 1989): 1.

109. Interviews with Senate Finance and Joint Committee staff, business representatives, November 1989.

110. "Packwood's Proposal Alienates Key Supporters, New Opposition Coalition Formed, *Tax Notes,* April 7, 1986, p. 6.

111. Interviews, November and December 1989.

112. "Banking Leaders Urge Retention of Loan Loss Reserve Deduction," *Tax Notes,* April 7, 1986, p. 8.

113. Lee Shepard, "Finance Committee Passes Timber and Oil Provisions with Few Changes," *Tax Notes,* April 14, 1986, p. 105.

114. The compromise depreciation plan would preserve the ACRS short lives and the 150 percent declining balance method, but would make productivity property eligible for the 200 percent declining balance method. "Finance Approves Depreciation Compromise Plan," *Tax Notes,* April 14, 1986, pp. 103–5.

115. Interview with Senate Finance staff, November 1989.

116. "Capitol Hill is Quiet while Lobbyists Mount Campaigns against Packwood Plan," *Tax Notes,* April 7, 1989, p. 5.

117. Interview with government staff member, November 1989.

118. Interview, November 1989.

119. Interview with Senate Finance staff member, November 1989.

120. Interview with congressional staff member, December 1989.

121. Interview with industry participant, November 1989.

122. Interview with industry participant, November 1989.

123. Laura Saunders, "Personalized Taxes," *Forbes,* June 1, 1987, p. 84.

124. Original members included Procter & Gamble, Philip Morris, IBM, the CEO Tax Group, the League of Women Voters, Bread for the World, the American Association of Retired Persons, the Consumer Federation of America, the National Association of Manufacturers, the National Federation of Independent Business, and the National Association of Wholesaler-Distributors. Nancy Davis, "The Coalition That Bob, Will, Bill, and Mary Built," *Association Management,* August 1986, pp. 63–69.

125. Senate Finance Committee, "Senator Bob Packwood's Statement to the '15/27/33' Coalition," May 16, 1989.

126. Interview with Senate aide, November 1989.

127. Mary Gael Timberlake, "Momentum for Finance Tax Bill Builds, but Undercurrents Could Spell Trouble," *Tax Notes,* May 19, 1986, p. 645.

128. American Retail Federation, "TRAC to Support Ways & Means Tax Reform Bill," *Federation Report,* 12, no. 48 (December 9, 1985): 1–2.

129. Interview with industry participant, November 1989.

Conclusion

1. Claus Offe, "Two Logics of Collective Action," in John Keane, ed., *Disorganized Capitalism* (Cambridge, MA: MIT Press, 1985), p. 180.

2. Philippe Schmitter, "Interest Intermediation and Regime Governability in Western Europe and North America," in Suzanne Berger, ed., *Organizing Interests in Western Europe* (Cambridge: Cambridge University Press, 1981).

3. David Plotke, "The Political Mobilization of Business, 1974–1980: Do Classes Have Interests?" paper presented at annual meeting of the American Political Science Association, Washington, DC, September 1988.

4. Dennis Quinn, "The End of the End of Ideology: The Reemergence of Ideology in Economic Policy," paper presented at annual meeting of the American Political Science Association, Atlanta, 1989.

5. Interview with industry representative.

6. Nancy Davis, "The Coalition That Bob, Will, Bill, and Mary Built," p. 64.

7. Ibid., p. 66.

8. Lindblom, *Politics and Markets.*

9. See Karl Marx, "The Eighteenth Brumaire of Louis Bonaparte," in Robert C. Tucker, ed., *The Marx-Engels Reader,* (New York: Norton, 1978), pp. 594–617.

10. David Vogel, *Fluctuating Fortunes* (Berkeley: University of California Press, 1989).

11. David Vogel, *Fluctuating Fortunes;* Thomas Edsall, *The New Politics of Inequality;* Graham Wilson, "American Business and Politics," in Allan Cigler and Burdett Loomis, eds., *Interest Group Politics,* pp. 227–31.

12. Joseph Pika, "Interest Groups and the Executive: Presidential Intervention"; Martha Joynt Kumar and Michael Baruch Grossman, "The Presidency and Interest Groups."

13. Jack Walker, "The Origins and Maintenance of Interest Groups in America," *American Political Science Review* 77 (June 1983), pp. 398–402.

14. Joseph Pika, "Interest Groups and the Executive: Presidential Intervention," p. 316; see also Kay Schlozman and John Tierney, *Organized Interests and American Democracy* (New York: Harper & Row, 1986) p. 322; Jeffrey Berry, *The Interest Group Society,* (Glenview, IL: Scott Foresman/Little, Brown, 1989), p. 152.

15. Martha Joynt Kumar and Michael Baruch Grossman, "The Presidency and Interest Groups"; Joseph Pika, "Interest Groups and the Executive: Presidential Intervention."

16. Howard Gleckman, "This Is Not the Last Chapter in Tax Reform, *Business Week,* September 1, 1986, p. 64.

17. What might affect our economic future? Reorganization of the international division of labor into trading blocks might be a first step. If international competition is reduced, a resurgence of capital-intensive manufacturing is possible. An alternative scenario is the further restructuring of the American economy. If labor-intensive sectors gain greater hegemony, we are likely to see a continuation of the tax code along the lines of the 1986 tax reform effort.

Index